Football, Politics and Identity

This book presents a series of fascinating case studies that show how the lives and bodies of clubs, players and fans around the world are enmeshed with politics.

It draws on original research in countries including England, Scotland, Ireland, Poland, Mexico, Algeria and Argentina and includes both historical and contemporary perspectives. It explores some of the most important themes in the study of sport, including sectarianism, migration, fan activism and national identity, and shows how football continues to be tied to political events, symbols and movements.

This is fascinating reading for any student or researcher working in sport studies, political science, sociology or contemporary history.

James Carr is Lecturer in Sociology at the University of Limerick, Republic of Ireland.

Daniel Parnell is Senior Lecturer in Sport Business at the University of Liverpool, UK.

Paul Widdop is Senior Lecturer in Sport Business Management, Leeds Beckett University, UK.

Martin J. Power is Senior Lecturer in Sociology at the University of Limerick, Republic of Ireland.

Stephen R. Millar is a Leverhulme Early Career Fellow in Ethnomusicology at Cardiff University and Visiting Research Fellow in Irish Studies at Queen's University Belfast, UK.

Critical Research in Football

Series Editors:
Pete Millward, *Liverpool John Moores University, UK*
Jamie Cleland, *University of Southern Australia*
Daniel Parnell, *University of Liverpool, UK*
Stacey Pope, *Durham University, UK*
Paul Widdop, *Manchester Metropolitan University, UK*

The *Critical Research in Football* book series was launched in 2017 to showcase the inter- and multi-disciplinary breadth of debate relating to 'football'. The series defines 'football' as broader than association football, with research on rugby, Gaelic and gridiron codes also featured. Including monographs, edited collections, short books and textbooks, books in the series are written and/or edited by leading experts in the field whilst consciously also affording space to emerging voices in the area, and are designed to appeal to students, postgraduate students and scholars who are interested in the range of disciplines in which critical research in football connects. The series is published in association with the *Football Collective*, www.footballcollective.org.uk.

Available in this series:

Russia and the 2018 FIFA World Cup
Edited by Richard Arnold

Football and Popular Culture
Singing Out from the Stands
Edited by Stephen R. Millar, Martin J. Power, Paul Widdop, Daniel Parnell and James Carr

Football and Discrimination
Antisemitism and Beyond
Edited by Pavel Brunssen and Stefanie Schüler-Springorum

Football, Politics and Identity
Edited by James Carr, Daniel Parnell, Paul Widdop, Martin J. Power and Stephen R. Millar

For more information about this series, please visit: www.routledge.com/sport/series/CFSFC

Football, Politics and Identity

Edited by James Carr, Daniel Parnell, Paul Widdop, Martin J. Power and Stephen R. Millar

Routledge
Taylor & Francis Group
LONDON AND NEW YORK

First published 2021
by Routledge
2 Park Square, Milton Park, Abingdon, Oxon OX14 4RN

and by Routledge
52 Vanderbilt Avenue, New York, NY 10017

Routledge is an imprint of the Taylor & Francis Group, an informa business

British Library Cataloguing-in-Publication Data
A catalogue record for this book is available from the British Library

Library of Congress Cataloging-in-Publication Data
Names: Carr, James, editor. | Parnell, Daniel, editor. | Widdop, Paul, editor. | Power, Martin J., editor. | Millar, Stephen R., editor.
Title: Football, politics and identity / Edited by James Carr, Daniel Parnell, Paul Widdop, Martin J. Power and Stephen R. Millar.
Description: Abingdon, Oxon ; New York, NY : Routledge, 2021. | Series: Critical research in football | Includes bibliographical references and index. | Identifiers: LCCN 2020055459
Subjects: LCSH: Soccer—Political aspects—Case studies. | National characteristics—Political aspects—Case studies. | Soccer—Social aspects—Case studies. | Nationalism and sports. | Sports spectators—Social conditions.
Classification: LCC GV943.9.P65 F66 2021 | DDC 796.334—dc23
LC record available at https://lccn.loc.gov/2020055459

ISBN: 978-0-367-43355-0 (hbk)
ISBN: 978-1-032-01232-2 (pbk)
ISBN: 978-1-003-00262-8 (ebk)

Typeset in Goudy
by Apex CoVantage, LLC

Contents

Contributors

John Bell is Research Associate with INCORE at Ulster University, Northern Ireland. His research focuses on the football fan culture surrounding the Northern Irish international football team. He has previously worked as a Research Associate for the Institute for Conflict Research in Belfast, Northern Ireland.

Paul Bell holds an MA in Terrorism and Political Violence from Queen's University Belfast, Northern Ireland. He is a qualified journalist and has written for Northern Irish publications such as the *Carrickfergus Times* and *Ballymena Guardian*. Paul has experience covering both Irish League and Northern Ireland international football matches.

Paul Breen is Senior Lecturer with the University of Westminster, UK. He writes and researches on language, culture and politics with a portfolio of published work across both academic and media fields. His output has included works of fiction relating to football and society.

Pavel Brunssen is a PhD candidate in the Department of Germanic Languages and Literatures at the University of Michigan, USA, where he is also pursuing a graduate certificate in Judaic Studies at the Frankel Center for Judaic Studies. His main research interests are antisemitism and antigypsyism in European football fan cultures. Pavel co-founded a magazine called *Transparent*, which focuses on the political aspects of soccer fan cultures of which he was editor-in-chief until 2017.

James Carr lectures in the Department of Sociology, University of Limerick, Ireland. In 2016, he published his first book *Experiences of Islamophobia: Living with Racism in the Neoliberal Era* (London and New York: Routledge) which focused on anti-Muslim racism in Ireland. In addition to other scholarly publications, James has also authored the *European Islamophobia Report* submissions on Ireland for 2015-20 has been the contributor to the *Yearbook of Muslims in Europe* for Ireland across the same period.

Robert Claus is working and publishing on diversity and anti-discrimination in sports and fandom, right-wing extremism and combat sports.

Leonie Cornips is Senior Researcher at the NL-Lab, Humanities Cluster (KNAW), in Amsterdam, the Netherlands, and Professor of Language Culture in Limburg at Maastricht University, the Netherlands. Her research is in sociolinguistics. Topics are language variation, national and regional identity construction through language practices, bidialectal child acquisition and multilingualism.

Matt Deighan is a doctoral researcher at Ulster University, Northern Ireland. His work examines identity politics and football in Northern Ireland. Matt is a former NI youth international footballer; he currently coaches an underage Irish league team and lectures in the sociology of sport at Dublin City University and Ulster University.

Philip Dine is Personal Professor and Head of French at the National University of Ireland Galway, Ireland. His research focuses on representations of the French colonial empire and its cultural legacies in fields ranging from children's literature to professional sport and sport and identity construction in France and the Francophone world.

Danny Fitzpatrick is Lecturer in Politics and International Relations at Aston University, UK. He is a co-founder of the Football Collective and co-convenor of the Political Studies Association Sport and Politics specialist group.

Mateusz Grodecki is Assistant Professor at the Institute of Philosophy and Sociology, the Maria Grzegorzewska University, Poland. His research interests focus on nation studies and sociology of sport, in particular on football studies and football fandom culture. He is a principal investigator in the research project 'The Character of National Ideologies of Football Supporters' funded by the National Science Centre, Poland.

Melissa Mora Hidalgo teaches classes in Chicana/o studies and women's, gender and sexuality studies at California State University, Fullerton, and CSU Long Beach, USA.

Sean Huddleston has been an educator at secondary, special needs and higher education levels for the last 18 years. Sean's main academic focus has been the analysis of politics, history and identity. Sean has been a member of Football Collective since its early conception and was the primary organiser of the 2018 Football Collective conference held at Hampden Park, Glasgow.

Radosław Kossakowski is Associate Professor in Sociology, Director of the Institute of Sociology and Chair of the Scientific Council of Sociology at the University of Gdańsk, Poland. His research interests include sociology of sport, football studies, qualitative methods and masculinities studies.

Katie Liston is Senior Researcher in the Sport and Exercise Sciences Research Institute at Ulster University, Northern Ireland. Katie is a former international athlete, with honours in football and rugby as well as national honours in Gaelic football. Katie also holds national titles with football clubs affiliated to the Irish Football Association and the Football Association of Ireland, and she was chairperson of Crusaders Strikers WFC.

Anthony May is Assistant Professor in Sport and Event Management at Coventry University, UK. His research is in topics related to sport, policy, politics and management. He is a member of the editorial board of the journal, *Managing Sport and Leisure*.

Stephen R. Millar is a Leverhulme Early Career Fellow in Ethnomusicology at Cardiff University, UK. His academic work concentrates on the interconnection between music and politics, the aesthetics of ideology, and how this is transmitted through popular culture. He is author of *Sounding Dissent: Rebel Songs, Resistance, and Irish Republicanism* (Michigan, 2020) and co-editor of *Football and Popular Culture: Singing Out from the Stands* (Routledge, 2021).

Daniel Parnell is an Associate Professor in Sport Business at the University of Liverpool Management School. Dan's research interests lie in business management, policy, and social and economic networks in sport. He serves as Co-Editor-in-Chief of the journal Managing Sport and Leisure and is the co-founder of The Football Collective, a global network of football scholars. He is also a co-editor of the Routledge Book series 'Critical Research in Football'. On top of this, Dan maintains extensive links within professional sport clubs, including being Head of Football Research at Dundee United FC and CEO of the Association of Sporting Directors. He tweets from: @parnell_daniel

Martin J. Power is a Senior Lecturer in Sociology and founding Director of the Popular Music and Popular Culture research cluster at the University of Limerick. He specialises in Urban Sociology, Inequalities and Social Exclusion, and the Sociology of popular music and culture. He is a fan of the Famous Glasgow Celtic.

Jim O'Brien is Senior Lecturer in Media and Visual Arts at Southampton Solent University, UK, and is Visiting Professor in Communication and Cultural Studies at The University of Vic, Spain. His current research projects include Sport, Globalisation and Identity, Football and Politics in Argentina, and Bob Dylan Studies, with particular reference to Dylan as Cultural Historian. He is also a fluent speaker of French and Spanish.

Peter Römer is Research Assistant in the Museum and Memorial "Geschichtsort Villa ten Hompel" in Münster, Germany, and works pedagogically in the field of Holocaust Education.

Lotte Thissen is Assistant Professor in the department of Health, Ethics, and Society at Maastricht University, the Netherlands. She is a trained cultural anthropologist specialised in multiculturalism, multilingualism, social relations and identity questions.

Giovanni Hortua Vargas is Professor at California State University and Pacific Oaks College, USA, and serves the community college known as Cypress College, USA. He teaches courses ranging from United States history to Latin American history to Xicanx (Chican@) studies and gender and sexuality in history. His research interests include, but are not limited to, music culture, race and the socio-political, sports culture (especially *fútbol*), topics on social justice, transnational sharing of culture and anything with oral tradition/history.

Paul Widdop is a Senior Lecturer in Sport Business Management, Leeds Beckett University, UK. His research explores social, economic and global networks on consumption and production of sport and popular culture. He has published widely in areas of sport and popular culture including articles in *Journal of Consumer Culture*, *Cultural Sociology*, *Cultural Trends*, *European Sport Management Quarterly*, *Political Behaviour*, *Electoral Studies*, and *Leisure Science*.

Introduction

Understanding the connection between football, identity and (P)politics

Martin J. Power, James Carr, Daniel Parnell, Paul Widdop and Stephen R. Millar

This collection of essays on football and (P)politics presents multidisciplinary scholarship from experienced and established academics together with dynamic, emerging scholars from across the globe. Football is one of the most hyper-commodified sports globally. As such, there has been increased investment in football, and it has gained traction within the academy with greater demand for football-related programmes in higher education and within the football industry. Moreover, in the current financial, political, social and cultural environment – football offers us one lens with which to view and analyse society and social issues. This book aims to contribute to that growing field (Hodges, 2018; Kossakowski et al., 2020; Rojo-Labaien et al., 2020), offering scholarship that directly engages with the world around us. The study of football may be one of the most fascinating lenses with which to view society. Indeed, football is both apolitical and political, at different points, degrees and contexts, which in turn makes almost every act political. From China's block out of Mesut Özil to the social activism of Marcus Rashford, to taking the knee, to being ownership neutral – football is a political heavyweight.

The book is the latest addition to the *Critical Research in Football* book series, which was launched by Routledge in close association with the Football Collective in 2017. Accordingly, it is pertinent to first introduce the Football Collective to the reader, as the group members played a fundamental role in cementing the foundations for people and ideas to organically grow and come to fruition, which in this case results in this volume.

In February 2016, several friends sat around a table in Manchester discussing the problems facing colleagues in academia. These included isolation, lack of resources, limited departmental support, increasing demands for teaching and learning, and an incessant narrative of publish in high-impact journals or perish if you can't do this. The industry was suffering from the marketisation of higher education, and many colleagues were on precarious contracts. The group agreed to extend collegiate support to develop a network of people interested in helping others interested in football research. This was where the Football Collective was born. Those in the group that day and in the conversations that followed – Hayton, Millward, Cleland, Rookwood, Doidge, Fitzpatrick, May, Hughson, Widdop and Parnell – developed an online platform and the first conference. The book series concept was developed at the inaugural Football Collective conference at FC United in November 2016 thanks to the support of Simon Whitmore of Routledge.

The *Critical Research in Football* book series was launched in 2017 to showcase the inter- and multi-disciplinary breadth of debate relating to 'football.' Thus far, the books series has attracted much interest from global football scholars. The first publication in the series covered fan activism, protest and politics in post-socialist Croatia (Hodges, 2018). The range of topics is vast, including fandom, consumption, fiction, history, migration, medicine, legacy, politics, activism and events. Indeed, the book series is steadily becoming a go-to place for football scholars to publish their research. While the predominant focus has been on association football, the series defines 'football' as broader than association football, with research on rugby, Gaelic and gridiron codes also featured. Books in the series are written and/or edited by leading experts in the field while consciously also affording space to emerging voices in the area and are designed to appeal to students, postgraduate students and scholars who are interested in the range of disciplines in which critical research in football connects.

This book's roots lie in the second annual Football Collective conference, which was hosted by the Popular Music and Popular Culture Research Cluster at the University of Limerick, Ireland, in November 2017 and focused on football, politics and popular culture. The conference organisers hosted a global cohort of almost 100 football researchers, academics and students from almost 20 countries who came together to interrogate the ways in which football, popular culture and (P)politics are entwined in contemporary global societies. Broad themes discussed included football and fan culture; migration; representations of football in popular culture; sexualities and gender identities; racism, anti-racism and Islamophobia; football and conflict; etc. It was here the conversation and foundations for this book and its partner volume, *Football and Popular Culture: Singing Out from the Stands*, were developed. The cases that ultimately are examined and presented in this volume therefore emerged from an assortment of national, political and cultural situations and from different ideological positions.

Putting football and P(p)olitics in context

While Politics is concerned with governments, governance, global capitalism and so on, *p*olitics "concentrates on the routine micro-politics of life and our everyday decisions" (Power et al., 2020a, p. 1). Politics and politics are intrinsically linked. Indeed, Janks (2012, p. 150) argues that:

> *the socio-historical and economic contexts in which we live produce different conditions of possibility and constraint that we all have to negotiate as meaningfully as we can. While the social constructs who we are, so do we construct the social. This dialectic relationship is fluid and dynamic, creating possibilities for social action and change.*

You have probably lost count of the number of times that you have heard that football and (P)politics have no business mixing. The editors of this volume unapologetically insist that football has always evidenced complex relationships with (P)politics and society (see, for example, Dunning et al., 2002; Spaaij et al., 2018). Because of its global appeal and strong ties to local allegiances, football is a hugely influential platform for billions of people across the globe. It offers a space for the public performance of communal identities, both for those demarcating dominant cultural values and for others who critique the status quo and celebrate their differences (see, for example, McKerrell, 2012; Jack, 2013; Millar, 2016; Herra, 2018; Marra and Trotta, 2019). When "a game matters to billions of people it ceases to be just a game. Football is never just football" (Kuper, 1996, p. 1).

One iconic incident at the Maksimir Stadium, Zagreb, in the former Yugoslavia on 13 May 1990 provided a highly potent example of the deep connection between football and politics. After a vote in Croatia for independence from the state of Yugoslavia, a riot occurred between the Bad Blue Boys Ultras of Dinamo Zagreb and the Delije Ultras of Crvena Zvezda. The Zagreb captain and future star of AC Milan, Zvonimir Boban, kicked a police officer who had allegedly been mistreating Croatian fans. Some observers argued that this act and the context in which it occurred symbolically marked the beginning of the end for Yugoslavia as a unified sovereign nation. Many of the combatants on the day would exchange the terraces for the front line in a brutal civil war that followed shortly afterwards (see Milekic, 2016 for an interesting discussion of this event. Also see Goldblatt, 2006). Indeed, Brentin (cited in Milekic, 2016) argues that the game, and these real and symbolic acts of violence, 'subsequently became one of the "founding myths of the Croatian nation", an event which is "deeply 'cemented' in social memory."'

Clubs, players and fans alike are entangled within politics – we all remember the 'Roman salute' given by Paolo di Canio in the game between Lazio and Livorno, for example. Clubs such as Celtic FC have been formed out of population upheavals and migration; others (explicitly or implicitly via their fans actions) such as Sporting Club de Bastia, FC Barcelona, Athletic Club Bilbao, Hapoel Taibe, Mtk Budapest, Ajax, and Rangers FC are/have been associated with independence or regionalist separatist movements and ethno-national and religious communities, while others still, such as Beitar Jerusalem, Lazio, St. Pauli and Livorno, have been affiliated with/used to promote political ideologies and parties (see Guerriero-Davies and Butler, 2018; Guerriero-Davies and Butler, 2019; Goldblatt, 2006; Sorek, 2002; Gehrmann, 1997; Doidge, 2013; Doidge, 2015; Carr et al., 2017; Bradley, 2004; Bradley, 2019; Webster, 2017; Taylor, 2006; Mayer, 2011; Brownfield Stein, 2017; Vantine de Lara Villela, 2017; de Brito d'Andréa, 2017). The continuing migration of people seeking refuge in Europe has seen football supporters raise their voices both in support of and in opposition to such migration (see Spaaij, 2015; Critchley, 2015; Conn, 2020; Horton, 2015). Racism and anti-racism continue to battle each other both on the pitch and in the stands and terraces (see Cleland and Cashmore, 2013; Cleland,

2014; Doidge, 2018). Broader contemporary international political controversies such as the prohibition of the Palestinian flag (see Stevens, 2016) and the wearing of symbols such as the British poppy (see Kelly, 2016) continue to spark controversy among player and fan communities alike. A very recent special issue of *Managing Sport and Leisure* (Power et al., 2020b) focused on football and (P)politics. Rookwood (2020) gave us insights on the politics and impact of 'international' football tournaments among 'countries' not recognised by football's established governing bodies. Dart (2020) examined the role football plays in the lives of those living under Israeli occupation in Palestine. Choluj et al. (2020) focused on the 'Against Modern Football' (AMF) movement in Poland, while Torchia (2020) highlighted how the utopian political goal of creating a community through the FC United football club is repeatedly constrained. Carr and Power (2020) explored the politics of female participation in football when that participation is policed by community members observing behaviour(s), while Ahn and Cunningham (2020) examined the politics of FIFA's Gender Initiatives. Thus, even from this brief review, we can clearly see that the myriad of connections between football and (P)politics is endless.

Structure, content and themes

A key aim of this collection is to provoke a broad, interdisciplinary and critical discussion about (P)politics and/or association football. Our book offers less of a 'country overview' than some of the existing texts, such as *Football and Politics: The Palgrave International Handbook of Football and Politics* (2018), for example, offering perspectives from locales around the world, but not claiming to be representative of an entire country. In some cases, it is bringing new case studies, in others it is interdisciplinary approaches, which, by extension, offer greater insight into broader methodological approaches. In the chapters that follow, football is analysed through a number of different perspectives, and the cultural and contextual interrogations provided illuminate new and dynamic ways of engaging with this subject matter. By inviting readers to understand and appreciate the power of football as a facet of identity (P)politics/(P)political involvement across cultural, social, national and international divides, our aim has been to make this collection international in scope.

The unique focus of this volume is identity, (P)politics and association football. It is organised into four main sections. There were multiple ways in which the material could have been organised; however, we chose a thematic approach. The first section of the book contains three chapters, which examine the politics of 'national' identity in a post-conflict scenario on a divided island. The chapters are based on data gathered from multiple sources and reflect multiple viewpoints.

Katie Liston and Matt Deighan's chapter opens the book and explores the lived realities of sport and identity politics in a divided society for Protestant/unionist/loyalist players that have represented Northern Ireland in youth/adult football. They argue that national team football plays a contrasting ideological and identity role for unionists in Northern Ireland, with the flag and anthem being identified as critical markers of a tendential unionism in the game. Crucially, the findings presented in this chapter suggest that the unintended outcome of intergroup contact in this setting is a muting of legitimate expressions of identity for one group and affirmation of the 'national' character of the other.

John Bell's chapter seeks to track how Northern Ireland's football fans have progressed from a situation where they were widely castigated for sectarian behaviour to one where they are winning awards for their behaviour. Drawing on Anthony Giddens' structuration theory, the chapter argues that while the Amalgamation of Official Northern Ireland Supporters' Clubs (AONISC) and the Irish Football Association have changed the 'rules' of what it means to be a fan within the stadium, outside this confine, sectarian fan behaviour persists, as the new 'rules' are more difficult to enforce in that setting. Ultimately, this chapter suggests UEFA and FIFA's current policy of selectively closing stadia as punishment for persistent 'offensive' fan behaviour does not in fact challenge these issues in the longer term.

Completing this trio of chapters, Sean Huddleston and Paul Breen argue that two decades after the 1998 Good Friday Agreement, Northern Irish society remains divided and is exemplified by the culture and practices that surround support for and endorsement of Ireland's two 'national' football teams. Huddleston and Breen argue that there has been little reflection on how football serves as a mirror for the 'post'-conflict divide that remains evident in Northern Irish society. Their chapter ultimately argues that unless such reflection occurs, the building of a shared society in Northern Ireland, with genuine equity of symbols, identities and political aspirations, remains some way off.

Section 2 of the book contains four chapters which focus on the political contexts and history of four countries and how football has been used to construct/reflect ideological identity in those countries through specific actions, symbols of remembrance, colonial and postcolonial aspirations and class populism.

Over the last decade, the rituals of military remembrance in British football have grown exponentially. In that context, Danny Fitzpatrick's case study of UK football explores the performance and projection of remembrance and how this impacts upon notions of collective identity. Fitzpatrick begins by theorising the relationship between football, military remembrance and British nationalism since the end of World War I, before examining the antecedents to the contemporary spectacularisation of military remembrance in football. Ultimately, this really important work asks one core question: why does football 'remember' and whose interest does this remembering serve?

Philip Dine's chapter offers an overview of Franco-Algerian relations on and off the football field since the 1920s, a decade that saw an unprecedented expansion in sporting participation and spectatorship on both sides of the Mediterranean. Dine clearly shows how football was mobilised by both coloniser and colonised in the last 50 years of France's presence in Algeria: as a focus for a distinctive settler identity; as a site of inter-ethnic contestation and often violent confrontation during the war of independence 1954–1962; and, crucially, as the most striking mechanism by which Algeria asserted its aspirations to nationhood.

In Chapter 6, Jim O'Brien argues that the political contexts and history of football in Argentina is critical to an understanding of the game's growth and development in the country. The core of his analysis in this chapter is an examination of the parallels and paradoxes between the mass movement of Peronism and the sub-cultural mores/mass populism of football. O'Brien ultimately argues that the political and class-centred cleavages at the core of Argentinian football's identity have framed an interlocking synthesis of nationhood, ethnicity and society, which continue to impact upon the game's contemporary landscape, at both the club and national levels.

Pavel Brunssen, Peter Römer and Robert Claus examine the new transnational racism that developed in Europe during the peak of the refugee crisis of 2014–2016. They argue that in order to understand contemporary right-wing politics, we must understand the triple strategy that it is pursuing: spreading their ideas, gaining representation in parliaments, and obtaining physical superiority over antifascist groups. The chapter argues that football fans played a crucial role in this process between 2014 and 2016, with right-wing Ultras and hooligans not only displaying their worldview in the stadiums but also on the streets, in the process facilitating the entrance of right-wing politicians to public spaces that otherwise would not have been available to them.

Section 3 contains two chapters, which are concerned with how the politics of language is used to reflect/enforce a particular identity. Melissa Mora Hidalgo and Giovanni Hortua Vargas, two US-based scholars, educators and fútbol fans of Latin American descent critique the persistent use of a homophobic and misogynist term by Mexican fans during national and club matches on both sides of the US-Mexico border. In this chapter, they unpack the controversial chant, drawing from an interdisciplinary combination of humanist and cultural studies fields and methods. The chapter provides key historical and cultural contexts for understanding the power of the particular word and how it is rooted in misogynist, masculinist and mythical narratives of Mexican nationalism.

Lotte Thissen and Leonie Cornips' chapter focuses on a regional derby game played in Maastricht, between MVV Maastricht and Roda JC. In this chapter, the authors focus on how regional politics of place-making and (un)belonging were played out before, during and after the match. Using sociolinguistic, anthropological and human geographical theories, their contribution to the volume addresses how language practices before and during the game produced centre and periphery dynamics (Győri Szabó, 2012).

The final section of the book consists of two chapters, which are concerned with the politics of 'grassroots' identity in football. First, Mateusz Grodecki and Radosław Kossakowski examine the mobilisation of social capital by 'grassroots' football supporters in Poland in the process of rescuing/rebuilding their football clubs. In doing so, this chapter fills an important gap in the study of football fan activism. Utilising a case study of Lechia Gdańsk, Odra Wodzisław and Hutnik

Kraków, Grodecki and Kossakowski's analysis reveals three main ways that social capital is utilised by supporters: a call to arms, appropriable social organisation and intentional social organisation.

Finally, Daniel Parnell, Danny Fitzpatrick, Anthony May and Paul Widdop examine the political economy of grassroots football. Although scholarship on football is well established, it has focused on the elite professional level; in terms of its governance and/or spectatorship and grassroots football, scholarship has largely been ignored. More recently, there has been increased interest in grassroots football; however, the paucity of academic research belies the prominent position of grassroots football in the cultural life and leisure of contemporary Britain. This chapter argues strongly that little value is placed on grassroots football, and indeed, wider grassroots sport, by the central government, which is in keeping with the wider neoliberal ideology that has achieved a global hegemonic position.

We explicitly acknowledge that this collection of essays on football and (P)politics is far from exhaustive. We are keenly aware that the 11 chapters presented here offer particular takes on very specific issues and are as varied as the authors who have written them. Even as we worked on the conception of this project and brought it to fruition, we could have included chapters that focused on very recent examples, not to mention the reams of historical cases that are worthy of examination. But a volume such as this had the potential to be limitless, and yet still incomplete. As editors, we trust that this book builds upon the work already included in this book series and offers a variety of insights from global football contexts, in turn providing scope for current and future scholars to contribute their work on football and (P)politics both to this series and to the wider academic literature.

References

Ahn, N.Y. and Cunningham, G. (2020) Standing on a Glass Cliff?: A Case Study of FIFA's Gender Initiatives. *Managing Sport and Leisure*, 25(1–2), 114–137.

Bradley, J. (2004) *Celtic Minded: Essays on Religion, Politics, Society, Identity and Football*. Glendaruel: Argyll.

Bradley, J. (2019) *Celtic Minded 4: Essays on Celtic Football Culture and Identity*. Glendaruel: Argyll.

Brownfield Stein, A. (2017) The Political Pandora's Box of Israeli Football Fans. Paper presented at the *Football, Politics and Popular Culture Conference*, University of Limerick, 24 November.

Carr, J. and Power, M. (2020) More than a Club, More than a Game: The Case of Diverse City. *Managing Sport and Leisure*, 25(1–2): 99–113.

Carr, J., Power, M. and Millar, S. (2017) More than a Game: Football, Politics and Popular Culture. *RTE Brainstorm*, 8 November. [online] available: www.rte.ie/brainstorm/2017/1106/917757-more-than-a-game-football-politics-and-popular-culture/ (accessed 14 October 2020).

Choluj, K., Gerard, S. and May, A. (2020) The Interdependence Between a Football Club and its Ultra-Fandom in Relation to 'Modern' Football: A Case Study of Legia Warsaw. *Managing Sport and Leisure*, 25(1–2), 64–79.

Cleland, J. (2014) Racism, Football Fans, and Online Message Boards: How Social Media Has Added a New Dimension to Racist Discourse in English Football. *Journal of Sport and Social Issues*, 38(5), 415–431.

Cleland, J. and Cashmore, E. (2013) Football Fans' Views of Racism in British Football. *International Review for the Sociology of Sport*, 51(1), 27–43.

Conn, D. (2020) 'Refugees Welcome': Bohemians Team Up with Amnesty for New Away Kit. *The Guardian*. 12 February. [online] available: www.theguardian.com/football/2020/feb/12/refugees-welcome-bohemian-fc-team-up-with-amnesty-for-new-away-kit (accessed 11 October 2020).

Critchley, M. (2015) Refugee Crisis: English Football Fans Say #RefugeesWelcome in Show of Solidarity. *The Independent*. 12 September. [online] available: www.independent.co.uk/sport/football/premier-league/refugee-crisis-english-football-fans-say-refugeeswelcome-show-solidarity-10498214.html (accessed 11 October 2020).

Dart, J. (2020) Palestinian Football and National Identity under Occupation. *Sport and Leisure*, 25(1–2), 21–36.

de Brito d'Andréa, C.F. (2017) Mapping Brazilian Antifa Ultras: An Overview through Facebook Pages. Paper presented at the *Football, Politics and Popular Culture Conference*, University of Limerick, November 23rd.

Doidge, M. (2013) 'The Birthplace of Italian Communism': Political Identity and Action amongst Livorno Fans. *Soccer and Society*, 14(2), 246–261.

Doidge, M. (2015) *Football Italia: Italian Football in an Age of Globalisation*. London: Bloomsbury Academic.

Doidge, M. (2018) The Role of Activism and Football in Supporting Refugees. In T.F. Carter, D. Burdsey and M. Doidge (Eds.), *Transforming Sport Knowledges, Practices, Structures* (21–35). London: Routledge.

Dunning, E., Murphy, P. and Waddington, I. (2002) Towards a Sociological Understanding of Football Hooliganism as a World Phenomenon. In E. Dunning, P. Murphy, I. Waddington and A. Astrinakis (Eds.), *Fighting Fans: Football Hooliganism as a World Phenomenon* (1–22). Dublin: University College Dublin Press.

Gehrmann, S. (1997) *Football and Regional Identity in Europe*. New Brunswick, NJ: Transaction Publishers.

Goldblatt, D. (2006) *The Ball is Round: A Global History of Soccer*. New York: Riverhead Books.

Guerriero-Davies, T. and Butler, M. (2018) *Political Football Clubs: The Right*. 13 November. [online] available: www.thefootballfaculty.com/2018/11/13/political-football-clubs-part-2-the-right/ (accessed 28 October 2020).

Guerriero-Davies, T. and Butler, M. (2019) *Political Football Clubs: The Seperatists*. 8 April. [online] available: www.thefootballfaculty.com/2019/04/08/political-football-clubs-part-iii-the-separatists/ (accessed 28 October 2020).

Győri Szabó, R. (2012) Identity and Soccer in Corsica. *Soccer & Society*, 13(1), 36–55.

Herra, E. (2018) Masculinity, Violence, and Deindividuation in Argentine Soccer Chants: The Sonic Potentials of Participatory Sounding-in-Synchrony. *Ethnomusicology*, 62(3), 470–499.

Hodges, A. (2018) *Fan Activism, Protest and Politics: Ultras in Post-Socialist Croatia*. London and New York: Routledge.

Horton, H. (2015) Football Fans Wave Banner Saying 'Refugees Not Welcome'. *The Telegraph*. 14 September. [online] available: www.telegraph.co.uk/news/worldnews/middleeast/israel/11863420/Football-fans-wave-banner-saying-Refugees-not-welcome.html (accessed 11 October 2020).

Jack, M. (2013) On the Terrace: Ritual Performance of Identity and Conflict by the Shamrock Rovers Football Club Ultras in Dublin. *Ethnomusicology Review*, 18, 1–6.

Janks, H. (2012) The Importance of Critical Literacy. *English Teaching: Practice and Critique*, 11(1), 150–163.

Kelly, J. (2016) Western Militarism and the Political Utility of Sport. In A. Bairner, J. Kelly and J.W. Lee (Eds.), *The Routledge Handbook of Sport and Politics* (277–292). London and New York: Routledge.

Kossakowski, R., Nosal, P. and Woźniak, W. (2020) *Politics, Ideology and Football Fandom The Transformation of Modern Poland*. London and New York: Routledge.

Kuper, S. (1996) *Football Against the Enemy*. London: Pheonix.

Marra, P. and Trotta, F. (2019) Sound, Music and Magic in Football Stadiums. Popular Music, 38(1), 73–89.

Mayer, T. (2011) *Football as an Arena of Arab Ethno-National Identities: The Case of Modern Israel*. Unpublished thesis (M.A.), Brandeis University. [online] available: https://bir.brandeis.edu/bitstream/handle/10192/13/Mayer_082011-1.pdf?sequence=1 (accessed 15 October 2020).

McKerrell, S. (2012) Hearing Sectarianism: Understanding Scottish Sectarianism as Song. *Critical Discourse Studies*, 9(4), 363–374.

Milekic, S. (2016) 1990 Football Riot Becomes National Myth in Croatia. *Balkan Transnational Justice*. [online] available: https://balkaninsight.com/2016/05/13/1990-football-riot-remains-croatia-s-national-myth-05-12-2016/ (accessed 14 January 2020).

Millar, S. (2016) Let the People Sing? Irish Rebel Songs, Sectarianism and Scotland's Offensive Behavior Act. *Popular Music*, 35(3), 297–319.

Power, M., Widdop, P., Parnell, D., Carr, J. and Millar, S. (2020a) Football and Politics: The Politics of Football. *Managing Sport and Leisure*, 25(1–2), 1–5.

Power, M., Widdop, P., Parnell, D., Carr, J. and Millar, S. (2020b) *Managing Sport and Leisure*, 25(1–2), 1–137.

Rojo-Labaien, E., Rodríguez Díaz, E. and Rookwood, J. (2020) *Sport, Statehood and Transition in Europe: Comparative Perspectives from Post-Soviet and Post-socialist Societies*. London and New York: Routledge.

Rookwood, J. (2020) The Politics of ConIFA: Organising and Managing International Football Events for Unrecognised Countries. *Managing Sport and Leisure*, 25(1–2), 6–20.

Sorek, T. (2002) The Islamic Soccer League in Israel: Setting Moral Boundaries by 76 Taming the Wild. *Identities: Global Studies in Culture and Power*, 9, 445–470.

Spaaij, R. (2015) Refugee Youth, Belonging and Community Sport. *Leisure Studies*, 34(3), 303–318.

Spaaij, R., De Waele, J.M., Gibril, S. and Gloriozova E. (2018) Football and Politics: Between the Local and the Global. In J.M. De Waele, S. Gibril, E. Gloriozova and R. Spaaij (Eds.), *The Palgrave International Handbook of Football and Politics* (3–17). London and New York: Palgrave Macmillan.

Stevens, S. (2016) Celtic Fans Pledge to Match Any UEFA Fine for Palestinian Flag Display and Donate Proceeds to Charity. *The Independent*. 22 August. [online] available: www.independent.co.uk/sport/football/european/celtic-fans-pledge-match-any-uefa-fine-palestine-flag-display-and-donate-proceeds-charity-a7203566.html (accessed 11 October 2020).

Taylor, M. (2006) Global Players? Football, Migration and Globalization, c. 1930–2000. *Historical Social Research*, 31(1), 7–30.

Torchia, D. (2020) Creating and Managing Community in a Community Football Club. *Managing Sport and Leisure*, 25(1–2), 79–98.

Vantine de Lara Villela, M. (2017) Industrialization, Proletariat and the Popularization of Football in Brazil: The Case of Bangu Athletic Club. Paper presented at the *Football, Politics and Popular Culture Conference*, University of Limerick, November 23rd.

Webster, J. (2017) Incestuous Love, Hermetically Sealed Hate, and the Return of the Old Firm. Paper presented at the *Football, Politics and Popular Culture Conference*, University of Limerick, 24 November.

Chapter 1

'Show respect to our anthem'

Identity politics and national team football in Northern Ireland

Katie Liston and Matt Deighan

Introduction and context

Football can unite and divide people at one and the same time, especially in divided societies. In September 2017, safety concerns were the main reason why neither national anthems nor flags were (dis)played at a (Women's) World Cup qualifying game, held in Mourneview Park, Lurgan, between Northern Ireland (NI) and the Republic of Ireland (RoI). This is the home venue of the Glenavon Football Club. A credible paramilitary (loyalist) threat was made against a club worker (and his family) were the Irish national flag – the tricolour – to be hoisted there. This resulted in the suspension of normal pre-match protocols. Six months later, underlying identity politics was again exposed, in relations between the two Irish football associations. The 'switch' is premised on the dual eligibility of those born in NI. Senior NI manager Michael O'Neill was cited as claiming that the Football Association of Ireland (FAI) 'only ever approach one type of player: Catholic' (*The Telegraph*, 10 March 2018). O'Neill also called for a gentleman's agreement that would prevent the FAI from approaching any representative NI player between the ages of 17 and 21. It is unclear if this agreement was ever reached. Other incidents too – involving domestic football north and south – have unmasked the depth and scope of identity politics involved, including national anthem protests (Figures 1.1 and 1.2). The question of precisely how football (dis)unites people is therefore a matter of debate.

Such sporting examples are not unique on the island of Ireland. The histories of modern athletics (Liston and Maguire, 2020) and football/soccer (Moore, 2015) reveal protracted identity cleavages, connected with partition. But all-island teams exist(ed) too, some 60 or so sports governed on a 32-county basis. Historically, the IFA administered football on the island (played in Dublin and Belfast mainly) before the Leinster branch separated in 1921, establishing the FAI. Consequently, footballers have represented both associations, illustrating that sporting nationalism is multifaceted and multi-layered (Cronin, 1999). At least 39 male players represented the IFA *and* FAI between 1908 and 1950, when the two associations competed separately, and an all-island team was informally constituted to play Brazil in 1973. Since the 1998 Good Friday Agreement

Figure 1.1 IFA Cup final 2018 Cliftonville FC.

Source: Courtesy of Albert Thomas.

Figure 1.2 FAI Cup final 2019 Allan Manus.

(GFA) however, 'switches' have mainly been 'southern' moves, from NI to the RoI, in the men's game especially (eg Darron Gibson, James McClean, Shane Duffy, Marc Wilson, Michael Duffy, Daniel Devine, Paul George, Liam McAlinden and Eunan O'Kane).[1]

NI manager Michael O'Neill is correct, historically speaking, if he meant to indicate that fewer players have *first* represented RoI and then declared for NI, not *vice versa*. Relations between the two associations are noticeably tense concerning this. In 2009, the IFA described it as a 'banana skin' and needed to ask why some players would rather play for the RoI. We argued previously that this required a necessary distance from the interests and values of either association and from unhelpful compressions of identity politics and sport. For the decisions of players to declare for the RoI were intimately connected with the contested context of football and of life in general in NI. The habitat of national team football plays a critical role in such decisions because intergroup contact often occurs first through the game, which likely plays a contrasting identity-affirming role for nationalists and unionists.

Here, we focus on the accounts of unionist national team players, which reveal how the fortunes of NI have become internalised as part of their habitus, and whose actions continue to reconstruct an imagined national character (Anderson, 1991). Though more work is required on the utility of the Protestant-Unionist-Loyalist (PUL) analytical unit, especially for those who are neither unionist nor loyalist, here the heuristic 'unionist' is used as an inductive tool because it was the label of choice for interviewees, even if in reality, three were much closer to loyalism.[2] This tag guided us in exploring deeply sedimented aspects of their habitus: as British and Ulster Orange men, as the established group in NI football, sharing intra-group habitus codes and fantasy shields (Elias, 2013), but with a contested sense of place and 'home' different to other British citizens.

Our two interview cohorts (unionists and nationalists) represent the post–Good Friday Agreement (GFA) generation, the first to be born into and live in relative peace. Nonetheless, they remain trapped in positions, often of mutual fear and distrust, born of the cycle of violence and negative peace, of persistent structural disadvantage, especially in urban interface areas, in which 'Northern Ireland has yet to be at peace with the idea of peace' (Brewer, 2018: 271). Football is ideologically and practically enmeshed in this complex knot. For the evidence is clear, especially in post-conflict societies, that sport might not only reflect wider social divisions but also play a role in reinforcing these. To interpret these unionists' accounts, we first need to understand unionist identities, the ways in which these are broadly reflected in/of football in NI, and the relevance of habitus and habitus codes (Maguire and Poulton, 1999) as sensitising concepts.

Unionisms in NI

Often misrepresented as a homogenous bloc, fissures within unionism have existed prior to and since the early 1920s. Six of the nine counties of the ancient Ulster province became *de facto* unionist after partition, given the total hegemony of the Stormont parliament and the exclusion of nationalists from positions of power: politically, in civic society and in other prominent occupations. These fissures were/are often revealed through sportive and non-sportive events alike – for example, unionist/loyalist protests following the 2012 decision of Belfast city council to restrict the flying of the Union Flag to 18 designated days and historical local rivalries between Irish league football clubs with strong unionist traditions (eg Bleakney and Darby, 2018; Bairner and Shirlow, 1998). While unionists are generally committed to the maintenance of the constitutional link with Britain, loyalists (those with 'harder' views [Todd, 2018]; across rural, single-identity towns and urban-interface loyalisms [Brewer, 2018], for some of whom sectarianism is acceptable) proffer a stronger ideological commitment to the political and perceived monocultural entity of NI. This sometimes means confrontation with the British government. Conventionally speaking, loyalism includes those unionists who use/advocate militancy to defend the union, drawn disproportionately from working classes and encompassing political and civic interests. Loyalism was connected with the political organisation of paramilitarism in the 1970s (McAuley, 2005). Simply stated, there are three unionist concerns (ranging from broad to narrow): *ideological* fears about the continued dilution of unionist/British identities, *moral* fears about further political concessions (eg the place of the Irish language) and *political* fears about British betrayal (eg loyalist meetings that opposed the Brexit 'Betrayal Act' [*Belfast Telegraph*, 7 November 2019]). A sense of treachery is now especially acute, given the approach taken by the current British prime minister towards the introduction of a (hard or soft) border on the island/in the Irish Sea and the implications of this for what unionists perceive to be 'our wee country.'

Of the academic work on the unionist identity continuum, two main interpretations exist. One is that unionism, in its widest varied guises and encompassing loyalism, is a form of (British) state-centred political value system (Aughey, 1989), in which identity politics *per se* is of lesser analytical importance than any real connection with the state. Though accepting this characterisation, a second view is that unionisms do carry some 'identity and national resonances' (Todd, 2018: 137), which are a key reference point for loyalty to the (British) state, but more than this, 'culture assumes greater importance in Loyalist conceptions of identity than class' (Brewer, 2013). Consequently, 'unionism and loyalism always represented traditions, repertoires and ideal types' (Todd, 2018: 2). There are those Protestants who share views with Catholic nationalists on social issues such as equal marriage or reproductive rights, and there are unionists/loyalists whose religious beliefs are less important than other cultural practices, such as bands/parades, that provide for the expression of communal identity, public space, territoriality and ethnic solidarity (Bell, 1990).

Given its global scope, association football is a powerful sport in terms of identity formation/reinforcement worldwide. One could therefore anticipate a spectrum of unionist identities in the game. Moreover, in divided societies like NI, it has been a dual agent of separation and a contentious point of ethno-national-religious contact, given its changing class (and, more slowly, gender) composition. It is a social site in which real, imaginary and embodied ideas about the 'national character' are activated and become viscerally important. In short, identity politics in football in NI trump connections with the British state, making it a complex Gordian knot (Deb, 2019).

The Gordian knot of 'our wee country'

We set out to unravel more of the hidden crevasses of ethno-national tensions in NI, in which the sense of collective identification was/is low and 'there is no ideological mortar . . . holding things together' (Gormley-Heenan and Aughey, 2017: 501). Since the GFA, incentives were removed for inter-communal conflict, but disputes over the flying of flags in particular continue to act as 'a lightning rod' for Protestant unease (Nolan, 2014: 13). Our previous work highlighted that nationalist players were caught in a double bind in international football: generating a habitus mismatch managed through a flexible sporting identity (Liston and Deighan, 2019). Protestant-Unionist rugby union and hockey players too, who represented 32-county sports that have compromised historically on flags and/or anthems, exemplified similar habitus practices. In one rugby union club in NI, the symbolic power of flags, music and sporting attire was used sparingly, and banter was a cultural tool to goad fellow club members but 'not to display genuine sectarian exclusion' (Kavanagh, 2019: 492).

Though the composition of the IFA is more mixed than ten years ago, officially it has not changed its position on the national anthem, requiring a change in their article of association, or flag. There are safety concerns among some on the IFA Council, following previous death threats, and neither of the two main political parties – Sinn Féin or the Democratic Unionist Party – supports a change to the anthem. One does not want to normalise NI and the other to negate the union. As a result, we concluded (Liston and Deighan, 2019) that the football idiom 'Our Wee Country' – which emerged out of the rebranding of the IFA in 2010/2011 – was a shield for unionists mainly, projecting an imagined charisma, protecting a state of mind and an ideological place. This begged a series of other questions: What are the experiences of unionist players in national team football? How did the fantasy shield operate for them? And how did these players respond to intergroup contact via football?

Football, habitus and imagined charisma

Historically speaking, national team football in NI was/is a tendentially unionist game as is Irish league football. Being the only major team sport to follow the contours of partition, today the IFA and FAI have demarcated imagery, symbolism and anthems. Though nationalists are more involved in the game, as players, employees and board members of the IFA, for instance, the hegemonic unionist identity dominates nonetheless, not least because sectarian attitudes are deeply embedded in club football (Wilson, 2005). This incorporates the unionist identity spectrum, including loyalism as an everyday culture and ideology, with all of its attendant ontological insecurities (McAuley, 2016).

The national character of unionists is intimately connected to football, one of the few team sports that keep alive the imagined charisma of NI.[3] So too in different ways does the broad curriculum in NI, in the segregated teaching of history (Gallagher, 2017), religion, geography and English,[4] the maintenance of old buildings (their flags and statues) and new sporting achievements that affirm NI. Most IFA league grounds are located in Protestant spaces (Bairner, 2001), including the aforementioned Glenavon FC, which reflects a unionist/loyalist social climate. Football remains highly contentious therefore and has played a critical role in the promotion of the we-image (Elias and Scotson, 2008) of NI since its formation.[5] For many years, the position of unionists as the established group (Elias and Scotson, 2008) gave them succour, but demographic, political and social changes have led to a gradual equalisation of power relations with nationalists. Indeed, for the first time, more nationalist than unionist MPs were elected in the most recent 2019 Westminster general election, and increasing support was shown for a non-aligned 'middle ground' political party, Alliance.

The resulting discrepancy between these imagined and actual positions – part of what Brewer (2015) calls a problem of expectations – has entailed a strategy on the part of many unionists that pursues a fantasy image of 'greatness,' through, we contend, the medium of football. This fantasy group image is connected with deeply rooted habitus codes of unionisms, some of which is nostalgic, but other dimensions reveal ethno-religious and class-based assertiveness/defensiveness. Examining these habitus codes also permits investigation of why contact situations in national team football in NI are not necessarily bearing positive fruit, unequivocally speaking, in terms of overcoming political, religious and cultural differences.

Research design and methods

Nine unionist players were interviewed, aged 18–25 years, part of the first post-conflict generation, who had played on national youth teams, and one as a senior international (see Table 1.1).

In most cases, they attended Protestant-controlled second-level schools, played for Protestant-associated football teams, were socialised into unionist/loyalist communities and saw themselves as British first and foremost. While each of the interviewees bore, in him, a group habitus, subtle differences existed within this group, as will be illustrated. Three acknowledged a Northern Irish identity layer, one as primary. All were passive anti-Catholics at the very least, six conforming to a secular anti-Catholic group, and some with a staunch defence of the union and attacks on republicanism (Brewer and Higgins, 1999). Data analysis was fluid. First- and second-order coding permitted the emergence of key themes informed by sensitising concepts and crosschecked for accuracy by both researchers. While

Table 1.1 Interview sample

Pseudonym	*Self-identified nationality*	*Political identity*	*Locale*	*Community*	*School*	*Club team*
Gareth	British B/ Northern Irish NI	Unionist U	Urban U	Protestant P	Integrated I	Protestant-associated P
Mark	B	U Loyalist L	Rural Single-Identity Town RSIT	P	P	P
Charles	B	U	Urban-Interface UI	P	P	P
Richard	B	U	U	P	P	P
Daniel	B	U/L	RSIT	P	P	P
Alan	B/NI	U	RSIT	P	P	I
Owen	B	U	UI	P	P	P
Michael	NI/B	U	UI	Mixed M	P	P
Simon	B	U/L	RSIT	P	P	P

the activities of the Orange Order were 'off limits,' a good rapport was established overall, based around the second author's shared experiences of football in NI in particular. As a result, original insights were generated into the operation of football as a fantasy shield, the Janus-faced ideological symbolism of the national team and the effect of segregated socialisation practices.

Findings: football as a fantasy shield

Like their nationalist counterparts, unionists were acutely aware of the role of national team football in bolstering future career prospects. Richard articulated a clear view shared by all nine: the NI team was a 'shop window.' Closely intertwined with this career exposure was a personal ambition to 'make it,' as a professional footballer: 'You know you're going to have to play against top, top players in other countries. It's only going to benefit you as a player and as a professional' (Gareth).

Yet unionists had much deeper ideological motivations that aligned with their we-image – namely, a cultural affinity with British/NI habitus codes and a sense of patriotism. All nine players cited national representation as a *primary* motivating factor that *affirmed* their national character and added succour to this. In Mark and Gareth's words: 'Playing for Northern Ireland meant a lot to me. . . . It meant a lot to my family, to my local area, to my local clubs that I played for, to my school,' and 'It's a big, big privilege to walk out with your teammates and *your country*.'

All nine regularly attended NI games from a young age, having positive experiences. Accordingly, they were already attached, ideologically and emotionally, to the venue for international home games, prior to becoming representative players themselves.

> I didn't miss a Northern Ireland game for six years. I was a season ticket holder. . . . I can still remember my seat [identifying details omitted]. . . . I don't think I am ever going to forget that. . . . I loved it.
>
> (Michael)

Windsor Park (WP) thus enhanced British/unionist imagery and symbolism for them. Reflecting on his early experiences of this site, Owen recalled that 'there used to be more Blue than Green,' and Gareth too indicated that the crowd atmosphere had changed over time. It was 'hostile. . . . There was a lot more sectarianism.' Charles acknowledged that he participated in sectarianism there, singing 'no surrender' during the national anthem 'without fully knowing why.' In fact, attending international matches at WP was akin to other cultural activities such as the Orange Order,[6] 12 July celebrations and marching bands. Charles illustrated this as follows: 'My culture would be things like the Union Jack, the lovely Union Jack . . . the 12th July, the marching parades, the Orange Order, *going to Windsor*, the Titanic and your North Coast.' WP was home, sportively speaking, and in cultural and ideological terms, an embodiment of the imagined NI.

Yet, on entering the national football system, these players had to actively fit into a culturally familiar but now communal environment, with nationalist teammates. At the outset, cliques emerged, mainly along club lines. One consequence was that groups sought out and found confirmatory ethno-religious symbols and cultural codes as a strategy of identity demarcation and, ultimately, of acceptance. For unionists, 'if they played for Cliftonville or Newhill then obviously you knew they were a Catholic or if they played for the Shankhill or Greenisland then they were probably Protestant' (Daniel). Accurate or not, such perceptions protected the purity of clubs thought to be unionist or nationalist preserves.

Additional signifiers included first names (eg William versus Seán, assumed to identify British/Ulster unionist or Irish nationalist), schooling and cultural activities. Mutual support for Glasgow Rangers FC and the NI senior side was also central to establishing a shared cultural language among interviewees.[7] Divisions soon started to emerge, and the exposure to discordant identity politics generated individual and social challenges. Next we focus on how unionist players looked, Janus-faced, to their (sporting and political) futures, as one means of dealing with such challenges, but were (inevitably) drawn to the past.

NI football as Janus-faced

Like Janus, the ancient Roman god, national team football was an important transition for unionists. Their interview accounts show some positive, still limited, changes in perceptions of nationalists (resulting from intergroup contact) and a willingness to consider the perspective of 'the other.' Cliques established initially along the lines described above did soften, and some acknowledged that they would benefit, personally, from a greater understanding of nationalist/Irish culture. Such softening did not extend to their own we- or group image, however, especially in terms of habitus codes and national character symbols. The decision of nationalist teammates to bow their heads during the national (and royal) anthem – God Save the Queen – as a form of protest was deemed as especially disrespectful by all nine.

Michael's views reveal an 'othering' of nationalists through his pronoun use: 'If you're proud enough to stick on the jersey then just stand there and show respect to *our* anthem.' The anthem was a particularly contentious habitus code, and those who objected to it were positioned as lacking patriotism towards NI, not dissimilar to responses to Kaepernick's taking-the-knee-protest in the US (McDonald, 2020). But subtleties existed.

Two of the nine players were open to changing the anthem to be more inclusive. However, they warned that the majority of supporters would not receive this warmly. The remaining seven saw no need to change it:

> I don't see any reason why it needs to be changed. It's been part of a load of people's identity for *years upon years upon years* and to take that away from people probably wouldn't be the wisest thing to do.
>
> (Simon, emphasis added)

Internal conflict centred on these habitus codes of flag and anthem and players' responses to the 'banana skin' of dual eligibility also revealed slim differences. Four regarded nationalists who 'go south' as misusing the system. Though national teams are already known as flags of convenience to display talents on an international stage (Maguire and Stead, 1996), our previous interviews (Liston and Deighan, 2019) also show that cultural factors and identity politics had a role in nationalist players going 'down south,' perhaps not fully understood by unionist interviewees here:

> It does seem like they're abusing that system, especially if they're born in Northern Ireland, and they've gone up through the Northern Irish system, through years and years and years . . . using the facilities, the coaching, that sort of thing, and then *all of a sudden* declaring themselves Irish, and playing for down south.
>
> (Charles, emphasis added)

Although not necessarily agreeing with the switch, three had a more pragmatic sportive perspective. Here, broader awareness of the competitive labour market of professional football was also evident (Roderick, 2006). One said:

> It's a shame that they are developed here and decide to go elsewhere but you can look at the other side with players like Oliver Norwood who is an English guy who maybe went through the English youth system and has been developed there. He's now playing for Northern Ireland, so you can look at it both ways.
>
> (Alan)

The presence of English-born players within the NI national team system magnified further the contested sense of place and 'home.' Three of the four, who saw nationalists as abusing the talent system, felt the same about English-born players:

> To be honest I don't agree with it (the presence of English players) at all. . . . They are not good enough for England so they come and use Northern Ireland as a stepping stone to further their club career.
>
> (Mark)

Such players were seen as waving, if not abusing, flags of convenience.

Yet a third perspective emerged that showed some appreciation of the habitus mismatch for nationalists who 'go south' and their subsequent treatment, best summed up by Owen. In his words:

> It's a shame because you are missing out on good players that you would like to see playing for Northern Ireland. But obviously it's difficult because some of them have grown up in difficult areas where it wouldn't be acceptable to play for Northern Ireland so they could get abused for it. It's annoying to miss out on them but it doesn't irritate me as much as it would other people.

Showing greater reflexivity than others, Owen added that a 'lot of people [meaning PULs] think because they are going to play for the Republic *it gives them a chance to be sectarian towards them*' (emphasis added). Although sectarianism was previously directed at nationalist players at WP, two interviewees now accepted that 'there is no reason at all why Catholics cannot play for Northern Ireland' (Richard). There was a limit to this, however, because the national team still represented a unionist desire to maintain cultural and constitutional links with Britain. Any attempts to penetrate this fantasy shield – that is, bowing of the head during the national anthem or suggestions of a compromised flag or anthem, as in rugby union, hockey or the Commonwealth Games, resulted in a peremptory dismissal of 'the other' who, unwilling to accept the status quo, simply did not belong to 'our wee country.' These affective elements affirmed centripetal notions of a British NI in the face of centrifugal forces of nationalism, as did segregated socialisation and cultural practices.

'As you were': segregated socialisation

Cultural differences were manifested mainly along ethno-religious lines because 'ethnicity is the invoking of culture in claims about identity' (Nic Craith 2003: 3). Like many in NI, inter-generational socialisation occurred for interviewees in segregated communities.

> It's just the way I have been brought up. I've always been taught the British way . . . was brought up through a Protestant school, live in a Protestant area, go to a Protestant church.
>
> (Simon)

All nine players experienced this from a young age, hailing from communities infused with British-oriented symbols – for example, the Union Flag on kerbstones, lampposts and walls, much more prominent than Ulster or NI flags. Consequently, these players felt a stronger cultural affinity to the union. Alan highlighted some awareness of this: 'It's probably because I have grown up with the Union Jack flag flying around my area that I would identify myself more so with the Union Jack than the Northern Irish flag or the Tricolour.'

Families also played a significant role in the early inculcation of a British-oriented national habitus. Each interviewee confirmed that a significant male family member (eg father/uncle/grandfather) encouraged them to take part in British/unionist cultural activities such as playing/marching bands, 12 July activities, the Boys Brigade, the Orange Order and/or playing for and/or supporting football clubs with a known traditional British/unionist ethos (eg Glasgow Rangers, Linfield or Crusaders FC).

The segregated schooling system also moulded this British national character by exclusively promoting some sports. This led to a paradoxical situation for two interviewees who had represented a 32-county Ireland in another sport. Though one (anonymous) remarked that his school 'made such a big deal about playing for Ireland,' neither acknowledged a sense of 'Irishness,' both describing themselves as 'proud British citizens,' thereby separating sportive from civic nationalism and nationality. These two emphasised that a 32-county governance model could not be replicated in football. As one explained: 'Football is . . . a more heated game and the fans, there's more tension and it's not as friendly as them other sports (such as cricket and rugby).' Such was the socio-economic patterns attached to ethno-religious fuelled tension in the game.

For all but Gareth, who attended an integrated school, football was a point of first contact with nationalists. One clear example of the distillation of this intra-group socialisation was Michael's first insight at 13 years old into life in a divided society, via football. As he put it:

> I never understood it. I was a bit blinded by the whole thing. I couldn't really understand it. . . . So I was naive and didn't know the whole ins and outs of the conflict. It wasn't until I started to get into my teens that I sort of started to see the divisions.
>
> *Interviewer: Where did you see it?*
> Michael: Suppose at Crusaders vs Cliftonville was the first time that I saw it.
>
> *Interviewer: Where you watching or playing?*
>
> Michael: Watching. It was when I first started going to Crusaders matches seeing these two sets of fans trying to kill each other. I was sort of thinking 'what is going on here'? I have memories as a young boy standing in the terrace where there was this old metal cage fence in the middle of stand holding the two sets of fans away from each other. So this fence is holding them back but they're still spitting on each other and giving abuse about people who have died.

This first contact manifested itself further on the playing pitches, competing against nationalists.

> When you get told on a Thursday that you're going to be playing the likes of Sunnyside, or Cliftonville, you know, everyone kind of perks up a bit, because they're the Catholic teams, and we're a Protestant team. . . . It's a Protestant versus Catholic thing.
>
> (Charles)

Joining a unionist-oriented football club was therefore part of the process of inculcating and evoking we- and they-images. Football had taken on added symbolic and cultural significance from a young age. It was already a fantasy shield of choice for unionists, only enhanced/deepened through national team representation.

Conclusion

Three main themes emerged from the interviews conducted here. These not only affirm the findings of previous work (Liston and Deighan, 2019) but they point to the challenges of making identity politics less salient in sport in post-conflict societies, a point affirmed since in other work published after our interviews (e.g., Mitchell, Somerville, Hargie and Simms, 2020). First, the socialisation of interviewees (family, education, religion and community life) was explicitly unionist in orientation. Second, the dream of a future professional football career was the closest they came to sharing cultural interests with 'the other' and *vice versa*. A third and critical finding was that national football was Janus-faced: playing a contrasting ideological and identity role. For unionists, NI representation was the clearest articulation of their identities, and WP (now the *National* Stadium) was equally, if not for some, more ideologically and culturally important than other activities. Prominent by its absence was any (changing) philosophy around the tendential hegemony of unionism in the game and, to a lesser degree, anti-Catholicism, exhibited, for instance, through 'no surrender' during the anthem. For pragmatic career reasons, unionists acknowledged the benefits of 'mixed football,' but crucially, the national team provided a fantasy shield for them: projecting 'their' imagined national character and preserving important habitus codes (anthem and flag). This also reflected contemporary concerns regarding the place of NI within (a potentially fragmenting) United Kingdom and the impetus given towards Irish unity (real and imagined) by the outworkings of Brexit. Since these interviews were completed, a withdrawal date was agreed, a new Conservative leader/British prime minister was elected, a power-sharing Stormont executive was restored and a global COVID19 pandemic was declared. In March 2021 a group which includes representatives of loyalist paramilitaries withdrew support for the Good Friday Agreement. Still, a number of other questions arise from this work.

Though some commentators see a growing support for middle-ground politics as indicative of positive change in NI, the evidence here suggests that unionists show continued opposition to compromise, especially when faced with the prospect of a united Ireland or if concessions would further dilute the real or perceived jurisdiction of NI within the UK. When invited to consider the impact of prior socialisation on their footballing experiences, only one of our interviewees (Gareth) demonstrated a pronounced capacity for self-reflexivity and relative detachment; others, much less so and by degrees. By extension, if people do not comprehend their own identities and socialisation processes very clearly, it would seem that the chances of having a clear grasp of the identities of other (minority/ outsider) groups are rather reduced.

Today, contact between ethno-religious groups in national team football results in an overall reinforcement rather than dissolution of differences. This contrasts somewhat with the incremental steps taken by the IFA, through its Football for All (good relations) work, the decision by all Home Nations on the voluntary wearing of armbands on Armistice Day owing to tensions around the Earl Haig poppy symbol (eg Kelly, 2012), and the actions of some NI supporter groups to shift the public football narrative in a more positive direction. Yet the precise workings of the national team as a fantasy shield for unionist supporters warrants further examination, especially in terms of any changing we-images and we-ideals. The collective evidence generated by our two rounds of interviews suggests that *male* unionist players avoid what are perceived to be potentially divisive issues in their interactions with nationalist teammates. In fact, religious belief was for some unionist interviewees a 'no-go area' as were Orange Order activities. This reflects a more deep-seated anti-Catholicism (Brewer and Higgins, 1999: 252), involving mainly cultural dimensions here, which defines group boundaries and 'helps to create and rationalise social closure.'

In evaluations of shared education in NI (eg Hughes and Loader, 2015), feelings of awkwardness and (passive and active) avoidance were shown to exist about addressing differences, and that undermined its potential effectiveness. More questions might therefore be asked about the entrenchment of avoidance norms in football in NI, particularly around contentious habitus codes such as the flag and anthem, and about the actions of national team coaches who, in seeking to manage the 'problem,' potentially inflame differences – for example, by encouraging/constraining players to learn/mouth the anthem or directions not to drop heads during it. Further insights into the operation of the different modes of commonsense reasoning that might sustain anti-Catholicism in football (such as distortion, deletion, distance and denial) are also required, given that talk about Catholicism among Protestant players is talk about identity in NI and *vice versa*.

Sportive and legal rights remain closely intertwined too, as the ongoing DeSouza case demonstrates for citizenship. Though the GFA recognises the birth right of people in NI to identify and be accepted as Irish or British, or both, the British Home Office's position, flowing from the British National Act 1981 and currently upheld by the Upper Tribunal in October 2019, is different. For the

Home Office, the right to identify does not mean a right to choose citizenship. With citizenship come questions of national team nomenclature, sporting jurisdiction and eligibility that have long been imposed by British government and sports officials since the 1930s (Liston and Maguire, 2020).

Finally, the overall outcome appears to be that commonsense notions about Catholics and Protestants are given a social reality in national team football, especially when more sensitive – and arguably the most critical – issues are avoided, wilfully or otherwise. This is partly reflective of a lack of wider political consensus, including the failure of the Commission on Flags, Identity, Culture and Tradition (established in June 2016) to deliver findings, at a cost of almost £750,000. Their brief was perhaps 'too big,' having taken on not only flags and murals but also language, identity, media and sports emblems (McCormack, 2019). Yet the IFA also bears responsibility to its' youth and adult national team players, male and female, even if the flag and anthem might be perceived as inimical to institutional/organisational harmony. The unintended outcome of the status quo is a muting of legitimate expressions of identity, a limited development of the skills associated with understanding and respecting difference, but also a narrowing of the scope to deal with post-conflict tensions and the narratives of those that might propagate it. Some may actively resist any change to the status quo – whatever that might be – and others are likely to seek to depoliticise it, instead continuing to promote the myth that football is above politics. If the 1998 GFA is more a liberal-inspired elastic bandage over deep-seated wounds than a permanent multi-level suture (Vaughan-Williams, 2006), then it is difficult to see how a new NI in footballing terms breaks down sedimented habitus codes (see also Tonge and Gomez, 2015). For, as apartheid has shown, it is impossible to have normal sport within an abnormal society.

Notes

1 Besides Alex Bruce, Patrick and Shane McEleney, Johnny Gorman, Gerard Doherty and Tony Kane have played for *both* Irish football associations at youth level. Declan Rice, former Irish underage player, who also played senior friendlies for RoI, made his senior debut for England in a UEFA 2020 qualification game in March 2019. Evelyn Carnegie, a Catholic from Newry, represented the RoI in the 1990s while Laura 'Shaka' Hislop, a Protestant from Shankill Road, Belfast, represented the same team from 2003 to 2009. Christine Drain represented both NI and RoI in the women's code.

2 These three displayed the clearest understanding between unionism and loyalism. They may have used the former as a label because of the negative connotations between loyalism and paramilitarism/crime.

3 There is also netball, played by women, whose success does not ignite the national character in the same way, and the Commonwealth Games.

4 Examples of such autonomy include: the Norman invasion from an English/British perspective and the reign of Henry VIII over Great Britain (but much less so, Ireland), the Reformation over the Gospel, the geography of the British Isles, and Shakespeare over Seamus Heaney.

5 Other sports that fulfilled this function included track and field athletics, which, historically speaking, became directly embroiled in questions of identity, recognition and jurisdiction following partition (see Liston and Maguire, 2020). Prominent unionist

politicians intervened directly with the British Olympic and Amateur Athletic Associations in the late 1920s and early 1930s on behalf of a nascent NI Amateur Athletics Federation to ensure that the six-county jurisidiction was legitimated.

6 The Orange Order or Loyal Orange Institution is a mainly cultural organisation dedicated to furthering the aims of Protestantism and maintaining a British connection.

7 As one public example of this, Jordan Jones, former NI Under-19 player, signed a pre-contract agreement with Glasgow Rangers FC on 5 January 2019, tweeting that it was a 'dream come true' and an 'unbelievably proud day for me and my family.' National women's player Demi Vance was also described in a club announcement as being 'a Rangers fan all her life' (https://rangers.co.uk/news/women/rangers-sign-demi-vance/).

References

Anderson, B. (1991) *Imagined Communities: Reflections on the Origin and Spread of Nationalism*, 2nd edition. London: Verso.

Aughey, A. (1989) *Under Siege: Ulster Unionism and the Anglo-Irish Agreement*. London: Hurst & Co.

Bairner, A. (2001) *Sport, Nationalism and Globalization: European and North American Perspectives*. Albany: State University of New York Press.

Bairner, A. and Shirlow, P. (1998) 'Loyalism, Linfield and the Territorial Politics of Soccer Fandom in Northern Ireland', *Space and Polity*. 2 (2): 163–177.

Bell, D. (1990) *Acts of Union: Youth Culture and Sectarianism in Northern Ireland*. London: Palgrave Macmillan.

Bleakney, J. and Darby, P. (2018) 'The Pride of East Belfast: Glentoran Football Club and the (re)Production of Ulster Unionist Identities in Northern Ireland', *International Review for the Sociology of Sport*. 53 (8): 975–996.

Brewer, J. (2013) 'Culture, Class and Protestantism in Urban Belfast', *Discover Society*. Issue 2 November 2013, available at https://discoversociety.org/2013/11/05/culture-class-and-protestantism-in-urban-belfast-2/

Brewer, J. (2015) 'Peace Processes', in Wright, J. (ed.) *International Encyclopedia of the Social and Behavioral Sciences*, 2nd edition. Oxford: Elsevier, pp. 648–653.

Brewer, J. (2018) 'The Sociology of the Northern Irish Peace Process', in Armstrong, C., Herbert, D. and Mustad, J. E. (eds.) *The Legacy of the Good Friday Agreement: Northern Irish Politics, Culture and Art after 1998*. London: Palgrave Macmillan, pp. 271–289.

Brewer, J. and Higgins, G. (1999) 'Understanding Anti-Catholicism in Northern Ireland', *Sociology*. 33 (2): 235–255.

Cronin, M. (1999) *Sport and Nationalism in Ireland: Gaelic Games, Soccer and Irish Identity since 1884*. Dublin: Four Courts Press.

Deb, A. (2019) 'Identity: Northern Ireland's Gordian Knot', *UK. Const. L. Blog*. 17 October, available at https://ukconstitutionallaw.org/2019/10/17/anurag-deb-identity-northern-irelands-gordian-knot/

Elias, N. (2013) *Studies on the Germans: Power Struggles and the Development of Habitus in the Nineteenth and Twentieth Centuries*. Collected Works of Norbert Elias Vol. 11. Dublin: UCD Press.

Elias, N. and Scotson, J. (2008) *The Established and the Outsiders*. Collected Works of Norbert Elias Vol. 4. Dublin: UCD Press.

Gallagher, A. (2017) 'Addressing Conflict and Tolerance through the Curriculum', in Bellino, M. and Williams, J. (eds.) *(Re)Constructing Memory: School Textbooks, Identity, and the Pedagogies and Politics of Imagining Community: Vol III. (Re)Constructing Memory: Education, Identity, and Conflict*. Netherlands: Sense Publishers, pp. 191–207.

Gormley-Heenan, C. and Aughey, A. (2017) 'Northern Ireland and Brexit: Three Effects on "the Border in the Mind"', *The British Journal of Politics and International Relations*. 19 (3): 497–511.

Hughes, J. and Loader, R. (2015) '"Plugging the Gap": Shared Education and the Promotion of Community Relations through Schools in Northern Ireland', *British Educational Research Journal*. 41 (6): 1125–1142. DOI:10.1002/berj.3206

Kavanagh, T. (2019) '"It'd Just Be Banter": Sectarianism in a Northern Irish Rugby Club', *Cultural Studies ↔ Cultural Methodologies*. 20 (5): 485–495. DOI:10.1177/1532708619886330.

Kelly, J. (2012) 'Popular Culture, Sport and the "Hero"-ification of British Militarism', *Sociology*. 47 (4): 722–738.

Liston, K. and Deighan, M. (2019) 'Whose "Wee Country"?: Identity Politics and Sport in Northern Ireland'. *Identities*. 26 (2): 203–221. DOI:10.1080/1070289X.2017.1392103

Liston, K. and Maguire, J. (2020) 'The "Great Game" and Sport: Identity, Contestation and Irish-British Relations in the Olympic Movement', *Journal of War & Culture Studies*. Online First. DOI:10.1080/17526272.2020.1864873

Maguire, J. and Poulton, E. (1999) 'European Identity Politics in Euro 96: Invented Traditions and National Habitus Codes', *International Review for the Sociology of Sport*. 34 (1): 17–29.

Maguire, J. and Stead, D. (1996) 'Far Pavilions? Cricket Migrants, Foreign Sojourns and Contested Identities', *International Review for the Sociology of Sport*. 31 (1): 1–23.

McAuley, J. (2005) 'Whither New Loyalism? Changing Loyalist Politics after the Belfast Agreement', *Irish Political Studies*. 20 (3): 323–340.

McAuley, J. (2016) *Very British Rebels? The Culture and Politics of Ulster Loyalism*. London: Bloomsbury.

McCormack, J. (2019) 'Dr Dominic Bryan: NI Flags Commission's Brief "too big"', 27 June, available at www.bbc.co.uk/news/uk-northern-ireland-48786758

McDonald, M. (2020) 'Once More, With Feeling: Sport, National Anthems, and the Collective Power of Affect', *Sociology of Sport Journal*. 37 (1): 1–11.

Mitchell, D., Somerville, I., Hargie, O. and Simms, V. (2020) 'Can Sport Build Peace After Conflict? Public Attitudes in Transitional Northern Ireland', *Journal of Sport and Social Issues*. Online First. DOI. ORG/10/1177/0193723520958346.

Moore, C. (2015) *The Irish Soccer Split*. Cork: Cork University Press.

Nic Craith, M. (2003) *Culture and Identity Politics in Northern Ireland*. London: Palgrave Macmillan.

Nolan, P. (2014) *Northern Ireland Peace Monitoring Report No.3*. Belfast: Community Relations Council. Available at https://cain.ulster.ac.uk/events/peace/docs/nipmr_2014-03_full.pdf

Roderick, M. (2006) 'A Very Precarious Profession: Uncertainty in the Working Lives of Professional Footballers', *Work, Employment and Society*. 20 (2): 245–265.

The Telegraph (2018, March 10) 'Martin O'Neill Disappointed at Suggestions Republic of Ireland Target Catholic Players from the North'.

Todd, J. (2018) 'Unionism and the Paradoxes of Identity Change', *Irish Political Studies*. 33 (1): 136–143.

Tonge, J. and Gomez, R. (2015) 'Shared Identity and the End of Conflict? How Far Has a Common Sense of "Northern Irishness" Replaced British or Irish Allegiances since the 1998 Good Friday Agreement?', *Irish Political Studies*. 30 (2): 276–298.

Vaughan-Williams, N. (2006) 'Towards a Problematisation of the Problematisations that Reduce Northern Ireland to a "Problem"', *Critical Review of International Social and Political Philosophy*. 9 (4): 513–526.

Wilson, R. (2005) *Football for All: A Baseline Study*. In association with Irish Football Association. Belfast: Democratic Dialogue http://cain.ulst.ac.uk/issues/sport/docs/wilson1205.pdf

Chapter 2

From 'Billy Boys' to 'Ulster Boys'?

Sectarianism, Northern Ireland supporters and the emergence of the 'Green and White Army'

John Bell and Paul Bell

Introduction

To date, the literature on sport in Northern Irish society has tended to discuss its divisive nature, with a particular focus on the Northern Ireland international football team as a Durkheimian 'totem' of Ulster Protestantism, which is most visibly manifest in the sectarian behaviour of a section of supporters during matches. Yet, as the chapter will shortly outline, this body of work tends not to have kept up to date with developments in the fan culture over the past 15 years, which have included Northern Ireland supporters being awarded the 'Brussels International Award' by UEFA in 2006 for their efforts to challenge sectarianism at matches (UEFA, 2009) and the awarding of the *Grand Vermeil* medal to supporters of both Northern Ireland and the Republic of Ireland for their behaviour during the EURO 2016 tournament in France (BBC, 2016).

This chapter aims to take into account the rather Kantian concern of Michel Foucault that we need a 'reflective relation to the present' (Faubion, 1994, p. 313). How did Northern Ireland football fans progress from being widely castigated through the arts and in the media to winning awards for their behaviour? How has the current *doxa* (Bourdieu, 1977), that Northern Ireland fans are a 'peaceful' and 'fun-loving' bunch been established?[1] This chapter seeks to explore these questions by drawing upon interview data from 25 Northern Ireland supporters and Irish Football Association (IFA) staff in relation to the joint fan/IFA *Football for All* initiative to challenge sectarianism at Northern Ireland football matches.

Drawing upon the structuration theory of Anthony Giddens, the chapter argues that the Amalgamation of Official Northern Ireland Supporters' Clubs (AONISC) and the IFA have altered the allocative and authoritative resources and 'rules' of what it means to be a fan within the confines of the stadium itself. Yet, outside the stadium, issues still exist with regards to sectarian fan behaviour where the new 'rules' on what it means to be a supporter are more difficult to enforce. This research suggests that greater attention needs to be paid to internal dynamics within supporter groups. Fan activism can actively challenge sectarian behaviour at matches within stadia, given the means of social control over a designated group of supporters within a delineated geographical space. In line with Giddens, and contra to key tenets of Foucault's *oeuvre*, surveillance is not always constraining, but can be enabling, particularly in terms of challenging individuals engaging in inappropriate behaviour. This chapter suggests that the current policy of UEFA and FIFA to close parts of stadia if 'offensive' fan behaviour occurs does not challenge these issues in the longer term, nor does such a policy empower the majority of supporters who do not behave in this way (see also Millar, 2016).

Irish football in context

The popular Marie Jones play *A Night in November* is representative of how the media has historically portrayed Northern Ireland supporters and is reflective of earlier academic work, which developed this focus on sectarianism in an attempt to explain fan behaviour within the context of the ethno-national divide and political violence between Ulster Protestants and Irish Catholics between the late 1960s and the Good Friday Peace Agreement of 1998 (Sugden and Bairner, 1993, 1994; Sugden and Harvie, 1995; Bairner, 1997, 1999).

The main protagonists during the three decades of violence were the British state and pro-state Protestant paramilitaries, the Ulster Defence Association (UDA) and the Ulster Volunteer Force (UVF), who wanted Northern Ireland to remain part of the United Kingdom, and the Irish Republican Army (IRA), which was the largest republican paramilitary group conducting a guerrilla warfare campaign for a 32 county all-Ireland state. During this conflict, often euphemistically referred to as the 'Troubles,' almost 4,000 people were killed and more than 40,000 injured (McKittrick et al., 1999).

The sectarian behaviour of a section of Northern Ireland supporters has been linked to the 'siege mentality' within 'Ulster loyalism,' which is reported to have been exacerbated during this tumultuous period of violence (Aughey, 1989). Thus, working-class Protestant males took to the football terraces from the mid-1980s onwards to voice their frustrations over the loss of the local unionist-dominated government in Belfast in 1972; the 'sell-out' of the Anglo-Irish Agreement in 1985; the Downing Street Declaration of 1993 and the wider processes of deindustrialisation, job losses and their increasing detachment from political unionism (Sugden and Bairner, 1993; Bairner, 1997). The highest-profile incident in terms of sectarian fan behaviour came in 2001 with the treatment of Celtic FC player Neil Lennon, who was booed by a section of the home crowd (his own fans) every time he touched the ball in a match against Norway (Reid, 2008). For 'hard-line' Ulster loyalist supporters of the Northern Ireland team, by signing for Celtic, a club with distinct Irish roots, he was perceived to be a 'proxy warrior' for Irish republicanism (Hoberman, 1984, p. 6; Sugden and Bairner, 1993). In August 2002, Lennon retired from international football following a death threat he received, allegedly from the Loyalist Volunteer Force (LVF) (Bairner, 2003).

Using Jennifer Todd's (1987) typology, Bairner (2005) argues that the identity most clearly expressed at Northern Ireland football matches is an 'Ulster Loyalist' as opposed to a more 'moderate' 'Ulster British' one. In this context, the literature refers to Northern Ireland fans wearing the colours of red, white and blue to symbolise their political attachment to the union with Great Britain (Shirlow, 2005), while the regular singing of songs with anti-Catholic sentiments such as the 'Billy Boys' led to a 'sectarian atmosphere' at Windsor Park, which alienated the vast majority of Catholics and even 'moderate' Protestants from attending matches (Fulton, 2005, p. 149; see also Millar, 2015).[2]

Yet there are several limitations underpinning the literature. The work is dated and has tended to overlook the development of the *Football for All* (FFA) campaign from the year 2000 onwards (which gained impetus after the treatment of Neil Lennon), which was a joint fan/IFA initiative to try and promote a more 'family-friendly atmosphere' at matches and challenge sectarianism in the stadium. This failure to keep pace with developments in the dynamics of football fandom in Northern Ireland is most likely related to a more significant limitation of the work to date – that it is based on little or no empirical data. While much of the work asserts generally accepted truisms (that Northern Ireland fans tend to be drawn from the pro-Union and 'Protestant' community), as Oscar Wilde (1891, p. 3) wrote, 'Even things that are true can be proved.' Although there has been research conducted with northern Catholic footballers with regards to the 'eligibility' issue (Hassan et al., 2009; Liston and Deighan, 2018; McGee and Bairner, 2010; Murray and Hassan, 2017), there is a lack of empirical data on Northern Ireland supporters themselves (see Bell et al., 2020). This lack of empirical work on Northern Ireland football fans was one of the reasons for the development of the lead author's doctoral thesis, which aimed to investigate the culture of Northern Irish international football fandom (Bell, 2017).

Methodology

The chosen methodology for the research included semi-structured interviews with fans themselves (21 supporters) and IFA staff (4). Interviews were conducted between January and February 2016 in the aftermath of Northern Ireland's qualification for the EURO 2016 tournament in France. A purposive selection strategy was selected to guide the recruitment of interviewees (Denzin and Lincoln, 2005). While most supporters were from male (19) and Protestant backgrounds (18) (which reflects the dominance of Protestant males among the fanbase of the team, see Bairner, 1997), to achieve maximum variation, the sample also included Catholic fans (3), female fans (2), and a range of ages (between 18 and 67 years). The sample also included those who were not members of supporters' clubs (12) as well as members of supporters' clubs (9) and those who had been involved in the *Football for All* initiative (5) as well as those who had no involvement (16).

The website of the IFA provided online information on supporters' clubs based in Northern Ireland. Contact was made with ten clubs who were asked if a member would be interested in participating in the research. However, a combination of 'snowball' and 'opportunistic' sampling was used to access those fans who were not members of supporters' clubs, as they are typically more difficult to access (Denzin and Lincoln, 2005). An 'interview schedule' was developed, which asked fans to consider their historical experiences of supporting Northern Ireland; why they were supporters of the team; their thoughts on symbolic issues such as flags, emblems and anthems; and finally, their knowledge and experience of the *Football for All* campaign.

All interviews were digitally recorded with the prior informed and written consent of the interviewees. All names used in this chapter are pseudonyms to protect the anonymity of interviewees. NVivo 10 was utilised to input, code and analyse the data. However, despite attempts to improve the validity of the data, all material from interviews is co-constructed through dialogue between participant and researcher (Rubin and Rubin, 2005). Case studies such as this are also context dependent, which reduces their transferability to other contexts (Yin, 2009). However, there are similarities in football fandom across national boundaries, which suggest that the findings of this chapter are relevant for football in other countries, particularly within the current policy context of both UEFA and FIFA closing stadia in the event of 'offensive' fan behaviour. This is particularly the case in Scotland, given the close historic links with Northern Ireland and similar challenges facing the football authorities there with regards to fan practices that draw upon musical or cultural references associated with particular ethno-national identities (see Millar, 2015, 2016). The introduction and eventual overturning of the 'Offensive Behaviour at Football' Act in Scotland also indicates that there can be difficulties implementing policy responses to fan behaviour that is deemed 'offensive' (Waiton, 2018).

Research findings

A song for 'Ireland' or 'Ulster'?

Fan recollections of attending Northern Ireland matches have, historically, reflected the dominant trend within the literature to suggest that prior to the violence of the 'Troubles,' the support base of the Northern Ireland team was more mixed in terms of attracting both Protestants and Catholics (Hassan, 2002). Several fans suggested that this was due to a wider recognition among the fanbase of an 'Irish' dimension to their identity. Paul recalled attending matches in the late 1960s when *'in those days you used to sing "Ireland" and all. . . . It wasn't "Northern Ireland". It was "Ireland, Ireland," and "we'll support you ever more"'* while Gareth noted that the '[match] programmes up to about the '70s *would have said Ireland on it.'*

Tony, who first watched Northern Ireland lose 4–0 to Scotland at a packed Windsor Park in 1959, noted that he would have attended matches with Catholic friends and, even into the early and mid-1970s, he reflected that '. . . *I would have went in mixed company to international football. A group of us* [Protestants and

Catholics] *would have went*.' Even if we accept at face value that sectarianism from the terraces was for all intents and purposes less likely to be openly articulated before the violence of the 'Troubles,' this should not lead us to ignore that on various occasions the 'stocks of knowledge' (Schutz, 1967) or 'cultural capital' (Bourdieu, 1977) associated with being a Northern Ireland fan drew upon wider unionist cultural reference points. Indeed, Paul, who attended the World Cup in Spain in 1982 and was there the night Northern Ireland defeated the hosts 1–0 in Valencia, remembered Northern Ireland fans singing '*It's a boy, it's a boy*' at the match in honour of Prince William, who had been born four days before the game.

That said, undoubtedly the violence of the 'Troubles' created an atmosphere wherein political identities and loyalties became more significant in the context of displays by supporters at matches. Fans noted that as the 'Troubles' progressed throughout the 1970s and 1980s, the attitudes of a section of fans changed, first with regards to what was deemed to be acceptable to wear to matches and second to what songs were sung from the terraces. Several fans recalled elements within the fanbase in the early days of the 'Troubles' rejecting the team colours of green and white. George, who would later become a key driver of the FFA campaign, recalled being 'beaten up' in 1981 alongside a Catholic friend and fellow fan for wearing a green-and-white scarf in a pub after a Northern Ireland match. He recalled, '*. . . that was still, em, still in the middle of the Troubles and you didn't wear green and white. . . . Cos, they were Catholic colours, you know?*' Nor was George alone in this experience:

> *I remember actually being at a match and wearing a green rosette and having a green and white scarf and having it ripped off me. . . . As a kid, I was only about 14/15. Cos in those days they all wore red, white and blue scarves like. There was very little green and white.*
>
> (Paul)

> *That's right. You used to wear Linfield scarves, or Glentoran scarves or Crusaders scarves. They would have wore* [sic] *anything bar green and white.*
>
> (Jamie)

Jamie's point about the emerging trend within a section of the Northern Ireland fanbase between the 1970s and 1990s of wearing red, white and blue colours associated with Ulster unionism and loyalism was a common one discussed at length by many fans, a trend that several fans themselves admitted taking part in. Steve commented, '*When I first came I probably went along with the flow, you know what I mean? You were going to the match and you would tend to wear a Linfield scarf.*' Similarly, Chris reflected upon the apparent predominance of the red, white and blue colours on the terraces as the 'Troubles' progressed:

> *I mean I remember going to Windsor, and it was, it was all red, white and blue. But that's what it was. That's who you were. It was . . . but back then,* [pause],

with the Troubles and all on, we didn't know any different. We, you know, you just weren't aware. You knew, you were young like, you knew there was another side [Catholics]. *You didn't know some of the other side as such were playing in your team either, you know?*

(Chris)

Within this context, some fans reflected upon taking part in singing sectarian songs at matches:

Well, I remember you know, ironically I remember being at Windsor Park and singing 'The Sash' and the 'Billy's'. At that time those songs – because you are talking about the height of the Troubles, you know, [19]*70s. . . . And yet you, when you went, we were singing 'We're up to our necks in fenian blood' and flipping Pat Jennings is standing there, you know? I actually go on* [the] *Our Wee Country website and I posted a thing saying 'Look, I think it's time that we look at this here'. Because how can you talk about singing 'Up to your necks in fenian blood' whenever you have Catholic players in your starting eleven, in your team like?*

(Paul)

I know, and he's standing there in front of you and he's won 120 odd caps for Northern Ireland . . .

(Jamie)

Yeah. And yet, as a kid – it just seemed to be the thing, you know?

(Paul)

Michael, one of three Catholic Northern Ireland fans interviewed, reflected upon attending matches in the 1990s:

. . . but the atmosphere then – I suppose you don't quite pick up on it for another couple of years – I remember one of the flags they were selling outside the ground at one of the first games I was at had 'Proud to be a Prod' written on it. Em, and it was Northern Ireland football, and I couldn't understand why my dad wouldn't get me one of the football flags at that time. And I suppose even, it was basically, we had two chants then – it was the 'Billy Boys' and 'The Sash'. Really. From what I can remember as a kid. You didn't have the 'Away in a Mangers' . . .

Brian recalled matches in the late 1980s as *'a dark period for Northern Ireland football'* when attendances were as low as 2,000 and Celtic players Anton Rogan and Allen McKnight received abuse from a section of the home crowd. Yet the abuse that Rogan and McKnight received would arguably be surpassed by the experience of Neil Lennon in the early 2000s.

The 'enemy within'? The development of football for all and the Neil Lennon 'incident'

The preceding section noted that a number of Northern Ireland fans themselves admitted taking part in practices at matches that they suggested that, on current reflection, they did not fully consider at the time. George remembered 'belting out' the 'Billy Boys' beside Catholic friends without really questioning what he was doing, a theme echoed by Paul who referred to being a *'kid'* singing such songs as *'it just seemed to be the* [done] *thing.'* Chris suggested that *'we didn't know any different'* in terms of singing particular songs. A home match against the Republic of Ireland in November 1993, one week after the Shankill bomb and Greysteel massacre, has become particularly infamous for the 'sectarian atmosphere' (Moore, 2015), even inspiring the production by local playwright Marie Jones referred to at the beginning of the chapter (Privas, 2010).

Such comments from supporters suggest that their fandom at this point was based upon their 'tacit knowledge,' which they now struggled to fully explain verbally; they were caught up in the 'flow' of praxis (Giddens, 1993). Such practices were associated with a narrow form of 'ethnic fan' nationalism (Ben-Porat, 2014), wherein ideals of 'hegemonic masculinity' also played a part (Connell, 1995). However, some supporters disagreed with such behaviour at the time, although they felt 'powerless' to challenge it. Tony recalled that on the night Neil Lennon was booed by a section of Northern Ireland fans against Norway in February 2001, he was *'angry and embarrassed'*:

> *We were in the Kop stand*[3] *and these three or four guys to my right, who my son* [name removed], *knew to see, and knew by name I think, were giving Neil Lennon a hard time. And yes, Northern Ireland were playing badly that night, so the crowd wasn't as vociferous, or weren't making as much noise as they maybe do now. And yes, when the crowd were quiet, these few guys were shouting towards Neil Lennon because he played for Celtic. And the stewards were very slow to remove them. In fact, ourselves* [sic] . . . *told the stewards that if they didn't remove these guys, we would remove them – but we wouldn't remove them as quietly as they would remove them.*

Although the treatment of Neil Lennon was an uncomfortable experience for those supporters who disagreed with what was being sung in their name, the real significance of the event lay in fan representatives' subsequent 'knowledgeability' (Giddens, 1984) that spatial distribution and surveillance in the stadium were key elements in dominating or dictating the atmosphere that they had previously ignored (Foucault, 1977):

> *I was in the north stand at that stage, and although we had 11 supporters' groups... we were in all different parts of the stadium. And I said, 'Well, what we really*

> *need to do is get all of our clubs together in the one place and have this singing section.' Some people don't like a singing section – but have us all in the one place. So we got, it was 800* (tickets) *that we got into the Kop and another 200 in to the North Stand...Because* (at) *the Neil Lennon one, we didn't. There's 50 guys booing, we couldn't do anything, cos there was maybe 15 of us here, 20 there, 30 at another, you know, so you couldn't really – the fans weren't coordinated. So, sectarianism was given, like, the opportunity to thrive because there was no one - whereas if you had 800 people anywhere in a football stadium all singing the same stuff, the rest join in.*
>
> (George)

The Amalgamation of Official Northern Ireland Supporters' Clubs (AONISC) thus began booking out these seats within which they would place their own members, who had agreed to sign up to new anti-sectarian 'rules' of football fandom (on social 'rules,' see Winch, 1958), which discouraged the singing of sectarian songs and attempted to 'produce' an atmosphere that they dictated. The block-booking of supporters together was targeted on those specific parts of the stadium where most of the sectarian singing was coming from (including the North Stand and the West Stand/Kop behind the goal). The rationale associated with the block-booking of match tickets was twofold. First, the new regulations required fans to supply their names and addresses to purchase tickets; thus, if someone was to engage in sectarian behaviour within the stadium, it would be much easier to identify them and remove them from the stadium or ban them from future matches. Second, the block-booking of tickets assisted the coordination of efforts to challenge those singing sectarian songs:

> *For me, it was 2001, Czech Republic away. Em, that's when 'Sammy McIlroy's Green and White Army' started there like...I was at that match, it was an away game, and for me that's where it really started to be embedded – 'Sammy McIlroy's Green and White Army' – it was a chant like no other – you could sing it for like 30 minutes, you know! 'Sammy McIlroy's Green and White Army.' And it just, it almost became like a trance like...There was about 500 fans at that game, right? And we must have chanted at that match, we got beat 3-1, eh, and for two-thirds of the match we must have just shouted 'Sammy McIlroy's Green and White Army'!* (Laughs)
>
> (IFA 3)

The creation of a new canon of non-political songs such as 'We're Not Brazil . . .' and 'Green and White Army' indicates that Back et al. (2001) were correct to challenge Bloch's (1974) assertion that 'you cannot argue with a song.' Essential to ensuring that the singing of these new songs was promoted among the wider fan collective in the stadium was the 'analytical arrangement of space' that is characteristic of panopticism in a disciplinary society (Foucault, 1977, p. 203). In this regard, a small number of supporters with megaphones were placed within the North Stand and Kop and could survey what songs were being sung, drawing upon the rest of the crowd to 'correct' any (mis)behaviour when appropriate (including any attempts to sing the 'Billy Boys,' promoting alternatives such as 'Ulster Boys' instead). As argued by Bell et al. (2020, p.982, drawing on Bourdieu 1977), "those AONISC members, such as George, who were directing the crowd in song, are reminiscent not only of the ultra cheerleaders, whose role tends not to be referred to in the Northern Irish literature. . . but of . . . [those] 'spokesmen', who are granted 'tacit delegation' of the group's authority, constantly recalling the collective to the values that it officially recognises:"

> *you would start a chant and you would see everybody around you, look over the Kop, and you would see it spreading across, you know? And, then you would look down the north stand and you would see them gradually, and the ambition was, or the objective was to get the far side of the north stand right down all singing, whether it was `Stand up for the Ulstermen', or whatever it was, you know, whatever the thing was, or `Green and White Army', you know? Just trying to get everybody. So, it started in this wee hub.*
>
> (George)

The difficulties with challenging sectarianism were inherently linked to Northern Ireland fans feeling like separated individuals and *FFA* worked to give them a collective 'voice' through spatial redistribution. Foucault's analysis of the simultaneous individualising and collectivising of surveillance seems pertinent; those who opposed sectarian singing became a collective whose songs were 'normalised' in the routine match-day behaviour of fans (Giddens, 1993), while those engaging in sectarian singing in the stadium were individualised, differentiated and judged (Foucault, 1977):

> *To me those significant steps, risks that Northern Ireland fans took, started to change. Cos the troublemaker had to stop then. The troublemaker was isolated. . . .* [The] *Billy Boys were smothered out. . . . So they gave up. . . . So I think it was a useful, skilful tool.*
>
> (Steve)

However, while aspects of Foucault's *oeuvre* are useful in analysing the initial development of *FFA*, there are limitations to viewing *FFA* in purely Foucauldian terms. Indeed, the 'docility' or 'submission' required within the *FFA* campaign was of those engaged in sectarianism, not of the crowd in general. *FFA* sought to energise and utilise the agency of the majority of fans, not to make them Foucault's (1977) 'docile bodies.' Nor were the techniques used within *FFA* practised on the crowd by an external authority; the 'normalising gaze' was from within the crowd (fans) rather than outside it (police, stewards or CCTV). Giddens is therefore correct when he suggests that Foucault's conceptualisation of surveillance is too restrictive. While both convincingly argue that power is not merely 'possessed' and tends to reside in the collective, Giddens' assertion that surveillance is not only constraining but also enabling appears to be more relevant to an analysis of *FFA*. Although those fans who wished to engage in sectarian singing may have felt restricted in terms of their actions, those opposed to this behaviour felt empowered and were given a voice to challenge it.

A more useful conceptualisation of the reported changes that were implemented within *FFA* is Giddens' (1984) definition of social 'structure' as rules and resources that are open to change. Through the spatial organisation of fans and the role of AONISC members in the early stages of the campaign, there was a capability, in Giddens' terms, to control and command the behaviour of others. Indeed, certainly two of the three key features that Giddens associates with authoritative resources appear to be relevant in this regard: the organisation of social time-space and the organisation and relation of human beings in mutual association.

That members of the AONISC became aware of the significance of their spatial distribution within the confines of the stadium itself also played a significant role in the ability to hold effective displays involving the wearing of green shirts, green wigs, green face paint, flags and card displays – in other words, to gain control over the distribution of allocative (or material) resources (Giddens, 1984). All these practices were conducted under the auspices of the 'Sea of Green' initiative, which aimed to encourage supporters to wear the team colours to the match, rather than Rangers or Linfield tops (red, white and blue).

Efforts on these two fronts (in terms of manipulating vocal utterances and visual symbolism) led to the creation of the 'Green and White Army' (GAWA), the name given to the Northern Ireland fans by themselves, the IFA and the media in the early 2000s in the aftermath of the treatment of Neil Lennon. Like the Scottish 'Tartan Army' before them (Giulianotti, 1995), the 'rules' of being a 'member' of the GAWA focused upon non-sectarianism (they were, however, not necessarily apolitical) and 'having a laugh,' primarily through self-deprecating songs such as 'We're not Brazil, we're Northern Ireland.' The humour of fans helps to promote internal 'solidarity' within the GAWA (Pearson, 2012) and transmits the message to listeners that Northern Ireland fans are interested in verbally 'abusing' only themselves and not others through sectarian discourse (see Fine, 1984; Seckman and Couch, 1989; Filick et al., 2016; Sharpe and Hynes, 2016).

However, despite the challenging of sectarian singing in the stadium itself, fans suggested that it was much more difficult to do this in bars/pubs pre- and post-match as the spatial organisation and control of supporters is much less coordinated; this is the private 'backstage' area where social norms tend to be more relaxed and less formal (Goffman, 1959).

It should also be noted that the 'stocks of knowledge' (Schutz, 1967) associated with the Northern Ireland team also retain a linkage with wider unionist norms and practices. The anthem played before Northern Ireland matches remains 'God Save the Queen,' the anthem of the United Kingdom. While some supporters felt that it made 'the hairs stand up on the back of your neck' (Steve and Stewart), others felt it was not in keeping with the ethos of inclusion that the 'Football for All' campaign had espoused. Many supporters, even those from Protestant and unionist backgrounds, advocated an alternative, such as a *'Northern Ireland national anthem'* (Brian).

An issue in relation to the anthem is that following the third line of 'God save our Queen,' prior to the line 'Send Her victorious,' a small group of supporters still shout out the Ulster loyalist slogan 'No surrender'(on loyalist and republican song 'add-ins,' see Millar, 2016). Some fans spoke of their embarrassment and even anger at those who engage in the shout, referring to it as making them feel *'ashamed'* (Steve) and *'I just cringe when I hear it'* (Gareth).

Although it is difficult at this juncture to ascertain if a change in anthem would encourage more northern Catholics to support the Northern Ireland team, it became apparent throughout the research that it was one issue that most fans and IFA staff felt had been overlooked in the attempts to encourage more members of the northern nationalist and Catholic community to join them within the 'ranks' of the GAWA.

Conclusion

This chapter has argued that the literature on Northern Irish football fandom has overlooked the developments that have taken place within Northern Irish international football fan culture in the past 15 years. The cessation of the violence of the 'Troubles' provided the space for less aggressive fan practices to emerge, wherein Northern Ireland fans along with the IFA, changed the 'structure' of Northern Irish fandom by manipulating the allocative and authoritative resources and 'rules' associated with supporting the side, which led to the creation of the transformed 'social system' commonly referred to as the 'Green and White Army' (GAWA). The spatial distribution and organisation of fans in the stadium within the context of surveillance were crucial in the significance of the emergence of the GAWA fan culture. Yet viewing 'surveillance' in purely constraining terms and only originating from an external source (CCTV, police, stewards) ignores the enabling potential for 'lateral surveillance' among fans themselves (Giddens, 1984; Dixon, 2014).

However, in line with structuration theory, the 'structural continuity' of the fan collective is always open to change, as it is continually (re)created and brought into being through fan practices (Bell et al., 2020). The GAWA continues to face challenges (both inside and outside the stadium) from within the fanbase from those who wish to (re)assert more narrow forms of ethnic fan practices. Power relations and the control of resources therefore remain important in internal struggles for legitimacy within the GAWA and who defines which fan practices are deemed to be (un)acceptable (Bell et al., 2020).

There are lessons that can perhaps be learnt from the creation of the GAWA for other footballing contexts. A difficulty that both supporter- and organisational-led approaches to inappropriate fan behaviour (such as racism and xenophobia) face is that they do not directly address behaviour *in situ* and tend to ignore the significance of the spatial distribution of supporters in the stadium, which this chapter has suggested is crucial to creating the 'atmosphere' at a football match. Through their partnership with the IFA, Northern Ireland fans had access to the resources that supporter initiatives on their own tend to lack, while the fact that FFA's aims were more circumscribed than achieving long-term attitudinal change and involved empowering fans themselves to challenge other fans gave the campaign credibility.

While a noble endeavour, if we wait until everyone is converted by 'educated professionals' to a more positive attitudinal disposition to the many 'others' in society, we may be waiting a long time. As Giddens (1984) suggests, a change in *praxis* can in fact change the social 'rules' of acceptable behaviour (and vice versa). This implies that, as in FFA, one doesn't have to start with attitudes, but rather can focus on practical behaviour and the spatial distribution of supporters in the stadium. This would provide a rejoinder to the rather simplistic responses to 'offensive' fan behaviour that have thus far been adopted by UEFA and FIFA. From 1 June 2013, UEFA (2016) enacted new regulations that allowed for the partial or full closing of football stadia in the event of 'offensive' fan behaviour. Conceivably, under these guidelines, the entire support base of a team can be punished for the actions of just a handful of individuals. Partial and full stadium closures in the aftermath of small groups of supporters engaging in inappropriate behaviour, in the longer term, not only punishes the innocent along with the guilty, but it also fails to adequately empower fans to actively challenge such behaviour within their midst.

Notes

1 See 'Northern Ireland are homeward bound but their fans are leaving on a high'. Available online at: https://www.theguardian.com/football/blog/2016/jun/25/northern-ireland-fans-wales-euro-2016 (accessed March 10th 2021).

2 The 'Billy Boys' song initially emerged in Glasgow in the 1920s and was associated with the members of an infamous Scottish Protestant razor gang led by Billy Fullerton (Reid, 2008). The main controversy with the song, sung to the tune of the American civil war song 'Marching through Georgia,' is that it contains the sectarian and anti-Catholic line 'We're up to our knees in fenian blood.'

3 Also known as the 'Alex Russell Stand.'

References

Aughey, A. (1989) *Under Siege: Ulster Unionism and the Anglo-Irish Agreement*. New York: St. Martin's Press.

Back, L., Crabbe, T., and Solomos, J. (2001) *The Changing Face of Football: Racism, Identity and Multi-culture in the English Game*. Oxford: Berg.

Bairner, A. (1997) '"Up to their knees"? Football, sectarianism, masculinity and Protestant working-class identity', in Shirlow, P., and McGovern, M. (eds.), *Who Are 'The People'? Unionism, Protestantism and Loyalism in Northern Ireland*. London: Pluto Press, 95–113.

Bairner, A. (1999) 'Soccer, masculinity and violence in Northern Ireland: Between hooliganism and terrorism', *Men and Masculinities*, 1(3), 284–301. https://doi.org/10.1177/1097184X99001003003

Bairner, A. (2003) 'Political unionism and sporting nationalism: An examination of the relationship between sport and national identity within the Ulster unionist tradition', *Global Studies in Culture and Power*, 10(4), 517–535. https://doi.org/10.1080/714947401

Bairner, A. (2005) 'Sport, Irishness and Ulster Unionism', in Bairner, A. (ed.), *Sport and the Irish: Histories, Identities, Issues*. Dublin: University College Dublin, 157–171.

BBC (2016) *EURO 2016: Irish Football Fans Awarded Medal of City of Paris*. Available at: www.bbc.co.uk/news/world-europe-36661166 (accessed 10 December 2019).

Bell, J. (2017) *Green and White Army: The Structuration of a Social System?* PhD Thesis, Ulster University, UK. Available at: https://ethos.bl.uk/OrderDetails.do?uin=uk.bl.ethos.714501

Bell, J., Somerville, I., and Hargie, O. (2020) 'The structuration of a sporting social system? Northern Ireland fans, Football for All and the creation of the Green and White Army', *International Review for the Sociology of Sport*, 55(7), 975–990. https://doi.org/10.1177/1012690219862917

Ben-Porat, A. (2014) 'Who are we? My club? My people? My state? The dilemma of the Arab soccer fan in Israel', *International Review for the Sociology of Sport*, 49(2), 175–189. https://doi.org/10.1177/1012690212458506

Bloch, M. (1974) 'Symbols, song, dance and features of articulation, or is religion an extreme form of traditional authority?', *Archives Europennes de Sociologie*, 15(1), 55–81. https://doi.org/10.1017/S0003975600002824

Bourdieu, P. (1977) *Outline of a Theory of Practice*. Cambridge: Cambridge University Press. https://doi.org/10.1017/CBO9780511812507

Connell, R.W. (1995) *Masculinities*. Berkeley: University of California Press.

Denzin, N.K. and Lincoln, Y.S. (eds.) (2005) *The Handbook of Qualitative Research*. 3rd ed. First published, 1994. Thousand Oaks, CA: Sage.

Dixon, K. (2014) 'The role of lateral surveillance in the construction of authentic football fandom practice', *Surveillance and Society*, 11(4), 424–438. https://doi.org/10.24908/ss.v11i4.4585

Faubion, J.D. (ed.) (1994) *Power: The Essential Works of Michel Foucault 1954–1984, Volume Three*. Trans. by Robert Hurley and Others. Reprint, 2002. London: Penguin Books.

Filick, R., Ţurcan, A., Thompson, D., Harvey, N., Davies, H., and Turner, A. (2016) 'Sarcasm and emotions: Comprehension and emotional impact', *The Quarterly Journal of Experimental Psychology*, 69(11), 2130–2146. https://doi.org/10.1080/17470218.2015.1106566

Fine, G.A. (1984) 'Humorous interaction and the social construction of meaning: Making sense in a jocular vein', *Studies in Symbolic Interaction*, 5(1), 83–101. https://doi.org/10.1177/089124189018003004

Foucault, M. (1977) *Discipline and Punish: The Birth of the Prison*. Trans. by Alan Sheridan. Reprint, 1991. London: Penguin Books.

Fulton, G. (2005) 'Northern Catholic fans of the Republic of Ireland soccer team', in Bairner, A. (ed.), *Sport and the Irish: Histories, Identities, Issues*. University College Dublin, 140–156.

Giddens, A. (1984) *The Constitution of Society: Outline of the Theory of Structuration*. Facsimile of 1st ed., 2013. Cambridge: Polity Press.

Giddens, A. (1993) *New Rules of Sociological Method: A Positive Critique of Interpretive Sociologies*. 2nd ed., with a new introduction. Originally published, 1976. Cambridge: Polity Press.

Giulianotti, R. (1995) 'Football and the politics of carnival: An ethnographic study of Scottish fans in Sweden', *International Review for the Sociology of Sport*, 30(2), 191–224. https://doi.org/10.1177/101269029503000205

Goffman, E. (1959) *The Presentation of Self in Everyday Life*. Reprint, 1990. London and New York: Penguin Books.

Hassan, D. (2002) 'A people apart? Soccer, identity and Irish nationalists in Northern Ireland', *Soccer and Society*, 3(3), 65–83. https://doi.org/10.1080/714004886

Hassan, D., McCullough, S., and Moreland, E. (2009) 'North or south? Darron Gibson and the issue of player eligibility within Irish soccer', *Soccer and Society*, 10(6), 740–753. https://doi.org/10.1080/14660970903239933

Hoberman, M. (1984) *Sport and Political Ideology*. Austin: University of Texas Press.

Jones, M. (2006) *A Night in November*. First published, 1995. London: Nick Hern Books.

Liston, K., and Deighan, M. (2018) 'Whose "wee country"?: Identity politics and sport in Northern Ireland', *Identities: Global Studies in Power and Culture*, 26(2), 203–221. https://doi.org/10.1080/1070289X.2017.1392103

McGee, D., and Bairner, A. (2010) 'Transcending the borders of Irish identity? Narratives of northern nationalist footballers in Northern Ireland', *International Review for the Sociology of Sport*, 46(4), 435–455. https://doi.org/10.1177/1012690210380584

McKittrick, D., Kelters, S., Feeney, B., and Thornton, C. (1999) *Lost Lives: The Stories of the Men, Women and Children Who Died as a Result of the Northern Ireland Troubles*. Edinburgh: Mainstream.

Millar, S.R. (2015) 'Musically consonant, socially dissonant: Orange walks and catholic interpretation in West-Central Scotland', *Music and Politics*, IX(1), 1–23. http://dx.doi.org/10.3998/mp.9460447.0009.102

Millar, S.R. (2016) 'Let the people sing? Irish rebel songs, sectarianism, and Scotland's Offensive Behaviour Act', *Popular Music*, 35(3), 297–319. https://doi.org/10.1017/S0261143016000519

Moore, C. (2015) *The Irish Soccer Split*. Cork: Cork University Press.

Murray, C., and Hassan, D. (2017) '"They're just not my team": The issue of player allegiances within Irish football, 2007–2012', *Soccer and Society*, 19(5–6), 687–703. https://doi.org/10.1080/14660970.2017.1399607

Pearson, G. (2012) *An Ethnography of English Football Fans: Cans, Cops and Carnivals*. Manchester: Manchester University Press.

Privas, V. (2010) 'Monological drama to reshape the Northern Irish identity: *A Night in November* by Marie Jones', *Estudios Irlandeses*, No. 5, 68–80. Available at: https://cain.ulster.ac.uk/estudiosirlandeses/privas10.pdf (accessed 10 December 2019).

Reid, I.A. (2008) '"An outsider in our midst": Narratives of Neil Lennon, soccer and ethno-religious bigotry in the Scottish Press', *Soccer and Society*, 9(1), 64–80. https://doi.org/10.1080/14660970701616761

Rubin, H.J. and Rubin, I.S. (2005) *Qualitative Interviewing: The Art of Hearing Data*. Thousand Oaks, CA: Sage.

Schutz, A. (1967) *Phenomenology of the Social World*. Trans. by G. Walsh and F. Lehnert. Paperback ed., 1972. Evanston, IL: Northwestern University Press.

Seckman, M.A., and Couch, C. (1989) 'Jocularity, sarcasm and relationships: An empirical study', *Journal of Contemporary Ethnography*, 18(3), 327–344. https://doi.org/10.1177/089124189018003004

Sharpe, S., and Hynes, M. (2016) 'Black faced, red faces: The potentials of humour for anti-racist action', *Ethnic and Racial Studies*, 39(1), 87–104. https://doi.org/10.1080/01419870.2016.1096405

Shirlow, P. (2005) 'Sport, leisure and territory in Belfast', in Bairner, A. (ed.), *Sport and the Irish: Histories, Identities, Issues*. Dublin: University College Dublin.

Sugden, J., and Bairner, A. (1993) *Sport, Sectarianism and Society in a Divided Ireland*. Leicester University Press.

Sugden, J., and Bairner, A. (1994) 'Ireland and the World Cup: "Two teams in Ireland, there's only two teams in Ireland"', in Sugden, J., and Tomlinson, A. (eds.), *Hosts and Champions: Soccer Cultures, National Identities and the USA World Cup*. Aldershot, Hampshire: Arena, 119–139.

Sugden, J., and Harvie, S. (1995) *Sport and Community Relations in Northern Ireland*. Coleraine: Centre for the Study of Conflict, University of Ulster.

Todd, J. (1987) 'Two traditions in Unionist political culture', *Irish Political Studies*, 2(1), 1–26. https://doi.org/10.1080/07907188708406434

UEFA (2009) *Tous ensemble Wins Supporters Award*. Available at: www.uefa.com/insideuefa/stakeholders/european-union/news/newsid=938049.html (accessed 10 December 2019).

UEFA (2016) *Disciplinary Regulations*. 2016 Edition. Geneva: UEFA. Available at: www.uefa.org/MultimediaFiles/Download/Regulations/uefaorg/UEFACompDisCases/02/37/00/86/2370086_DOWNLOAD.pdf (accessed 10 December 2019).

Waiton, S. (2018) 'Criminalizing songs and symbols in Scottish Football: How anti-sectarian legislation has created a new "sectarian" divide in Scotland', *Soccer and Society*, 19(2), 169–184. https://doi.org/10.1080/14660970.2015.1133413

Wilde, O. (1891) *The Picture of Dorian Gray*. Reprint of the 1908 edition, 2001. Introduction by J.M.L Drew. Hertfordshire: Wordsworth Classics.

Winch, P. (1958) *The Idea of a Social Science and its Relation to Philosophy*. 8th Impression, 1973. Studies in Philosophical Psychology Series. London and New York: Routledge and Kegan Paul.

Yin, R.K. (2009) *Case Study Research: Design and Methods*. London: Sage.

Chapter 3

Two sides still at play 20 years after the Good Friday Agreement

Paul Breen and Sean Huddleston

Introduction

National pride is closely allied to political symbols, and Northern Irish society serves as an exemplar of how sport and politics are inextricably linked in the popular imagination. Armstrong and Mitchell (2001: 140) point to the role that social activities such as sporting events play in reinforcing a sense of national pride. However, in a divided society, even the most basic symbols can become contentious and be used as a vehicle for asserting ownership over the cultural terrain of a state. Northern Ireland is politically and demographically divided between the Christian denominations of Catholic and Protestant within a context where 'religious ascription has typically been seen as coterminous with national identity,' and Catholics see themselves as Irish rather than British (Nagle, 2012: 3). This means that there is significant support within the Northern Irish Catholic community for the Republic of Ireland's football team. This is a consequence of identifying with the notion of Ireland as a singular entity, which is more reflective of their long-held political aspiration of a united Irish state. As such, loyalty to the Northern Irish football team is seen as lukewarm at best.

However, this has not always been the case despite decades of conflict that arguably have their roots in the Anglo-Irish conflict of the early 1900s and the subsequent partition of Ireland into two states. It was only in the second half of the 20th century that the 'social significance of sport in Northern Ireland' (Hassan, 2002: 66) extended into the realm of political and cultural identification. Increasingly, 'ownership' of the national football team has become a crucial aspect of maintaining Protestant hegemony over a state that has seen considerable demographic change in the past half century. Many unionists still see their national team as being exclusively theirs since the working class unionist identity is inextricably linked to soccer (Bleakney and Darby, 2018). This linkage of a shared sport to a singular identity has helped cause a lack of 'sustained reflective dialogue' on the 'symbolic walls of the mind' that lie at the heart of this issue (Liston and Deighan, 2019: 216). Despite the increase in the Catholic population (Nolan, 2012; Hughes, 2013), Hassan (2002: 69) has observed that 'the popularity of soccer amongst Irish nationalists in Northern Ireland, far from questioning their sense of national identity, appears to provide many with an opportunity to express their support for the idea of Irish unification and engage in counter-hegemonic activity against the Northern Ireland State.'

This hardly seems like a recipe for the agreed society envisioned in the 1998 Belfast Agreement, signed into British, Irish and European law on Good Friday, 10 April 1998, after two years of formal negotiations between representatives of unionism and nationalism. This agreement established 'provisions for a new political and constitutional configuration in Northern Ireland, on the island of Ireland and between Ireland and Britain,' and cemented 'a strong equalisation policy' that had been in place since the late 1980s. Nagle (2012: 12) further describes the deal as recognising both nationalists and unionists' respective 'self-determination claims, the need to share political power, as well as "parity of esteem" for their cultural identities.' Parity of esteem though is a difficult construct to measure (O"Neill, 2003), and the agreement itself has been deemed a failure in taking on board 'overlapping, confused, or even contradictory identities' that 'slice through the alleged fault lines of conflict' (Vaughan-Williams, 2006: 518). Perhaps, nowhere is this more apparent than in the binary landscape of supporting 'the national football team,' which in itself is a loaded assertion since many Catholics also see Gaelic football rather than association football as their national game.

The situation is thus a complicated one and raises the question of whether or not it is possible to accommodate diversity within the support base and to have this reflected in the broader symbols associated with the Northern Irish football team. To date, that appears not to have been achieved to any substantive extent, and a scenario exists where, 20 years after the 1998 Belfast Agreement, sporting allegiances may be just as polarised as in those now-passed decades of conflict. It remains to be seen though if that could change, and whether or not there is scope for arrangements in which supporters, if not players, can strongly identify with teams from both parts of Ireland. For this to happen, a number of measures might have to be put in place regarding issues such as anthems and symbols, but even then as Roberts (2017) has pointed out, most Catholics would still probably identify more strongly with the Republic of Ireland regardless of any cosmetic changes.

However, an interesting challenge to this position comes in the existence of Catholic players such as Paddy McCourt and Niall McGinn. They have chosen to wear the colours of Northern Ireland, even in an era when they could self-select for the Republic (as others such as the infamous James McClean – of which more later – have done). This suggests that there may be hope for making the background environment of Northern Irish football more reflective of a broader society that has long since ceased to be 'a cold house for Catholics' (Trimble, 1998). For that to succeed though, Roberts (2017: 461) argues that it 'takes more than words' and cites the aforementioned Niall McGinn as saying that in some scenarios, such as the playing of the 'national' anthem, for Catholic boys it's a case of 'just put your head down and try to get through it' (ibid: 452), which seems a contradiction to the foundations of the 1998 Agreement.

Historical context

Much of Irish football's present-day divisions have resulted from the 'divorce' (Breen, 2014) of the island's two football associations in 1921, following the partition of Ireland into two states. Historically in Ireland, association football, had been the preserve of the Protestant northeast, even if two of the most recognisable clubs in that area, Belfast Celtic and Cliftonville, Ireland's oldest club, generally attracted a largely Catholic following (Roberts, 2017). In the aftermath of the split into two associations, the northern version retained a sense of righteousness in being true heirs to the title of the Irish Football Association (as the Football Association of Ireland were the ones who broke away), a sense that has continued to this day.

The Republic of Ireland football team's identity thus came to be based on a statist version of nationalism according to Cronin (1999: 124) in that it was formed around the boundaries of a political state – that is, the Irish Free State and later the Republic of Ireland – and that the FAI 'built its identity around the nation state, and not, as with the GAA, a mythical ideal of the nation.' Such a perspective mirrored the insular nature of southern Irish politics in the decades after partition, a situation changed gradually by entry into the European Union and a thaw in relations with Britain. However, by the late 1980s and early 1990s, the situation had changed radically, as noted in the *Irish Times* (30 June 1990), where they state that 'the Irish soccer team, with its extraordinary collection of polyglot Irish pedigrees, has given us a new pride in our multi-cultural Irishness, and put one more nail in the coffin of the old, exclusive . . . GAA-supporting, Fianna Fail-voting definition of "real" Irish-ness.' Despite such changes though, the situation within, and even the presence of the North, has always complicated whatever process Irish identity has undergone ever since partition.

Up until the 1990s, the Northern Irish soccer team had been the more successful of the two entities upon the island. They achieved qualification and some degree of respectability in three World Cup competitions as well as producing arguably the finest British footballer of his generation in terms of raw talent, George Best. Allied to this, when Northern Ireland played in the Spanish World Cup of 1982, they had a reasonable Catholic following, even though this was less than one year after the 1981 Hunger Strikes and the peak of the political conflict (Breen, 2014). Yet by the early 1990s football in the north became increasingly politicised as Ulster Loyalist identity became synonymous with support for Northern Ireland and an increasingly confident Catholic population found greater affiliation with the Republic of Ireland (Hassan, 2002). Further to this, the teams faced one another in qualification for major tournaments twice in the 1990s, exacerbating the sense of polarisation and creating what was to be deemed 'a bubbling cauldron of sectarian bile' (Roberts, 2017: 382) in which Northern Irish manager Billy Bingham was seen to play a key role and singled out for criticism in the southern media and the Irish parliament.

These years were characterised by some of the most vicious and pointless murders of the decades-old political conflict, including a bomb attack on a

Shankhill Road fish shop and the 'World Cup massacre' (Duggan, 2014), in which six civilians were murdered in a remote bar while watching the Republic of Ireland's match against Italy in the first round of FIFA's 1994 competition. This was also the era of instigating 'a lengthy, and often precarious, peace process' (Brown and Macginty, 2003: 85), which culminated in the 1998 Belfast Agreement. While there was some aspiration towards creating a harmonised 'Northern Irish' identity – one that accommodated respective pride in Britishness and Irishness within the one 'shared' identity (O'Neill, 2003), this actually served to reinforce the concept of two distinct communities defined by their political and religious affiliations. The 1998 Agreement also allowed for dual citizenship and gave Catholics in Northern Ireland who felt alienated by sectarianism and other issues surrounding the Northern Irish team to switch their allegiance (Hassan et al., 2009: 743). However, this has created a situation where a trickle of young Catholic players heading south at the start appears to have become a flood.

Hassan et al. (2009) have observed that 'no single explanation can be offered as to why talented young soccer players from Northern Ireland's Catholic community are choosing to play for Republic of Ireland teams' with a number of interlocking issues at play regarding these players and their choices. Cronin (1999: 124) highlights some of these issues and reasons as being the nature of the communities in which players reside, family allegiances and ties, political beliefs and affiliations, personal/national identities and sporting pragmatism (ie perceived increased chances of playing in better teams and better chances of playing in international tournaments). The perception of the IFA held by some nationalists in Northern Ireland (which has rarely been favourable) is also a factor in some of these players' decisions to declare for the Republic of Ireland (Hassan et al., 2009: 741; Roberts, 2017: 465–491).

The new century and persisting issues

The division in allegiances, and the factors underpinning them, appeared to reach a tipping point at the start of the 21st century. The treatment of Northern Ireland team captain Neil Lennon, particularly after he joined Celtic from Leicester City, confirmed to some in the Catholic community that anti-Catholic bigotry was rife and flourishing at Northern Ireland matches. Simon Kuper (2007) explains that when Lennon joined Celtic, some Northern Irish Protestants were unforgiving. To them, wearing the green-and-white hoops was a greater crime than being Catholic. During Northern Ireland versus Norway in Belfast's Windsor Park in March 2001, Lennon was abused by a section of his own crowd. They sang traditional anti-Catholic songs and chanted, 'We've Got a Provo on *Our*[1] Team' (Roberts, 2017: 408).

Such antagonism was directed towards Lennon because of what Clancy (2010: 86) describes as Glasgow Celtic's 'Irish origins and strong contemporary Irish links' and the fact that this Scottish football club continues 'to be a badge of Irish identity for many thousands of people.' The sectarian abuse of Celtic footballers by hardcore loyalist elements within the crowd, not just Neil Lennon, but also Anton Rogan and Allen McKnight previously (Roberts, 2017: 421) alienated Catholic supporters from going to matches and allowed the perception of Northern Ireland games as anti-Catholic events to grow. These incidents also resonated with other examples in Europe – for example, the problems faced by Bixente Lizarazu as a member of the French World Cup squad who was born a Basque but who chose to play for France. Lizarazu was subsequently put under 24-hour police protection after Basque paramilitary group ETA sent threatening letters to his parents' home (*Observer*, 04.03.2001).

For the Northern Ireland international side, the division that had gripped the country for so many decades was now being translated into support for the team. The Northern Ireland support, from the 1980s onwards, reflected an overt Protestant, unionist character that proved to be a difficult space for Catholic supporters to engage with (Sugden and Bairner, 1993: 78) and such a situation has continued through to the 21st century. On a positive note though, this situation strengthened the hand of some progressive figures working in football in Northern Ireland to tackle anti-Catholic bigotry and sectarianism, even if Lennon himself appeared to believe that not enough was done at the time, in practical terms, to ease the situation (Roberts, 2017: 409–412).

The outreach efforts of the IFA also saw initiatives with regards to refugees in Northern Ireland when, in 2003, the 'World United' football team was established by the IFA with the intention of giving 'immigrants the chance to meet other people from similar backgrounds, to get a foothold in Northern Ireland and to tackle racism in the process' (*Belfast Telegraph*, 10.01.2015). With the popularity of this initiative, Hassan and McCue (2013: 421) noted that 'by 2004 Northern Ireland was witnessing levels of inward migration it had never previously countenanced [and] . . . in considerable numbers availing of often comparatively higher wages and a better standard of living. Together with asylum seekers and refugees, predominantly from North Africa, these new arrivals formed the nucleus of early World United sides.'

Accordingly, diversity was increasingly becoming a feature of football in Northern Ireland, and further developments were to come with the appointment of a Catholic manager, Michael O'Neill, who has complimented the IFA on doing 'a great deal of work in making the games at Windsor Park inclusive' and that '*we*[2] want a team on the pitch which is inclusive of everyone' (*Independent*, 10.10.2015). He also went on to dispel cynicism about his appointment with the insinuation that he may have been given the job as a consequence of being a Catholic. His retort to that was simply that 'I'm not here to say Mass, I'm here to pick a team.' (*Belfast Telegraph*, 13.11.2015). Despite this change at the helm and many changes on the ground, there is still a long way to go in terms of realising Michael O'Neill's ambition of seeing every young Catholic born in Northern Ireland being passionate about playing for their country (Roberts, 2017: 466–468).

The James McClean factor?

Conversely, it is important to demonstrate examples that have had a negative impact on the possibility of Catholic/nationalist players declaring and playing for Northern Ireland. Four years after the signing of the Good Friday Agreement, Neil Lennon, from a strongly Catholic and nationalist background, captained the Northern Irish team while playing for the Glasgow Celtic football club in Scotland. However, he was forced to retire from international football at only 31 years of age due to death threats made against him prior to a friendly match against Cyprus. Almost a decade later, former Derry City players and then Northern Ireland internationals Paddy McCourt and Niall McGinn were sent bullets in the post (*and, as in the case of Neil Lennon, both were also Celtic players at the time*). Niall McGinn would later compound matters to an extent when he, possibly naively, announced that he had been a lifelong Republic of Ireland fan. These remarks proved especially ill judged due to their timing following a match in which he had been part of a Northern Ireland team beaten 5–0 by the Republic in a competition featuring all the 'nations' of Britain and Ireland (*Belfast Telegraph*, 27.05.2011). These remarks caused a social media furore among Northern Ireland supporters and would later prompt a public apology from the player, even though as a Catholic born in Donaghmore, he was probably voicing opinions shared by the majority of his community, but still not tolerated in the official narrative of the state.

Prominent football writers have highlighted other cultural factors that may have had a negative impact. Conall Cahill, for example, stated:

> As long as 'God Save The Queen' is played before Northern Ireland games, Irish Catholics born north of the border will stay away from Windsor Park and will choose to play for and support the Republic of Ireland instead of Northern Ireland. . . . Young people in the north are as secular as their southern counterparts in supporting the Northern Ireland football team, the playing of 'God Save The Queen' penetrates your consciousness and reminds you otherwise.
>
> (balls.ie)

Paul McVeigh, former Norwich City and NI international has also raised the question of 'what justifies the national anthem of England [God save the Queen] being played for Northern Ireland's football team?' and goes on to suggest that long as the authorities continue with this anthem, the Northern Irish football team 'will not have an identity of its own' and players from a nationalist background 'will continue to turn to the Republic' (ibid).

This alienation has also been evident in the women's game with Catherine Drain, a former Northern Ireland ladies international soccer player from the nationalist tradition who declared for the Republic of Ireland in February 1999, stating in an interview: 'I'm not ashamed to say it – you do feel more pride walking out in the Republic [of Ireland] jersey' (Hassan, 2002: 74). This is a feeling shared by former Derry City player, and current Republic of Ireland international James McClean who stated:

> You don't really feel at home. I think any Catholic would be lying if they said they did feel at home, seeing all those flags (Union Jacks) and hearing the songs and chants. For me, personally, I didn't feel part of it. I gave a piece – an article – not that long back and I was just describing how, as a Catholic in the squad, you don't feel part of the squad.
>
> (*Daily Mail*, 11.05.2012)

McClean probably best exemplifies an apparent political motivation in a young Irish nationalist footballer's decision to opt for the Republic, having provided very explicit indications of his allegiance and publicly expressing his Irishness in ways that are intimately bound up with the city of Derry where he grew up. McClean's identity is overtly nationalist, and his decision to declare for the Republic of Ireland was a logical extension of what he felt was his national identity. McClean himself elocuted this in an interview with the Irish *Independent* newspaper when he stated, 'Northern Ireland is not my country. Unless you're from where I'm from, Creggan [*traditional nationalist section of the city of Derry*] – which was a big part of The Troubles when I was growing up – unless you're from there, you don't really understand' (Hogan, 2015). McClean has also stated that playing for the Irish national team had been a personal, sporting ambition:

> Playing in the Aviva Stadium in Dublin in front of thousands of people and wearing that green jersey means so much to me and my team-mates

and that he feels

> very proud and very fortunate to have been given an opportunity to wear that jersey. I do everything in my power to give 100 per cent when wearing it.
>
> (*Irish Examiner*, 25.10.2016)

As a result of such a public expression of pride in his national identity, James McClean has stood out in terms of being a new bête noir for Unionism and Football. Some might argue that he has become the incarnation of an Irish national pride that is still treated with scorn across different classes and elements of mainstream British society. The treatment of McClean (with echoes of the historic treatment meted to former internationalist Neil Lennon), and subsequent pronouncements by public representatives on the unionist side, have arguably become new barriers to Catholic/nationalist acceptance of the Northern Ireland football team. Hassan (2002) provides important context behind players from Derry – that is, McClean – deciding to represent the Republic and the importance of geographical as well as historical factors. He sees a near tangible sense of rejection among Derry City FC fans of their location within Northern Ireland, propagated by their geographical and economic isolation in the state. The border separating Northern Ireland from the Republic of Ireland is to be found within four miles of the city centre yet is now virtually unrecognisable following the relaxation of border controls between countries in the European Union. As a result, the bond between Derry and certain parts of the Republic of Ireland, especially County Donegal, is very real. Exaggerated by their team's involvement in representative sport in the Republic of Ireland, nationalists in Derry now have to rely less on some mythical construction of Irish unity than might previously have been the case – rather, their association with parts of southern Ireland is both natural and inherently logical (ibid: 78).

In a similar manner, Shane Duffy (like other footballers Darron Gibson and James McClean, also born in Derry), initially capped by the north at various underage levels, has expressed very similar sentiments in suggesting it was a logical outcome of his own loyalties:

> It is a dream to play for the Republic of Ireland. . . . Everyone in my family is Irish and so am I. We are just living in Northern Ireland. I have always wanted to play for the Republic. I grew up supporting Ireland and so did everybody around me.
>
> (*Donegal Democrat*, 25.02.2010).

In recent times, more senior football players born in Derry City and the wider county have decided to represent the Republic of Ireland rather than Northern Ireland. James McClean, Shane Duffy, Darron Gibson, Eunan O'Kane are all senior players in the Ireland squad who hail from the same county and have represented the Republic of Ireland. This then gives rise to the conclusion that McClean (and others like him) were acting correctly in accordance with their consciences when deciding to declare for the Republic of Ireland. In similar cases, the unionist/loyalist reaction to these players' decisions are similar to how the French feel when they display the same sense of dismay when their 'home-grown players' – young men born in France but of Maghrebin or sub-Saharan family origin – decide to declare and play for the African countries of their parents (salutsunderland.com, 2012).

This nuance and contextualisation has been largely absent from unionist and loyalist examination. Members of the Democratic Unionist Party, on the conservative right wing of Britain's political spectrum, have been at the forefront of antagonism towards McClean's declaration for the Republic and other controversial gestures such as refusing to wear the poppy on his jersey during remembrance weekends. Gregory Campbell – the DUP MP for East Derry – in 2013, recommended that McClean should be sacked in response to the footballer tweeting about his love for the Republican song 'Broad Black Brimmer' (balls.ie). The DUP have been joined by other official unionist voices of opposition to McClean's viewpoints and politically motivated decisions. Billy Hutchison, leader of the Loyalist Progressive

Unionist Party, stated in the *Belfast Telegraph* that 'it was disgraceful that a Premiership player "earning £40,000 or £50,000 a week" for an English team then refused to wear a poppy.'[3] Herein, aside from the lack of tolerance for Irish nationalism, there is a perception that the only legitimate British identity is one that is accepting of militarism (see Kelly, 2017). Added to this, McClean has also become a target for the ire of Northern Ireland fans. When Northern Ireland made it three goals to nothing during their game against Greece on (08.10.2015), Windsor Park reverberated to a chorus of 'Are You Watching, James McClean?' (*Independent*, 10.10.2015).

As already mentioned, Northern Ireland is in an unenviable position of being a post-conflict society struggling to deal with the legacy of its past while also experiencing difficulties within the traumatic growing pains associated with being a new, multicultural society. McVeigh and Rolston (2007) have observed acutely,

> Instead of the promised post-GFA future 'free from racist and sectarian harassment' and grounded in human rights and equality, we find a state formation responsible for – and incapable of dealing with – frightening levels of racism and sectarianism. In terms of both racism and sectarianism, the Northern Ireland state, despite all its post-GFA gloss, remains part of the problem, not part of the solution.
>
> (McVeigh and Rolston, 2007)

Political leadership, within all these different societal aspects, therefore, must improve if Northern Irish society is to lessen its divisions of whatever variety.

There have been some notable high-profile commentators who have come out in support of the IFA on this issue. Former Northern Ireland footballer and assistant manager Gerry Armstrong, who later moved into a media career, has been consistent in his opposition to players from the North declaring for the Republic, particularly those players that he believes have not been allowed to make a decision at an appropriate juncture. He has stated: 'I think it is a problem because at 15 or 16, kids should be allowed to get on with their football and enjoy their football without another added pressure from a political point of view' (*BBC*, 10.10.2011).

Armstrong has even gone as far as accusing the FAI of poaching players from Northern Ireland and stating that some players have eventually 'returned' to play for Northern Ireland after declaring for the Republic and having expectations et al. falling through, although to date no evidence has been provided for such claims (*BBC*, 10.10.2011). Nevertheless, the reactions of Northern Ireland supporters to this perceived poaching of players by the Republic saw their fans launch a boycott of a friendly match in Dublin in 2011 between the island's two national sides (Storey, 2016: 7). Others have questioned Armstrong's version of events, however. Prominent Irish football writers, such as Cathal Dervan, have stated that they have not witnessed Football Association of Ireland (FAI) coaches at the side of matches in border areas such as Derry. He goes on to argue,

> The bottom line is if a person is good enough to get into the Republic of Ireland team, [the then coach] Giovanni Trappatoni will play him. It doesn't matter if he was born in Glasgow, Limavady, Coleraine, Ballymena or wherever. The Irish Football Association (IFA) have to accept this. This is legal, there is nothing illegal here in what the FAI are doing. The IFA have got to accept they are not bigger than the Good Friday Agreement.
>
> (*BBC*, 10.10.2011).

The deluge continues? Catholic players from the North and the South

There have also been fears within the IFA that there has been a 'player drain' to the Republic that has been gathering increasing speed in recent times. The IFA had hoped that the option of taking their case to the Court of Arbitration for Sport (facilitated by governing body FIFA) would break this perceived deadlock. However, the FAI has continually expressed confidence that the body would not change the current position especially when FIFA rules include a clause allowing players to change nationality once before they play a senior competitive match if they were born 'on the territory of the relevant association.' The Good Friday Agreement of 1998 provided Northern Irish people the opportunity to claim either British or Irish nationality but again, as reflected in attitudes surrounding the 'national' football teams, there remains a lack of hegemonic tolerance for nationalists' birthright to identify as being exclusively Irish.

On the sporting side, Hassan et al. (2009) have noted that the

> decision of young Catholics from Northern Ireland to turn their backs on the chance to represent the country of their birth at senior international level is a worrying trend for those governing the game there. Their decisions are essentially the product of socio-political issues where the views of significant others, including the player's perception of his role as a community representative, holds considerable sway.
>
> (pp. 752–753)[4]

Indeed, as observed with the likes of James McClean, Fulton (2005) has also suggested that the decision to declare for the Republic of Ireland is now another aspect of overt nationalism in the North:

> . . . this affiliation with the Republic of Ireland team also demonstrates a rejection of Northern Ireland as their support introduces a sense of aspirational nationalism, an allegiance to a 32 county independent Republic . . .

(and thereby) imposes a more complicated relationship between soccer and Irish sporting nationalism.[5]

For Smith (1991: 16), national identities 'fulfil more intimate, internal functions for individuals in communities' and are called upon to provide social linkage between individuals and classes by providing repertoires of shared values, symbols and traditions. Through such linkage, members develop a consciousness of shared heritage and cultural kinship. This consequently gives them a sense of communal strength and a perception of being strengthened by affiliation to a common national identity (ibid).

Tonge and Gomez (2015: 19) have noted that 'Northern Ireland may have become more secure as a political entity,' but in terms of its national identity, any shared sense of Northern Irishness 'has failed to flourish on a cross-community basis.' They go on to note that 'both communities do not look across to each other to redefine nationality, which is instead shaped by intra-communal debates over how best to express Britishness or Irishness.' Consequently, the possibility of growth in loyalty and connection with some Catholic players in the North and a Northern Irish identity has stymied attempts to create a 'cross-community' Northern Ireland team to a certain degree.

This sense of not accepting the conditions or subtext of the 1998 Agreement goes to the heart of what is partially to blame for the existing situation over how national identities are treated within Northern Ireland and how each side has totally different expectations of what the future holds. Since the agreement itself is shrouded in (necessary) ambiguity (Ruane and Todd, 2001; Breen, 2019), neither side needs to meet the other in the middle because conditions have been created where the two societies can exist in parallel. The contention only arises when they need to share space such as cross-community sporting events or public expressions of culture such as festivals and marches. Even a couple of decades after the signing of the 1998 Agreement, there still remains a challenge in creating the type of 'third space' advocated by Rapp and Rhomberg (2012). In the latter case, they appear to advocate a platform that entails a dilution of both cultures for which there seems no appetite on either side since they each feel considerable devotion to their own flags, emblems, cultural activities and even sporting affiliations (Hassan, 2002). Despite this, other cross-community sports have managed to strike a compromise, with rugby and boxing being among the most successful in creating conditions for the expression of personal and national identities that incorporate diverse expressions of identity. Boxing, as a sport of individuals, has created conditions where every fighter, nationalist or unionist, represents Ireland in the Olympic Games and Northern Ireland in the Commonwealth Games, thus formally recognising the society's shared British and Irish identities by effectively fighting under the flags of each state at different times (Cronin, 1997). Rugby union, as a team game more comparable to association football, has managed the same in other ways (Moore, 2015).

Comparison with Ireland rugby team

The controversy over Northern players declaring for the Republic of Ireland football team compares interestingly with the Irish rugby team and Protestant/unionist players who have played for this team. Indeed, in comparison with the football teams' situation, there is very little (if any) serious debate about Protestant/unionist players playing for an All-Ireland sports team (thus ignoring partition) and the creation of a Northern Ireland rugby team. There has also been an established coterie of important northern Protestant players in the Ireland team, thus possibly stymieing any debate about separate Ireland rugby teams (and reflection of national identity).

It may be useful to register the success of the Ulster rugby team in that this team, playing home games in Belfast and reflecting a long-established Protestant support, allows Northern Protestants to successfully juxtapose a British or Northern Irish identity, beside supporting or even playing for an All-Ireland rugby team. Trevor Ringland, a former Ireland rugby internationalist and former Ulster Unionist Party representative acknowledged this relationship recently when he stated that, 'Northern Ireland is actually as "British as Finchley" but also "as Irish as Cork" although our [Northern/Protestant/Unionist] Irishness is distinct from that of the Republic of Ireland' (*Belfast Newsletter*, 20.10.2017).

It should also be noted that the Irish Rugby Football Union (IRFU) has been arguably more successful in neutralising symbols and aspects that may appear alienating to Protestant players. The IRFU created its own flag after partition and also created a new anthem to be played before 'home' games after renditions of Amhrán na bhFiann (Tuck, 2003: 502), and this new anthem is the only anthem played when Ireland are playing away from home. Within this set of circumstances, players – Catholic/Protestant and Northern/Southern – have been consistently able to give specific explanations of a 'we – I balance' experience while representing 'their' Ireland (ibid: 511). Therefore, these teams have found a better means of reflecting the various layers of complexity that shape individuals' and communities' sense of national identity. The ability of rugby to allow players and supporters the room to compartmentalise and balance what are often seen as competing identities is possibly the key difference between the island's two football teams and one rugby team.

Conclusion

Some commentators have been brutal in their judgement on the IFA on this issue. Brendan Crossan, sports commentator for the *Irish News*, directly accused the IFA of refusing to acknowledge the complexities and realities of the situation facing them regarding player eligibility:

> . . . stamping your feet in frustration hasn't got the IFA anywhere. To use a football analogy, it's like playing long ball tactics and being frustrated by

> the outcome. Put simply, the IFA need better tactics. They should be asking themselves why so many young Catholic players don't want to play for the north. Indeed, the IFA would be better served if they carried out in-depth surveys/interviews with all the so-called 'defectors' to find out where they, as an association, are going wrong. Moreover, blaming the FAI for 'poaching' northern-born players is not a fair analysis of the situation.
>
> (*Irish News*, 17.03.2017).

Journalist and commentator Andrew Quinn, writing in the *Derry Journal*, also spelt out the predicament that Gerry Armstrong, and essentially the IFA and its supporters face:

> Gerry Armstrong is entitled to his opinion and it's a valid one but let's not shy away from the facts; the Northern Ireland football team needs a total facelift. If the IFA want to make declaring for Northern Ireland an attractive option for nationalists across the North then they must address the tough issues.
>
> (*Derry Journal*, 25.11.2011).

Criticism of a similar level and kind can be directed at unionist politicians and unionist-minded (ex and present) footballers, commentators et al. The refusal to recognise the belief of these players to follow their conscience and declare for their country has been typified by an obtuse attitude that ignores legitimate positions and concerns. Ironically, since the Good Friday Agreement was signed in 1998, and as the 2011 census found out, 20% of the population in Northern Ireland identify as Northern Irish (5% less than those who viewed themselves as Irish (*Guardian*, 12.05.2017). It is, therefore, significant that the Irish football association has refused to acknowledge or even attempt to cater for those fans and players who do not view themselves as unionist. While the desire to remove sectarianism from the stands has been largely successful (see Bell, 2017), the willingness to create a Northern Ireland team that can be represented by all people in the community appears to be far off even with so much relative success on the field in recent times.

Notes

1 '*Our*' in italics for emphasis within this paper and not used in original text.
2 '*We*' in italics for emphasis within this paper and not used in original text.
3 *Belfast Telegraph*, 4 January 2016.
4 Hassan, D., McCullough, S., and Moreland, E. (2009). North or south? Darron Gibson and the issue of player eligibility within Irish soccer. *Soccer & Society*, *10*(6), pp. 740–753. DOI:10.1080/14660970903239933, pp. 752–753.
5 Fulton, G. (2005). Northern Catholic fans of the Republic of Ireland Soccer Team. In Bairner, Alan (Ed.), *Sport and the Irish: Histories, Identities, Issues*. Dublin: UCD Press, p. 125.

References

Armstrong, G., and Mitchell, J. (2001). Players, patrons and politicians: Oppositional cultures in Maltese football. In Armstrong, G. and Giulianotti, R. (Eds.), *Fear and Loathing in World Football*. Oxford: Berg, pp. 137–158.

The Belfast Good Friday Agreement. (1998). *Agreement between the Government of the United Kingdom of Great Britain and Northern Ireland and the Government of Ireland*. Available at: www.gov.uk/government/uploads/system/uploads/attachment_data/file/136652/agreement.pdf (accessed 14 February 2016).

Bell, J. (2017). *Green and White Army: The Structuration of a Social System?* PhD Thesis, Ulster University, UK.

Bleakney, J., and Darby, P. (2018). The pride of east Belfast: Glentoran Football Club and the (re) production of Ulster unionist identities in Northern Ireland. *International Review for the Sociology of Sport*, *53*(8), pp. 975–996.

Breen, P. (2014). Irish football's long divorce. *The Football Pink*, Issue 6.

Breen, P. (2019). Healing past wounds with more than an elastic bandage – A small-scale evaluation of attitudes and aspirations of contemporary Northern Irish Catholics. *National Identities*, *21*(2), pp. 151–169.

Brown, K., and Macginty, R. (2003). Public attitudes toward partisan and neutral symbols in post-agreement Northern Ireland. *Identities: Global Studies in Culture and Power*, *10*(1), pp. 83–108.

Clancy, T. (2010). The big man, the footsteps, and the fissile saint: Paradigms and the study of saints' cults in Scotland. In Boardman, S. and Williamson, E. (Eds.), *The Cult of Saints and the Virgin Mary in Medieval Scotland*. Woodbridge, Suffolk: Boydell Press, pp. 1–20.

Cronin, M. (1997). Which nation, which flag? Boxing and national identities in Ireland. *International Review for the Sociology of Sport*, *32*(2), pp. 131–146.

Cronin, M. (1999). *Sport and Nationalism in Ireland: Gaelic Games, Soccer and Irish Identity since 1884*. Dublin: Four Courts Press, Ireland.

Duggan, K. (2014). Six men dead: The World Cup massacre. *The Irish Times Newspaper*, 15.06.2014.

Fulton, G. (2005). Northern Catholic fans of the Republic of Ireland Soccer Team. In Bairner, Alan (Ed.), *Sport and the Irish: Histories, Identities, Issues*. Dublin: UCD Press.

Hassan, D. (2002). A people apart: Soccer, identity and Irish nationalists in Northern Ireland. *Soccer and Society*, *3*(3), pp. 65–83.

Hassan, D., and McCue, K. (2013). The 'silent' Irish – Football, migrants and the pursuit of integration. *Soccer & Society*, *14*(3), pp. 416–428.

Hassan, D., McCullough, S., and Moreland, E. (2009). North or south? Darron Gibson and the issue of player eligibility within Irish soccer. *Soccer and Society*, 6, pp. 740–753.

Hogan, V. (2015). James McClean: I was hung out to dry over poppy issue. *The Irish Independent Newspaper*, 27.03.2015.

Hughes, J. (2013). *Is the Northern Ireland Peace Process Flagging?* London: School of Economics Politics and Policy Blog. Accessed at: http://blogs.lse.ac.uk/politicsandpolicy/archives/30225

Kelly, J. (2017). *Sport and Militarism: Contemporary Global Perspectives*. Butterworth, M. L. (Ed.). London: Routledge, pp. 149–162, Chapter 10.

Kuper, S. (2007). *Political Football: Neil Lennon*. Channel 4 News Blog. Accessed at: www.channel4.com/news/articles/sports/political+football+neil+lennon/882547.html

Liston, K., and Deighan, M. (2019). Whose 'wee country'?: Identity politics and sport in Northern Ireland. *Identities*, 26(2), pp. 203–221.
McVeigh, R., and Rolston, B. (2007). From Good Friday to Good Relations: Sectarianism, racism and the Northern Ireland state. *Race and Class*, 48(4), pp. 1–23.
Moore, C. (2015). *The Irish Soccer Split*. Cork: Cork University Press.
Nagle, J. (2012). The repositioning of Irish Nationalism in Northern Ireland – An examination of consociationalism and devolution in identity change. *Ethnopolitics Papers 2012/21*, pp. 1–28.
Nolan, P. (2012). *The Northern Ireland Peace Monitoring Report*. Presentation given at Chief Executives' Forum, Malone House, 20 February 2012.
O'Neill, S. (2003). Justice in ethnically diverse societies: A critique of political alienation. *Ethnicities*, 3(3), pp. 369–392.
Rapp, M., and Rhomberg, M. (2012). Seeking a neutral identity in Northern Ireland's political wall paintings. *Peace Review: A Journal of Social Justice*, 24(4), pp. 470–477.
Roberts, B. (2017). *Gunshots & Goalposts: The Story of Northern Irish Football*. London: Avenue Books, UK.
Ruane, J., and Todd, J. (2001). The politics of transition? Explaining political crises in the implementation of the Belfast Good Friday Agreement. *Political Studies*, 49(5), pp. 923–940.
Smith, A.D. (1991). *National Identity*. Reno: Penguin.
Storey, D. (2016). *Which boys in green? Identity issues in Irish soccer*. Available at: http://eprints.worc.ac.uk/5085/3/Sport%25204%2520Storey-3.pdf.
Sugden, J., and Bairner, A. (1993). *Sport, Sectarianism and Society in a Divided Ireland*. New York: St Martin's Press Inc.
Tonge, J., and Gomez, R. (2015). Shared identity and the end of conflict? How far has a common sense of 'Northern Irishness' replaced British or Irish allegiances since the 1998 Good Friday agreement? *Irish Political Studies*, 30(2), pp. 276–298.
Trimble, D. (1998). *Nobel Speech on Receiving the Nobel Peace Prize*. Available at www.nobel.se/peace/laureates/1998/trimble-lecture.html.
Tuck, J. (2003). The men in white: Reflections on rugby union, the media and Englishness. *International Review for the Sociology of Sport*, 38(2), 177–199.
Vaughan-Williams, N. (2006). Towards a problematisation of the problematisations that reduce Northern Ireland to a 'problem'. *Critical Review of International Social and Political Philosophy*, 9(4), pp. 513–526.

Chapter 4

'Poppies in the field'

The spectacularisation of military remembrance in British football

Danny Fitzpatrick

Introduction

On 12 November 2011, the English national football team played a friendly match against Spain at Wembley stadium. The fixture coincided with Remembrance Weekend, scheduled between Armistice Day and Remembrance Sunday – the two days in November each year when the United Kingdom (UK) pauses to remember the British and Commonwealth servicemen and women killed in conflict. In the days preceding, the English Football Association (FA) had requested permission from the sport's international governing body – the Fédération Internationale de Football Association (FIFA) – to allow the national team to wear shirts embroidered with red poppies – the familiar symbol of military remembrance – during the match. FIFA refused. The world governing body's decision rested on the assumption that the poppy represents a political symbol and as such contravened Law 4 of the Rules of the Game banning political, religious or commercial messages on shirts or equipment, which is designed to ensure 'the neutrality of the game' (FIFA, 2010).

The decision was met with a vehement response from both the British government and press. FIFA was lobbied by both Prime Minister David Cameron – who claimed it was 'absurd' and 'outrageous' to claim that 'wearing a poppy . . . is a political act' (BBC, 2011) – and Prince William, acting as president of the English FA, who requested, somewhat paradoxically, for the governing body to grant 'an exception in this special circumstance' despite stating that the poppy was a 'universal symbol of remembrance' with 'no political, religious or commercial connotations' (*Guardian*, 2011). The then minister for sport, Hugh Robertson, railed against FIFA, claiming that the poppy was 'not religious or political in any way . . . the British feel very strongly about this issue.' In a rather contradictory manner, he also maintained that 'wearing a poppy is a display of national pride, just like wearing your country's football shirt.' This short statement is doing a great deal of rhetorical work. Not only is Robertson claiming that the poppy is a symbol of national pride, identity and belonging, akin to support for the national football team, he is suggesting that both performative acts, and their symbiosis, are natural and apolitical. Similar sentiments were repeated during this spat with FIFA; Jack Wilshere, then a professional footballer for Arsenal and England, remarked at the time: 'the England team should wear poppies on Saturday. It's the nation's tradition and it would be disrespectful not to' (*Daily Mail*, 2011). In a recurrence of this debate in 2016, a journalist commented: 'Sport cannot be separated from remembrance because there has *always* been a link between the fields of battle and the fields of play' (Hitt, 2016: *my emphasis*).

These claims are ahistorical. The decisions taken about national commemoration, as opposed to private grief, are always political. At a mundane level, national commemoration is inherently political, as it involves the agency of both private and public institutions (including the state). But private grief can also be deliberately instrumentalised for political gain (Danilova, 2016). Collectivised grief, particularly at the national level, generates 'symbolic capital' (Bourdieu, 2018) that can legitimise purposive political action. From a Bourdieusian perspective (Rose-Redwood, 2009), the symbolic capital of private grief can be scaled up to consolidate or reinvent national solidarities (social capital). Military commemoration can invoke a mixture of feelings and emotions about both familial and collective memory and is inextricably linked to the politics of nationalism. Yet, the practices and narratives of military commemoration have the potential to be divisive as well as unifying. As recently as 1987, an IRA bomb killed 11 people at a Remembrance Sunday ceremony – sometimes referred to as the 'Poppy Day massacre' – in Enniskillen, Northern Ireland. The wilful blindness to this recent history of the poppy and military remembrance in the context of the territorial politics of the UK, let alone its wider relations in the world, is striking.

This type of ahistoricism will be familiar to critical observers of sportive nationalism (Brentin and Cooley, 2016). Sport constitutes a significant social ritual contributing to the conception of the nation as an 'imagined community' (King, 2003; Anderson, 2006 [1983]). Aside from war, sport is often the primary means through which a nation can attain its fullest expression (Sugden and Tomlinson, 1994). The interweaving of existing and new rituals of military remembrance into the cultural heritage of football constitutes an 'invented tradition' (Hobsbawm and Ranger, 2012 [1983]). Before 2011, the display of the poppy on the shirt of the national team had been a non-issue for the English FA. Indeed, when England played Brazil at the same time in November two years earlier, the embroidered poppies, that in 2011 were deemed to be sacrosanct in the traditional ritual of remembrance in Britain, were neither worn nor requested (Fox, 2014). The match against Spain in 2011 represented the 37th time the English national team had competed in an international game between 1 and 15 November since the end of World War I; in none of the 36 previous occasions did they take to the field with the adornment of the poppy (FA, 2019).

This presents a puzzle: why had the poppy been elevated to such a totemic symbol in English football in 2011, when previously it had been considered a non-issue? What were the antecedents to this change? This chapter interrogates these questions to analyse how football stadia have emerged as prominent sites of military commemoration and memorialisation. The English FA have themselves observed the change in practice, recognising 'greater focus . . . given to the level of support and respect shown by the national teams' (BBC, 2011) in recent years to military remembrance. The request to wear the poppy on the shirt was justified on the basis of this 'growing commitment . . . to show our respect and support' (BBC, 2011). This chapter traces the process of this 'growing commitment' to promote the use of football in the spectacle of military commemoration.

The concept of the spectacle (Debord, 1992 [1967]) lies at the heart of this analysis. Contemporary military remembrance is a spectacle: 'phenomena of media, culture, and society that embody the society's basic values, serve the enculturate individuals into this way of life, and dramatize the society's mode of conflict and conflict resolution' (Kellner, 1996: 458). The last 15 years have witnessed an increasing 'spectacularisation' of remembrance in British football. The spectacle of remembrance is consumed. This spectacularisation of military remembrance sees it embedded within the wider patterns of entertainment consumption in the 'Experience Society' (Schulze, 1992). Since the 1980s, there has been a growing emphasis on commoditisation of memory and 'spectacular' episodes of recent history in popular culture and entertainment: the Holocaust, World Wars I and II and the sinking of the Titanic. As these events move further into the past, they are less about *remembering* and more about *experiencing*. We cannot remember what we did not actually experience, but we can experience the ritual of remembrance. It is perhaps unsurprising that football came to play a bigger role in this process, given its position at the pinnacle of the modern mediated spectacle (Goldblatt, 2019). The enmeshment of remembrance and the sport-media-entertainment complex is essentially a 21st-century phenomenon.

Over the last decade particularly, the rituals of military remembrance in British football have grown evermore in publicity and ostentation, in stark relief to its origins of Victorian solemnity. They are often overtly militaristic. Military personnel in full uniform (both historic and contemporary) invariably accompany proceedings. Glasgow Rangers and Hearts have employed an artillery gun to commence the obligatory minute silence. The military heritage of World Wars I and II, such as a Mark IV tank and Spitfire plane, have been displayed outside stadia, at events such as the 'British Army Fun Zone' at the 2018 'Games of Remembrance' at Notts County (2018). Beyond silent reflection, fans are increasingly incorporated into this spectacle, active participants in the display of 'tifos' of giant poppies and messages of remembrance across entire terraces. Other invented traditions surrounding Remembrance Weekend – sometimes sardonically referred to as 'Poppy Season' and 'Poppy Pulooza' – in 2019 are so absurd they are almost beyond parody. Among the many examples included 'Poppy-Man': 'a man in a giant poppy suit and inexplicable clown shoes at Tranmere [a League One football club in Merseyside, England] was the moment it all became clear – this great festival of public respect has lost all sense of self-awareness' (Cooney, 2019). Football clubs have engaged in an 'arms-race' of remembrance in a bid to outdo each other with increasingly incongruous 'displays of pantomime respect' (ibid.). Moreover, the kitschness of these displays is embedded alongside the more conventional assemblage of other forms of commemoration, such as the minute silence.

A contingency of events is important in explaining this change. Military conflicts in the Falklands, the Gulf and, more recently, Iraq and Afghanistan – and the public's attitude to the involvement of British Armed Forces in those wars – have shaped the approach of military and political actors to the practice of remembrance. The incidence of notable anniversaries, particularly the centenaries of the start and end of World War I in 2014 and 2018, have undoubtedly provided added focus and prominence. But there is a broader, more underlying, process of reimagining the observable. UK football offers a useful case study to explore the performance and projection of remembrance and how this impacts upon notions of collective identity. In examining these trends, the chapter develops a novel theoretical account of the relationship between military remembrance, sport and politics in the UK since the end of World War I. It does so over four sections. The first theorises the relationship between football, military remembrance and British nationalism, identifying the points of tension as well as symbiosis. The second, as a corrective to the ahistorical accounts above, examines the antecedents to the contemporary spectacularisation of military remembrance in football. It identifies the 1927 FA Cup final and the Falklands War as critical junctures in the relationship between football, remembrance and nationalism. The third analyses the turn to history and commemoration in British football and society more generally, in order to understand the specific catalyst for change. The final section concludes by asking a core question: why does football 'remember,' and whose interest does this remembering serve?

The football-war-nation nexus

A nascent body of research has emerged in recent years that examines the politics of military remembrance in the UK (Danilova, 2016; Kelly, 2016). These studies are often situated in wider debates on the growing militarisation of popular culture in the contemporary post-9/11 era (Butterworth, 2014). Yet, despite the scholarly attention on the militarisation thesis, there have been few attempts to understand the growing links between association football and the military in the UK (cf. Penn and Berridge, 2018). To date, no research study has sought to explain, as well as document, this changing relationship. This chapter addresses this gap in the existing literature.

The duality of sacrifice and victory embodied by the poppy, resonates with the essence and history of football. The emotional appeal of sport is characterised by a range of dualities: life and death (Herzog, 2015), playfulness and seriousness (Critchley, 2017) and war and peace (Donnelly, 2011). Sport is inextricably linked to both conflict and unity, in both a metaphorical and literal sense. There have been long-established links between football and the military in the UK, in both war- and peacetime (Mason and Riedi, 2010). Football – which by the 1900s was the dominant feature of working-class male culture – was used by the government as both a mechanism for encouraging recruitment and a means of establishing morale within the British Army during the First World War (Fuller, 1990). As well as offering a conduit to appeal to the patriotic duty of working-class men to volunteer (before conscription in 1916), a number of 'Pals Battalions' comprised professional footballers exclusively, with several clubs suffering multiple fatalities to their players (Harris and Whippy, 2008).[1] These tragedies – along with the now much storied and celebrated images of Captain Wilfred Percy Nevill kicking a football 'over the top' and German and British troops playing a football 'friendly' during the Christmas Day truce of 1914 (Roberts, 2006) – has secured the place of football in the popular memory of the First World War (although the fact that the British Army sought to ban these 'truce games,' considering them to constitute 'near mutiny,' has been largely forgotten).

Even today, the lingua franca of football draws heavily on militaristic metaphors, precisely because of its development from 'battle-like encounters' (Dolan and Connolly, 2016: 190). A range of linguistic scholars have observed the cognitive parallels between military action and football (Lakoff, 1991). The vocabulary of football – as uttered by commentators, journalists, pundits and supporters – is dominated by military metaphors that tend to 'depict the activities in and around the football pitch in terms of an informal war zone' (Bergh, 2011), with its 'midfield generals' and forwards, described as 'humanoid tanks', adding 'heavy artillery to . . . [the] front line' (*The Telegraph*, 2016).

In the context of English football, this everyday military vernacular has often been accompanied by a tendency towards 'othering' in much of the popular discourse (especially in the tabloid press), and particularly with reference to the national team (Crolley and Hand, 2006). As Garland (2004) accounts, this can range from casual stereotyping and limited, monocultural understandings of Englishness to the nadir of the 'xenophobic, chauvinistic and jingoistic gutter journalism' exhibited by sections of the tabloid press during their coverage of Euro '96 (National Heritage Select Committee, 1996: 1). The association between football, the armed forces and the nation, while often implicit and 'banal' (Billig, 1995), is rendered explicit and 'hot' via the tabloid press at pivotal moments. A direct connection is sometimes made between the roles of the English football players and the British military, with exhortations to win matches in honour of 'our brave boys and girls . . . in Iraq and Afghanistan' (*Mirror*, 2010). Former conflicts are recast to narrate the vacillating performance and fortunes of the English national team; for example, in a report on the 2002 World Cup match between England and Argentina, the *Daily Star* invoked the *Sun*'s infamous headline about the sinking of the Argentinian battleship – the *General Belgrano* – during the Falklands War with 'Gotcha: foot of God sinks Argies' (8 June: 1).

Given the rhetorical links between war, nation and football, it is perhaps unsurprising that the remembrance of Britain's war dead has become a recurring feature of the British football calendar. However, as Wilson (2014: 197) observes, 'the manner in which these sites of memory frame the significance of the game in relationship to the war reveals wider assumptions about the contested memory of the conflict in Britain.' The framing of the relations between football and the military has not remained constant over time and serves as a useful lens through which to examine the nature of contemporary British identity and how this can be established, reinvented and contested. Despite the popular imagery of football and military life in the context of World War I, there were always important points of tension. The disdain heaped on the 'unpatriotic' FA and professional footballers for continuing with the 1914–1915 league season despite the advent of war is a case in point (Veitch, 1985). The instrumentalisation of football for military recruitment in this period relied more on the renunciation of football, rather than a celebration of its virtues. In a column headed 'Duty Before Sport,' *the Times* (1914) published the following announcement:

> This is no time for football. This nation, this Empire has got to occupy itself with more serious business. The young men who play football and the young men who look on have better work to do. The trumpet calls them, their country calls them, the heroes in the trenches call them. They are summoned to leave their sport, and to take part in the great game. That game is war, for life or death.

In terms of military commemoration, football played a largely peripheral role for much of its history. Several critical junctures in both the cultural heritage of football and the wider patterns of commemoration in British society can be identified over the last century that help explain the current nexus of football, military remembrance and British nationalism.

Critical junctures in the football-war-nation nexus: from 'banal' to 'hot'

1927 and 'Abide with Me'

The 1927 FA Cup final is a significant moment in this narrative, as it saw the introduction of several 'invented traditions' in the formal staging of national military commemoration in football. The 1927 showpiece between Arsenal and Cardiff City was notable in that it was attended by King George V and Britain's two 20th-century war-time prime ministers, David Lloyd George and Winston Churchill. It was the first time that 'Abide with Me' – a Christian hymn written by a Victorian clergyman in 1847 – was sung before the start of the final, reportedly at the behest of the king (Russell, 2008). The choice of hymn was notable; not only did it have connotations of the British establishment, due to its association with the Anglican Church and the monarchy, it had been sung in the trenches by Allied troops during World War I (Penn and Berridge, 2018). The timing of this innovation is also instructive. The 1927 FA Cup final was the first to broadcast on BBC radio (and recorded and later made available to purchase on record disc). It became one of the first 'mediatised rituals' (Cottle, 2006) in the age of mass public broadcasting, extending beyond the immediate spectators in attendance, to the radio audience at home. The nexus between football, military remembrance and national identity was crystallised in that moment at Wembley (then known as the Empire Stadium): 'a moment of remembrance that expressed the shared grief of a nation' (Hill, 2012: 12). Henry Garland (1957: 126), the hymn's historian, observed:

> There has been much boisterous singing of popular songs, but when 'Abide with me' was announced by the conductor, there fell on the vast crowd an immediate silence; compared with its moving intensity to the sudden silence at the Cenotaph on Armistice Day. It first struck me that it was out of place to sing a hymn so sacred as 'Abide with me' at a football match, but that feeling soon went as the Band of Guards played the opening chords. The volume of singing increased with each verse until the stadium became like the nave of a great cathedral. It was a deeply affecting experience bringing a lump to my throat and tears to my eyes.

This orchestrated, collective singing[2] of a restricted repertoire of 'national' songs, hymns (such as 'Abide with Me'), and music of the First World War, usually led by a marching military band, became embedded in the cultural fabric of football from the mid-1920s (Russell, 2014). It displayed the community-creating potential of football and the indispensable role of history, remembrance and memory in that process (Herzog, 2015).

The position of the military in football remained limited to these 'banal' (Billig, 1995) reference points for most of the 20th century. The place of military remembrance per se in football was virtually absent and has a much more recent heritage. The nature of military memorialisation is not fixed, therefore. There have been significant changes in popular attitudes towards the military, including the manner in which the war dead should be commemorated, over the last century. In the inter-war year (1919–1939), a two-minute silence was only observed on Armistice Day (11 November). There is no evidence of a two-minute silence at the only two football fixtures that took place on 11 November in 1922 or 1933 during this period (even though by the 1930s remembrance had become established in the calendar of British life [Noakes, 2015]). Following the end of World War II, the two-minute silence and other commemorative ceremonies were moved to the nearest Sunday after 11 November, thereafter referred to as Remembrance Sunday. This was prompted by the desire, on behalf of the British government, for military remembrance to be inclusive of both World War I and II, rather than have an exclusive focus on the former. The fact that professional football in Britain only began to be played on a Sunday from 1974 limited the connection between military commemoration and the national sport to very few opportunities. None were sought. Indeed, minute silences on or around Remembrance Sunday were only introduced in football at the turn of the millennium.

After 1945, the institution of 'Remembrance Sunday' served to strengthen the British myth of 'peacefulness,' which had emerged in the inter-war years (Lawrence, 2003). There has not been a single year that Britain has not been engaged in military conflict in the putative 'post-war' era; no other country has been engaged continuously in fighting over such a long period (MacAskill and Cobain, 2014). To date, 1968 and 2016 are the only years where no UK Armed Forces personnel have lost their lives as a result of conflict (MoD, 2019). In contrast to the conventional portrayals of the 'post-war' welfare state, Edgerton (2005) argues that it was equally driven by a logic of a 'warfare state'.[3] Regarding the latter, the Falklands War is a decisive moment. The conflation of the militaristic, nationalistic and sporting in the discourse on the Falklands was important in reshaping the relationship between all three thereafter.

The 'Falklands Factor'

The Falklands War reshaped public attitudes towards the military, driven by a media discourse that emphasised 'powerful myths of British identity from which a story of nationalism, bravery, and victory unfolded' (Maltby, 2016). Unlike much of the preceding post-1945 era, the Falklands War was fought outside the paradigm of the Cold War; it was predicated on the defence of sovereign territory against the aggression of a military dictatorship and framed (both by the government and the media) as a counterpoint to Britain's supposed domestic and international post-war decline (Jones, 2018). In a speech to a Conservative rally, Prime Minister Thatcher claimed, post-Falklands: 'Britain has re-kindled that spirit which has fired her for generations past and which today has begun to burn as brightly as before' (1983). The connection between the show of military strength and ultimate victory in the Falklands War in the prevailing context of the narratives of decline (including the fate of British football, both domestically and internationally) was not lost on the public. One Mass-Observation respondent suggested that 'the response of the great majority of people in Britain indicates a thirst for a glorious victory, perhaps because of our recent poor showing in football' (cited in Jones, 2018: 83).

As well as an electoral boost for the stuttering Conservative government in Thatcher's first term, the so-called Falklands Factor also entailed an upsurge in popular feeling about the role of the military as a crucial ingredient of British national identity (Hobsbawm, 1983; Barnett, 1982). The nexus between an increasing nationalist fervour, military victory and football was strengthened due to the coincidence between the tail end of the Falklands War and the English national team's participation in the 1982 World Cup. This meant the 'the stage was set for a conflation of politico-nationalist and footballing discourses' (Wren-Lewis and Clarke, 1983: 126–127):

> During the run-up to the 1982 World Cup the atmosphere undeniably changed. . . . A mood of patriotic optimism began to emerge. There can be

> no doubt that the news of British victories in the South Atlantic created the conditions for this mood. . . . The BBC team . . . were especially keen to identify 'a new national pride in the English team and their supporters'. With the English team's 3–1 victory over the French following two days after the first news of a British military triumph in Port Stanley, Jimmy Hill was able to speak of it as 'a time when pride and patriotism in this country is just reawakening.'

Victory in the Falklands War was interpreted, concluded Hobsbawm (1983: 19), '. . . as if we had won a World Cup with guns.' While such overt conflations of the sporting and the nationalistic dissipated after the end of the Falklands War, a more enduring shift in tone post-1982 can be detected. It marked a seminal moment in the civil-military relations of the UK, especially with regard to remembrance (Penn and Berridge, 2018). There were calls in the aftermath of the Falklands War in 1982 for the restoration of the two-minute silence to its original date of Armistice Day. Since the Falklands, there has been a concerted effort by successive British governments, as well as by the military itself, to promote military values and 'to legitimise the near-permanent state of war' (Penn and Berridge, 2018: 117). The participation of the British Armed Forces in conflict post-1982 – in the Gulf War (1990–1991), Bosnia (1992–1995), Kosovo (1998–1999), Sierra Leone (2000–2002), Afghanistan (2001–2014) Iraq (2003–2009) and Libya (2011) – prompted a reimagining of the role of military commemoration. However, it is only in the last decade that the instrumental role of football has been amplified in this context. This can be seen as a strategic response not only to the management of civil-military relations, but also to the perceived erosion of British national identity. The imbrication of sport and military remembrance is particularly powerful given that 'there is now an even greater uncertainty about what it means to serve one's country, at least in every arena outside of sport' (Ware, 2010: 1).

The relationship between football, military commemoration and nationalism is not deterministic. The growing prominence of military remembrance in football in recent decades should not be reduced to the engagement of the UK military in operations in the same period. Wider changes in the commemorative practices in British football and society – what Russell (2006) terms the 'commemorative turn' – are also important.

The 'commemorative turn'

The above discussion charted some of the changes and continuities in the nexus of football, the military and British nationalism. It also demonstrated, via the analysis of the introduction of 'Abide by Me' in the pre-match ritual of the FA Cup Final, how major professional sport events became seen as appropriate occasions for national mediations on the theme of death (Richards, 2014). So, while themes of the military and remembrance have been incorporated into the spectacle of football for just short of a century, they had been largely banal and implicit until the latter part of that period. As well as the conflation of militaristic, nationalistic and sporting discourses after the Falklands, 'football's culture of commemoration has altered both quantitatively and qualitatively from about 1985' (Russell, 2006: 3).

Commemoration of any kind was rare until the mid-1980s; the 1958 Munich air disaster and the death of Bill Shankly in 1981 being the notable exceptions. The Munich disaster was a particularly important historical marker and set the pattern for future commemorations in sport: 'In the immediate aftermath, the Football League ordered two minutes of silence at all games . . . together with the wearing of black armbands and the lowering of flags to half-mast' (Mitten, 2014). The narration of the Munich air crash went some way in constructing a football 'community' – what is often labelled the 'football family' in contemporary parlance. It was reported as a disaster of national and international significance and elided the communities of nation and football: 'the Daily Mail referred to it as "a black day for Manchester, for football, and for the British people"' (7 February 1958 cited in Mellor, 2004: 265). The interpretation of the disaster also revealed the affective power of football, which by the late 1950s was undoubtedly the *national* sport, to unify diverse groups of people across society. The Munich disaster demonstrated that, by the 1950s, football stadium not only had become important, and perhaps in some contexts the pre-eminent, 'emblem of locality' (Taylor, 1989: 93), but also a 'sacred place . . . analogous to a cathedral' (Bale, 1991: 131).

Notwithstanding the Munich disaster, other examples of commemoration in football were limited. On the rare occasions it did happen, commemoration was localised and relatively muted. As Russell argues, 'while football paid due respect to its dead, there was generally nothing distinctive about its public mourning in terms of frequency and style' (2006: 3). The shock of three footballing catastrophes in quick succession can be identified as a critical juncture: Heysel (1985), Bradford (1985) and Hillsborough (1989). The latter of these is particularly critical to a shift in the memorial culture of football. In the immediate aftermath of Hillsborough, both Sheffield Wednesday's home ground, as the site of the disaster, and Anfield, the home stadium of Liverpool fans who had been its victims, became huge shrines composed of flowers, club scarves and shirts, personal mementos, including teddy bears and photos. Observing the reaction to Hillsborough, Taylor (1989: 92) remarked how the pictures of these shrines impressed on him how football stadia had become sites of 'popular sanctification.' Bairner (2006) highlights the relatively restrained public reaction to the Ibrox Stadium disaster of 1971, against the outpouring of emotion for Hillsborough. Indeed, as Walker (2004: 180) notes, 'the Ibrox disaster has been much more the subject of popular inquiry and personal remembrance since the late 1980s than before.' Notwithstanding the sheer scale of loss, Hillsborough (in a similar vein to the Bradford City fire disaster at Valley Parade in 1985) may have had a more visceral impact because of its mediated nature: it was broadcast live on BBC Grandstand, the tragedy unfolding on screen in front of the nation (Taylor, 2013). Hillsborough signalled a general trend towards more explicit displays of commemoration in football.[4] However, it's important not to overstate the rapidity of change following these events. As late as 1998, Frank Keating (1999) remarked upon the lack of attention afforded by football to the death of World Cup–winning England manager Alf Ramsey, saying: 'Football is too manic these days to spare time for reflection, remembrance, or humanity, even in death.'

The emergence of football commemoration should be seen in context of 'a much wider shift in the nation's emotional ecology' (Russell, 2006: 10). Several studies have pointed to the 'new cultures of memorialisation and commemoration' following the death of Princess Diana (Russell, 2006: 5). It is notable that most sport fixtures, including the English and Scottish Premier League football season, were postponed on the day her death was announced, as well as the following Saturday when her funeral took place (BBC, 1997). The Labour government of the time intervened to apply pressure on the Scottish FA to reconsider its decision to continue with its scheduled fixture against Belarus (Miller, 1997). The decision to postpone was unprecedented: notwithstanding extreme weather, the football season had continued virtually uninterrupted in the post-1945 era, even in the aftermath of the death of King George VI and Sir Winston Churchill.

Why does football 'remember'?

It is in this context of a commemorative turn in both British sport and society, that we should consider the growing prominence of military remembrance in football. Since 1995, the 50th anniversary of the end of World War II, national commemoration has taken place on both Armistice Day and Remembrance Sunday. This change created the space for a more prominent role for military commemoration *within* football. The first minute silence for fallen soldiers took place in the 1999/2000 season. Since then, it has become a permanent fixture in the football calendar. The shift in the role of the national game in military commemoration after 2000 is likely to have been affected by the changes in remembrance practices and the football calendar, the role of particular actors (such as the Royal British Legion [RBL]) in lobbying for change, as well as wider trends in attitudes to commemoration in British society.

The institution of the minute silence for the war dead in football has been augmented over the intervening period. Whereas it was first introduced only to matches taking place on Remembrance Sunday, in the last decade, it has tended to cover professional football matches in all four divisions of the football league, as well as much of the amateur game, scheduled nearest to Remembrance Weekend. The presence of military personnel, in full uniform, as distinguished guests at professional football fixtures has become a more frequent sight in the same period. The hyper-mediatised nature of modern football is important when considering military commemoration. The advantage of football stadia as a 'memory hotspot' over other public spaces, such as market squares and war memorials, is that dutiful observance of the two-minute silence is almost guaranteed, which can be broadcast to millions at home and overseas. The more diverse range of commemorative practices that emerged in football post-Hillsborough shaped innovations in military commemoration: for example, the unveiling of the Heart of Midlothian memorial to 'fallen footballers' in Edinburgh in 2004 (Ramshaw, 2014); a special, limited-edition green 'military-style' Bolton Wanderers third strip during the 2014/2015 season, embossed with the words 'Lest We Forget,' from Laurence Binyon's poem 'For the Fallen' (Penn and Berridge, 2018); and the holding of dedicated remembrance services for the war dead at football stadia. What was the stimulus for this change?

The increasing use of commemorative silence in football – what the *Guardian* called 'imitations of armistice silences' (12 September 2002) – and wider society threatened the privileged status of Remembrance Weekend. By the late-1990s there were expressions of anxiety, particularly by the RBL as the self-referential 'guarantor of remembrance,' about whether 'the annual memorial to those killed fighting for their country was gradually waning' (Vallely, 2000). At this point the marginalisation of military remembrance – in the midst of the wider proliferation of other types of commemoration – was seized upon by parts of the tabloid press. The *Sunday Express* conducted a survey of 12- to 16-year-olds, finding that a quarter of those interviewed had 'no idea what Remembrance Sunday was for, believing it was to commemorate other historical figures such as Guy Fawkes (Chambers and Black, 2000). This unease was heightened after three-minute silences were held in the aftermath of the terrorist atrocities of 9/11, the 2004 Madrid bombings and the 7/7 London bombings, as well as the 2005 Asian Tsunami. So-called 'silence inflation' was perceived as a threat to the distinctiveness and centrality of military remembrance in the British polity.

The rising prominence of the poppy in football can be seen as part of a strategic response to this challenge. The reinvention of military commemoration in football should be understood according to a broader 'remembrance project,' driven by the RBL, which coheres around the central aim to reaffirm remembrance as a central plank of British public life via popular culture.[5] Football's collective acquiescence reveals the ulterior interests of its authorities and clubs in this project. The latest stage in this evolution of military commemoration in football is the reification of nations ('Cymru 'n Cofio'/'Wales Remembers'), sports ('Football Remembers') and individual clubs ('Arsenal Remembers'). There is an increasingly choreographed spectacularisation of military remembrance, which seeks to establish a discrete relationship between the football leagues and clubs and the military via the poppy. The ubiquity of pin badges sporting the club crest alongside the poppy worn by football managers is an example of this appropriation of remembrance.

The football clubs and authorities[6] are fully cognisant that they operate in a hyper-mediated landscape and are 'anxious to show a sense of social responsibility that, for all the genuine motives involved, is undoubtedly underlaid by an acute consciousness of image' (Russell, 2006: 14). There is a desire to reaffirm traditional links to community and nation in an era of globalised football.

An era where football is characterised by 'transnational circulation of labour, information, capital, and commodities' (Giulianotti and Robertson, 2004: 549) and post-national modes of consumption has arguably resulted in an increased need to denote local football identity (Johnes and Mason, 2003). The chairman of Arsenal, who are owned by American businessman Stan Kroenke, Sir Chips Keswick said:

> It's an honour for the club to be part of remembering those who have sacrificed so much for us. It's extremely important that we create legacies to remember those eight players who paid the ultimate sacrifice and show our respect for them and the many other servicemen and women who continue to serve.
>
> (Arsenal, 2018)

As Foster and Woodthorpe (2012: 53) argue, terrace cultures (including those involving memorial and remembrance) have come to adopt a crucial role in representing the nation and locality 'by actuating particularistic symbolism before global audiences.'

Military remembrance has evolved to form a crucial part of football's cultural political economy. The spectacle of remembrance in football is likely to continue to grow, as football becomes more of an important commodity for the media and other sponsoring interests to expand their markets and sustain their profits in an increasingly competitive global economy. The turn to commemoration provides useful 'moral lessons' of loyalty, duty, sacrifice and service of 'our heroes,' which contrast sharply with the 'the degradation of contemporary footballers' (Russell, 2006: 20–21). As Marina Hyde argues, in the discourse on 'sacrifice in the age of pampering':

> Each Remembrance Day we now seem to be reminded just how badly the present crop of moisturised millionaires would struggle in a muddy trench. . . . No social group is discussed in these terms more than footballers, who are forever being compared unfavourably with generations past who were conscripted into world wars. No profession doesn't know it's born like footballers don't know they're born.
>
> (*Guardian*, 9 November 2016)

Conclusion

We have come full circle. The instrumentalisation of football in the dominant nationalistic-militaristic discourse of the contemporary era rests on the denigration of the game rather than its extolment, just as it did at the start of the 20th century. In the modern spectacle of military remembrance, an antipathy to 'pampered millionaire footballers' is often juxtaposed with the reverence of the 'fallen soldier'. The decoupling of football from its traditional communities – epitomised by the caricature of the avaricious, immoral 'modern footballer' – is used to further sanctify the war dead and strengthen the communal bonds of a fracturing British nationalism. In the cosmopolitan, multinational English Premier League, particular opprobrium is reserved for the few professional footballers who have refused to wear poppy on their football shirts: James McClean, and to lesser extent, Nemanja Matic, have been subject to staunch criticism and pressure for choosing not to support the Poppy Appeal on the basis of British troops' respective involvement in Northern Ireland and the Balkans.

The potency of sport to foster imagined communities, especially national, is well documented (Brentin and Cooley, 2016). The imbrication of military remembrance and memories of war within the spectacle of the contemporary hyper-mediated landscape of football represents an important aspect of the reconstruction of British national identity. The growing 'rhetorical entanglement' (Sirvent and Reyburn, 2017) of sport and militarism has emerged during a period of existential challenge to the very notion of the UK as a unitary and union state. Part of this crisis is derived from the difficulty of expressing the purpose of the state at a time when the historic civic ideologies of Britain – of Protestant messianism, imperial adventure and the Keynesian welfare state – have been exhausted (Moran, 2017: 70). The turn of the new millennium signalled a renewed interest, on behalf of leading politicians, with the 'fuzzy' nature of British national identity (Mandler, 2006). In the early years of New Labour, Tony Blair sought to forge new 'a forward-looking modern patriotism' (2001) in an attempt to remould Britishness to account for a more multicultural society in an increasingly interdependent, globalised world. In the wake of the 7/7 London bombings and resurgent Scottish nationalism, Blair's successor, Gordon Brown, identified the task of establishing a clearer definition of Britishness as one the key goals of his premiership. Sport has played an increasing role in this endeavour. Despite the rhetoric of so-called progressive patriotism, the last two decades have witnessed a revival in martial values in the official discourse on Britishness. The exhaustion of the other common enterprises of the UK has seen the British state rely increasingly on military providentialism as the residual element of British national identity: 'the one civic ideology common to all parts of the Kingdom, and crossing partisan boundaries' (Moran, 2017: 83). It is in this context in which military remembrance derives its power: a civic ritual, with unparalleled affective capacity, which unites almost all. Of course, it is not unusual for memories of war and sacrifice to provide a unifying force across a nation's population. What is novel is the increasing role of sport – and particularly football in the UK context – in its memorialisation.

As Butterworth (2014: 207) argues, because live sporting events are unparalleled in their ability to attract tens of thousands of people to select locations, joined by a viewing public of millions beyond the stadium, and encourage passionate, groupish displays of public expression, 'they are uniquely suited to constituting fans as citizen-subjects, especially by identifying their fanship with spectacular displays of nationalism and patriotism.' The power of football in the modern spectacle lies in its apparent authenticity; there is 'a real crowd in a real stadium, where social relationships, networks, and identities established amongst those present offer an indissoluble humanity' (Goldblatt, 2019: 4). The crowd becomes the 'physical embodiment of the nation' (Fox, 2006: 226). The symbolic capital of this symbolic authenticity is irresistible to powerful political and economic forces. Stahl (2009: 31) observes the insidious, shaping effect of this spectacular 'militainment,' contrasting it with conspicuous propaganda:

> Whereas propaganda rationally engages with argument and narrative, the spectacle forgoes persuasion in favor of fostering disengagement. Whereas propaganda addresses an audience that matters, the spectacle presumes an audience that does not. And whereas propaganda seeks to answer the question of why we fight, the spectacle loses itself in the fact that we fight.

The instrumentalisation of football in the spectacle of military remembrance, however, risks undermining the meaning and solemnity of commemoration, as it becomes ever more obsessed with the highly mediated images and the appearance of dutiful respect – a simulacrum of remembrance – over actual thoughtful reflection: 'The spectacle, considered as the reigning society's method for paralyzing history and memory and for suppressing any history based on historical time, represents a false consciousness of time' (Debord, 1992 [1967]: 60).

Notes

1 Over the course of the First World War, Bradford City FC lost nine players, Everton FC lost five players, Manchester United lost two players and Newcastle United FC suffered the loss of seven players (Harris and Whippy, 2008).

2 The invented ritual of Abide with Me as the 'Cup Final hymn' represented the culmination of a larger movement of 'community singing' that had begun in 1925, with the establishment of the Community Singers Association, and popularised in the preceding 1926–1927 football season. Community singing was an elite-led movement, driven by the tabloid press and the *Daily Express* in particular. It was distinct from the spontaneous and sporadic outbursts of song that had been witnessed before at football: 'it was planned, structured and controlled by the organising bodies' (Nannestad, 2010: 4). In addition to the commercial motives of the British press, community singing movement can be seen as a strategy to promote social cohesion at a time of strife and division, in the wake of the 1926 General Strike. The term 'community' is crucial here. The collective act of singing provided a sense of belonging to a community; it creates the image of communion (for both active participants and the audience) in Anderson's conception of 'imagined communities' (1983). The *Daily Express* wrote of community singers that 'they will find that they are united by indissoluble bonds of cooperation and sympathy' (Russell, 2008: 126).

3 Britain continued to conscript men of service age until 1960 and was engaged in multiple conflicts, including the Korean War (1950–1953) and operations in early Cold War; notably in Greece, Palestine, Malaya, Egypt, Kenya, Cyprus and southern Arabia. Although the later Cold War (from the 1960s) saw the British force used less frequently, as the period of decolonisation came to an end, the eruption of violent conflict in Derry caused the British army to be deployed to Northern Ireland in 1969 (until 2007, when Operation Banner concluded, representing the longest continuous deployment in British military history).

4 There is a distinction to be made here between official and fan-led commemoration. The acts of commemoration in the immediate aftermath of the Hillsborough disaster – including the spectacular Anfield shrine covering vast swathes of the pitch and the 'The

Mile of Scarves' knotted between there and Goodison Park, the home of their local rivals Everton – were initiated by football fans. It was ten years before an official minute silence was observed at the FA Cup semi-finals in 1999, following pressure from by the Hillsborough Justice Campaign group. Hillsborough was notable for 'the mass involvement of ordinary people in the invention or re-invention of ceremonies and rites' (Russell, 2006: 10). The extension of commemorative practices set a precedent, with football fans of different clubs borrowing from and thus universalising the commemorative practices of Hillsborough to articulate their emotional response to death and mourning. Post-Hillsborough, new forms of memorial and sepulchral cultures in football, which challenge and subvert as well as build upon existing commemorative and ecclesiastical traditions, have emerged: the naming of spectator stands after deceased players and managers (Russell, 2006), memorial plaques and 'commemorative bricks' (Herzog, 2013), the scattering of ashes on the 'hallowed turf' or in club 'memorial gardens' (Cook, 2006), football-themed funerals (Huggins, 2012) and the erection of monuments to footballing 'greats' (Stride et al., 2013).

5 See Kelly (2012: 728) who documents the increase in militarisation as part of this broader 'remembrance project'. Prime-time Saturday evening programmes promote the 'support the troops' message: *X Factor 2008* and *2010* released a 'song for heroes'; *Dancing on Ice 2011* included 'Tickets for Troops' patron Lance Corporal Johnson Beharry VC as one of its 'celebrity' dancers. Additionally, serving soldier Katrina Hodge (nicknamed 'Combat Barbie') replaced the dethroned Miss England in the 2009 Miss World contest; active soldiers 'The Trio' released a Christmas 2009 album *Coming Home*; soldiers' partners, 'The Choir, Military Wives,' released a Christmas 2011 single; Prime Minister (Gordon Brown) and serving military personnel took centre stage at the grand finale of ITV's Britain's Best awards programme; an Oscar-like military award show labelled 'The Millies' emerged; *Sky News* initiated a military-inspired 'For Queen and Country' week; and a Sunday night prime-time 'Concert for Heroes' at Twickenham was screened live on BBC1 (12 September 2010).

6 This proliferation of memorialisation in football is not restricted to the UK. Herzog (2015: 198) shows that a multitude of diverse traditions, ceremonies and rituals are widely employed by clubs and associations throughout Europe and beyond, although he concedes that these trends have 'strong roots' in the UK.

Bibliography

Anderson, B. (2006 [1983]) *Imagined communities: reflections on the origin and spread of nationalism*. London: Verso Books.

Arsenal (2018) 'Arsenal remembers', 09 November 2018. Retrieved from: www.arsenal.com/news/arsenal-remembers

Bairner, A. (2006) '"In balance with this life, this death": mourning George Best', *International Review of Modern Sociology*, 32(2): 293–308.

Bale, J. (1991) 'Playing at home: British football and a sense of place', in J. Williams and S. Wagg (eds.), *British football and social change*. Leicester: Leicester University Press, 130–144.

Barnett, A. (1982) *Iron Britannia: why Parliament waged the Falklands War*. London: Allison and Bushy.

BBC (1997) 'Britain remembers'. Retrieved from: www.bbc.co.uk/news/special/politics97/diana/pauses.html

BBC (2011) 'Prince William demands Fifa U-turn on poppy ban'. Retrieved from: www.bbc.co.uk/sport/football/15643295

Bergh, G. (2011) 'Football is war: a case study of minute-by-minute football commentary', *Veredas-Revista de Estudos Linguísticos*, 15(2): 83–93.
Billig, M. (1995) *Banal nationalism*. London: Sage.
Bourdieu, P. (2018) 'The forms of capital', in Granovetter, M. and Swedberg, R. (eds.), *Handbook of theory and research for the sociology of education* (3rd ed.). Oxon: Routledge, 241–258.
Brentin, D. and Cooley, L. (2016) 'Nationalism and sport: a review of the literature', *Studies on National Movements*. Retrieved from: http://snm.nise.eu/index.php/studies/article/view/0306s
Butterworth, M.L. (2014) 'Public memorializing in the stadium: mediated sport, the 10th anniversary of 9/11, and the illusion of democracy', *Communication & Sport*, 2(3): 203–224.
Chambers, S. and Black, E. (2000) 'Lest we forget? Sadly, many young people never learned what Poppy Day means', *The Sunday Express*, 11 November 2000.
Cook, E. (2006) 'Saying goodbye our way', *The Guardian*, 19 August 2006. Retrieved from: www.theguardian.com/lifeandstyle/2006/aug/19/familyandrelationships.family
Cooney, G. (2019) 'Poppy displays hit new heights of absurdity while Jose anoints Liverpool as champions', *the42.com*, 11 November 2019. Retrieved from: https://the42.ie/4886529
Cottle, S. (2006) 'Mediatized rituals: beyond manufacturing consent', *Media, Culture & Society*, 28(3): 411–432.
Critchley, S. (2017) *What we think about when we think about football*. London: Profile Books.
Crolley, L. and Hand, D. (2006) *Football and European identity: historical narratives through the press*. London: Routledge.
The Daily Mail (2011) 'Now Germans back us to wear poppies as Cameron blasts "absurd" FIFA', *The Daily Mail*. Retrieved from: www.dailymail.co.uk/sport/football/article-2059198/FIFA-poppy-ban-Germans-England-wear-poppies-David-Cameron-blasts-FIFA.html
The Daily Star (2002) 'Gotcha, Foot of God sinks Argies', 8 June 2002. Retrieved from: www.sfgate.com/sports/article/Quick-kicks-2811143.php
Danilova, N. (2016) *The politics of war commemoration in the UK and Russia*. Basingstoke: Palgrave Macmillan.
Debord, G. (1992 [1967]) *The society of the spectacle*. Paris: Les Éditions Gallimard.
Dolan, P., and Connolly, J. (2016) 'Sport, unity and conflict: an enduring social dynamic', *European Journal for Sport and Society*, 13(3): 189–196.
Donnelly, P. (2011) 'From war without weapons to sport for development and peace: the Janus-face of sport', *SAIS Review of International Affairs*, 31(1): 65–76.
Edgerton, D. (2005) *Warfare state: Britain, 1920–1970*. Cambridge: Cambridge University Press.
FIFA (2010) 'Regulation 54.1', Equipment Regulations, *FIFA*, 1 April 2010. Retrieved from: www.fifa.com/ aboutfifa/officialdocuments/doclists/laws.html 2
Football Association (FA) (2019) '999 and counting'. Retrieved from: www.thefa.com/news/2019/10/30/08/45/england-1000-games-list-999-and-counting
Foster, L. and Woodthorpe, K. (2012) 'A golden silence? Acts of remembrance and commemoration at U.K. football games', *Journal of Sport and Social Issues*, 36(1): 50–67.
Fox, J. (2006) 'Consuming the nation: Holidays, sports, and the production of collective belonging', *Ethnic and Racial Studies*, 29(2): 217–236.

Fox, J. (2014) 'Poppy politics: remembrance of things present', in Sandis, C. (ed.), *Cultural heritage ethics: between theory and practice*. Cambridge: Open Book Publishers.

Fuller, J.G. (1990) *Troop morale and popular culture in the British and Dominion Armies 1914–1918*. Oxford: Clarendon Press.

Garland, H.J. (1957) *Henry Francis Lyte and the story of 'abide with me'*. Manchester: Torch Publishing.

Garland, J. (2004) 'The same old story? Englishness, the tabloid press and the 2002 football world cup', *Leisure Studies*, 23(1): 79–92.

Giulianotti, R. and Robertson, R. (2004) 'The globalization of football: a study in the glocalization of the "serious life"', *The British Journal of Sociology*, 55: 545–568.

Goldblatt, D. (2019) *The Age of Football*. London: Macmillan.

The Guardian (2002) 'When silence isn't golden', *The Guardian*, 12 September 2002.

The Guardian (2011) 'Prince William calls on Fifa to overturn ban on England shirt poppies', *The Guardian*. Retrieved from: www.theguardian.com/football/2011/nov/09/david-cameron-outrageous-poppy-ban

Harris, C. and Whippy, J. (2008) *The greater game: sporting icons who fell in the Great War*. London: Pen and Sword.

Herzog, M. (2013) '"Be a part of Ibrox forever". Clubgeschichten und Fanbiographien in den "commemorative bricks" und "memorials" der Fußballclubs Rangers und Celtic', in M. Herzog (ed.), *Memorialkultur im Fußballsport. Medien, Rituale und Praktiken des Erinnerns, Gedenkens und Vergessens*. Stuttgart: Kohlhammer.

Herzog, M. (2015) 'Rituals and practices of memorial culture in football', in Pyta, W. and Havemann, N. (eds.), *European football and collective memory*. London: Palgrave Macmillan.

Hill, J. (2012) 'Sport, history and imagined pasts', in Hill, J., Moore, K. and Wood, J. (eds.), *Sport, history, and heritage: studies in public representation*. Woodbridge, Suffolk: Boydell Press.

Hitt, C. (2016) 'The reasons why sport cannot be separated from remembrance', *Wales Online*. Retrieved from: www.walesonline.co.uk/news/wales-news/reasons-sport-cannot-separated-remembrance-12130659

Hobsbawm, E. (1983) 'Falklands fallout', *Marxism Today*, January 1983, 13: 13–19.

Hobsbawm, E. and Ranger, T. (2012) *The invention of tradition*. Cambridge: Cambridge University Press.

Huggins, (2012) 'Gone but not forgotten: sporting heroes, heritage and graveyard commemoration', *The Journal of Theory and Practice*, 16(4): 479–495.

Hyde, M. (2016) 'War, poppies and footballers: sacrifice in the age of pampering', 9 November 2016. Retrieved from: www.theguardian.com/football/blog/2016/nov/09/england-scotland-war-poppies-footballers-remembrance-day

Johnes, M. and Mason, R. (2003) 'Soccer, public history and the national football museum', *Sport in History*, 23(1): 115–131.

Jones, M. (2018) *War and British identity: a study of Mass Observers' perceptions of the use of British military force since 1982*. Unpublished thesis, Keele University.

Keating, F. (1999) 'Sir Alf departs a land unfit for heroes', *The Guardian*, 6 May 1999.

Kellner, D. (1996) 'Sports, media culture, and race – some reflections on Michael Jordan', *Sociology of Sports Journal*, 13: 458–467.

Kelly, J. (2016) 'Western militarism and the political utility of sport', in *Routledge handbook of sport and politics*. London: Routledge, pp. 277–292.

King, A. (2003) *The European ritual: football in the new Europe*. London: Routledge.

Lakoff, G. (1991) 'Metaphor and war: the metaphor system used to justify war in the Gulf', *Peace Research*, 23(2): 325–332.
Lawrence, J. (2003) 'Forging a peaceable kingdom: war, violence and fear of brutalization in post-First World War Britain', *Journal of Modern History*, 75(3): 557–589.
MacAskill, E. and Cobain, I. (2014) '"British forces" century of unbroken warfare set to end with Afghanistan exit', *The Guardian*, 11 February 2014. Retrieved from: www.theguardian.com/uk-news/2014/feb/11/british-forces-century-warfare-end
Maltby, S. (2016) 'Media-remembering the Falklands War: subjectivity and identification', *International Journal of Communication*, 10(2016): 642–659.
Mandler, P. (2006) 'What is "national identity"? Definitions and applications in modern British historiography', *Modern Intellectual History*, 3(2): 271–297.
Mason, T. and Riedi, E. (2010) *Sport and the military: the British Armed Forces 1880–1960*. Cambridge: Cambridge University Press.
Mellor, G. (2004) 'The Flowers of Manchester': The Munich Disaster and the Discursive Creation of Manchester United Football Club', *Soccer & Society*, 5(2): 265–284.
Miller, S. (1959–2003) 'Palace rejects funeral plea: silent tributes: nation to stop for one minute at the end of service', *The Guardian*, 3 September 1997. Retrieved from: https://theguardian.newspapers.com/clip/45217780/the-guardian/
Ministry of Defence (MoD) (2019) *UK Armed Forces deaths: operational deaths post World War II, 3 September 1945 to 28 February 2019*. Retrieved from: https://assets.publishing.service.gov.uk/government/uploads/system/uploads/attachment_data/file/789825/20190328_UK_Armed_Forces_Operational_deaths_post_World_War_II-O.pdf
The Mirror (2010) 'Gerrard: our frontline forces have inspired us', *The Mirror*, 11 June 2010. Retrieved from: www.mirror.co.uk/sport/football/news/england-captain-steven-gerrard-frontline-3355283
Mitten, A. (2014) 'Manchester remembers the Munich air disaster', *ESPN*, 6 February 2014. Retrieved from: www.espn.co.uk/football/blog/name/93/post/1854038/headline" www.espn.co.uk/football/blog/name/93/post/1854038/headline
Moran, M. (2017) *The end of British politics?* Basingstoke: Palgrave Macmillan.
Nannestad, I. (2010) 'Pack up your troubles: Football and community singing', *Soccer History*, 22: 3–7.
National Heritage Select Committee (1996) *Press coverage of Euro '96 football competition*. London: HSMO.
Noakes, L. (2015) 'A broken silence? Mass observation, Armistice Day and "everyday life" in Britain 1937–1941', *Journal of European Studies*, 45(4): 331–346.
Notts County (2018) 'Games of remembrance a huge success'. Retrieved from: www.nottscountyfc.co.uk/news/2018/november/games-of-remembrance-recap/
Penn, R. and Berridge, D. (2018) 'Football and the military in contemporary Britain: an exploration of invisible nationalism', *Armed Forces & Society*, 44(1), 116–138.
Ramshaw, G. (2014) 'Sport, heritage and tourism', *Journal of Heritage Tourism*, 9(3): 191–196.
Richards, B. (2014) '"Abide with me": mediatised football and collectivised mourning', in Bainbridge, C. and Yates, C. (eds.), *Media and the inner world: psycho-cultural approaches to emotion, media and popular culture* (pp. 19–33). London: Palgrave Macmillan.
Roberts, J. (2006) '"The best football team, the best platoon": the role of football in the proletarianization of the British Expeditionary Force, 1914–1918', *Sport in History*, 26(1): 26–46.

Rose-Redwood, R.S. (2009) 'From number to name: symbolic capital, places of memory and the politics of street renaming in New York City', *Social and Cultural Geography*, 9(4): 431–452.

Russell, D. (2006) '"We all agree, name the stand after Shankly": cultures of commemoration in late twentieth-century English football culture', *Sport in History*, 26(1): 1–25.

Russell, D. (2008) 'Abiding memories: the community singing movement and English social life in the 1920s', *Popular Music*, 27(1): 117–133.

Russell, D. (2014) '"See, the conquering hero comes! Sound the trumpets, beat the drums": music and sport in England, 1880–1939', *Sport in Society*, 17(3): 303–319.

Schulze, G. (1992) *Die Erlebnisgesellschaft [The experience society]*. Frankfurt: Campus.

Sirvent, R. and Reyburn, D. (2017) 'Uniforms and unanimity: reading the rhetorical entanglement of militarism and sport through mimetic realism', in Butterworth, M.L. (ed.), *Sport and militarism* (pp. 191–208). Oxon: Routledge.

Stahl, R. (2009) *Militainment, inc.: war, media, and popular culture*. New York, NY: Routledge.

Stride, C., Wilson, J.P. and Thomas, F. (2013) 'Honouring heroes by branding in bronze: theorizing the UK's football statuary', *Sport in Society*, 16(6): 749–771.

Sugden, J. and Tomlinson, A. (1994) *Hosts and champions: soccer cultures, national identities and the USA World Cup*. London: Ashgate Publishing.

Taylor, I. (1989) 'Hillsborough, 15 April 1989: some personal contemplations', *New Left Review*, 177(1). Retrieved from: https://newleftreview.org/issues/I177/articles/ian-taylor-hillsborough-15-april-1989-some-personal-contemplations.

Taylor, M. (2013) *The association game: a history of British football*. London: Routledge.

Thatcher, M. (1983) *Margaret Thatcher's Speech to Conservative Rally at Cheltenham, July 1983*. Retrieved from: www.margaretthatcher.org/document/104989

The Telegraph (2016) 'David Moyes' Victor Anichebe gamble beginning to look like lottery win for Sunderland', *The Telegraph*, Retrieved from: https://www.telegraph.co.uk/football/2016/11/20/david-moyes-victor-anichebe-gamble-beginning-to-look-like-lotter/

The Times (1914) 'Duty Before Sport', *The Times Digital Archive*, 3 September 1914: 6.

Vallely, P. (2000) 'Living in the nation's memory', *The Independent*, 11 November 2000.

Veitch, C. (1985) '"Play up! Play up! and Win the War!" Football, the nation and the First World War 1914–15', *Journal of Contemporary History*, 20(3): 363–378.

Walker, G. (2004) 'The Ibrox Stadium Disaster of 1971', *Soccer & Society*, 5(2): 169–182.

Ware, V. (2010) 'Lives on the line', *Soundings*, 45: 147–159.

Wilson, R. (2014) 'It still goes on: football and the heritage of the Great War in Britain', *Journal of Heritage Tourism*, 9(3): 197–211.

Wren-Lewis, J. and Clarke, A. (1983) 'The World Cup – a political football', *Theory, Culture & Society*, 1(3): 123–132.

Chapter 5

Football in 'French' Algeria and 'Algerian' France

From colonisation to globalisation

Philip Dine

Introduction

This chapter offers an overview of Franco-Algerian relations on and off the football field since the 1920s, a decade that saw an unprecedented expansion in sporting participation and spectatorship on both sides of the Mediterranean. As France's nearest and most assimilated colonial territory, Algeria was the jewel in the imperial crown and would only be surrendered belatedly and at appalling human cost. Football was mobilised both practically and symbolically by coloniser and colonised throughout the last half century of the French presence in North Africa: as a focus for a distinctive settler identity; as a means of asserting Algeria's aspirations to nationhood; as a site of inter-ethnic contestation and often violent confrontation; as a theatre for armed insurgency during the liberation war of 1954–1962; and as the most striking manifestation in the cultural sphere of nationalist sentiment, notably through the establishment in 1958 of the star-studded football team of the revolutionary Front de Libération Nationale (FLN). Football would also be central to post-independence representations of the Algerian state, as the victorious FLN sought both to legitimise its one-party regime and exert soft power within the Arab-Islamic world as well as more broadly. This exploitation of football, and particularly major international matches, as vehicles for the communication of state narratives in Algeria has continued until the present day (Bouandel and Amara 2019).

In a striking example of this process, the FLN's long-term communications strategy was clearly in evidence during the 2006 'state visit' to his parents' homeland of the most famous footballing product of the Algerian diaspora, Zinedine Zidane. Among the game's finest ever practitioners, Zidane had been an inspirational figure in France's historic home success in the 1998 FIFA World Cup. Having thereby established himself as a global megastar, this iconic player would shine at European giants Juventus and Real Madrid before coming out of international retirement to steer the French to another World Cup final in 2006. In the deeply symbolic setting of the Berlin Olympic Stadium, Zidane opened the scoring audaciously before being sent off in extra time in outrageously theatrical fashion and subsequently immortalised in everything from literature and fine art to YouTube clips viewed by millions. The star's complex representation in France and Algeria will be considered here, as will the broader impacts of migration between the two countries, including notably the makeup of Algerian national teams at the 2010 and 2014 World Cup competitions.

To discuss a century of sporting interactions between France and Algeria is also, inevitably, to engage with their broader relationship throughout history. The territory that became modern Algeria was invaded by a French expeditionary force in 1830 and then 'pacified' by means of often brutal military repression in the face of sustained indigenous resistance. Critically, it was in 1848, Europe's 'Year of Revolutions,' that the ephemeral Second Republic took the momentous step of incorporating the still embryonic colony into the French nation-state. Unlike other overseas territories, the so-called *trois départements* – the primary administrative divisions of colonial Algeria, based on the major cities of Algiers, Oran and Constantine – were proclaimed to be as inalienably integral to the 'one and indivisible' republic as any other French province. The territory thus saw its status permanently transformed, ceasing to be a colony at all in administrative and political terms. This was the legal fiction that underpinned the emergence of *Algérie française* or 'French Algeria' and which would, a century later, make decolonisation so politically problematic and so durably traumatic.

To this political reimagining was added the demographic reality of civilian settlement, which began in the wake of the 1848 Revolution and was to increase dramatically under the Third Republic (1870–1940), the long-lived regime that emerged from catastrophic military defeat in the Franco-Prussian war and was responsible for the creation of a recognisably modern France. Displaced populations from Alsace and Lorraine would be among the first French citizens to settle in North Africa, bringing with them the culture of the vine, among other regional traditions. This process of plantation and expropriation was made possible by the Warnier Law of 1873, which saw land traditionally held in common by indigenous Algerians pass into the private ownership of the incoming settlers. Thus, refugees from the country's eastern provinces would lead the way for subsequent waves of settlers not only from France, but also from neighbouring Italy and Spain, as well as the Balearic Islands and Malta. These Southern European migrants were typically impoverished families seeking a better life on the other side of the Mediterranean. In time, they would become naturalised French citizens; while their own winegrowing expertise would contribute to viticulture's establishment as a pillar of the emerging colonial economy.

This composite population transfer would transform Algeria into France's only real settler colony. By the onset of the war of independence in 1954, the territory numbered some one million 'Europeans,' more familiarly known by their nickname of *Pieds-Noirs* or 'black feet.'[1] Irrespective of their national origins, members of this community were full citizens of the republic, as were Algeria's approximately 30,000 Jews, whose presence in the territory dated from the 15th century and who, without consultation, had been made French by administrative decree in 1870. The remainder of Algeria's approximately ten million inhabitants was made up of 'Muslims,' as the official nomenclature designated the majority population of Arabo-Berber subjects. This subordinate position entailed a variety of duties to the 'mother country' [*la mère patrie*], notably including service under the French flag in two world wars, although few individual or collective rights. Coloniser and colonised were thus divided by their legal status, as well as by 'race,' religion and language. With the advent of modern sport as both a mass practice and a social spectacle after the Great War of 1914–1918, the two communities would be juxtaposed in new ways, with football destined to become the most contested of Algerian sporting sites.

The colonial period: settler identification and anticolonial mobilisation

Much as in 'metropolitan' France, football's rapid expansion in colonial Algeria had its roots in mobilisation during the First World War. Having been given their first taste of the game in allied army camps, returning Algerian soldiers served as sporting evangelists. The territory's first football leagues were established in 1919–1920, and over 100 clubs are estimated to have been in existence by the 1923–1924 season (Wahl 1992, p. 44). The majority of these associations were established by Europeans for the exclusive benefit of white players and spectators, serving as a mechanism for the celebration of their varied Mediterranean origins, together with a shared *Pied-Noir* identity. However, a minority of clubs were more inclusive in their recruitment practices, such as the Racing Universitaire d'Alger, founded in 1927. This association's racially mixed membership included the future Nobel Prize winner Albert Camus (1913–1960), who played for its junior side between 1928 and 1930, when tuberculosis cut short a promising career as a goalkeeper. As French Algeria's most celebrated literary spokesman, Camus often referred to the territory's favourite game, highlighting football's social and even philosophical importance, notably when he stated, 'Truly, the little that I know about morality, I have learnt on football pitches and theatre stages, which will remain my real universities' [Vraiment, le peu de morale que je sais, je l'ai appris sur les terrains de football et les scènes de théâtre qui resteront mes vraies universités] (Camus 2008, p. 607).

In his writing, Camus situated the game within a broader vision of inter-ethnic harmony in the colonial Algeria of the interwar years, as would subsequent apologists for *Algérie française*. While amicable exchanges across the colonial divide undoubtedly occurred both within and between football clubs, the game soon became a focus for inter-ethnic hostility and nationalist advocacy, as the rapid expansion that had occurred in European football in Algeria was mirrored by the simultaneous emergence of 'Muslim' clubs. A survey conducted 'discreetly' for the colonial governor-general's office in 1933 confirmed the existence of a thriving indigenous club scene, which was rightly suspected of serving as a focus for nationalist agitation (CAOM 1931–1941). This said, the game would be appealed to by a range of local political opinions. Thus, on the one hand, and as its name suggests, a club like the Union Sportive Franco-Musulmane de Sétif, founded in 1933, not only attracted Arabo-Berber players, but also administrators from among that community's French-educated and assimilation-minded elite. Revealingly, in 1937–1938, local pharmacist and leading reformist politician Ferhat Abbas served as the club's president. Indigenous *notables* were similarly involved as officials of the three departmental leagues, based in the major cities of Algiers, Oran and Constantine (Wahl 1992, p. 44). In contrast, the Mouloudia Club Algérois, the oldest indigenous club, founded in 1921, literally wore its revolutionary colours on its sleeve. Taking its name from the annual festival celebrating the birth of the Prophet, the club played in the green-and-red of the banned nationalist flag, also adopting the pan-Islamic symbols of the star and crescent.

In the 1930s, a combination of internal and external factors combined to raise the symbolic stakes in Algerian football. The increasingly vocal demands of the nationalist movement came into conflict with the determination of the settler population to preserve the colonial status quo, against a backdrop of global economic depression and the rise of totalitarianism on the other side of the Mediterranean. Violent clashes between the players and supporters of clubs drawn from the ever more hostile communities became a commonplace in Algerian football during this period. As early as 1928, the French authorities sought to avoid such inter-ethnic confrontation by banning exclusively Arabo-Berber teams and requiring that a minimum of three European players be included in any given side. However, this decree was widely ignored, and clashes between the communities occurred throughout the following decade, with nationalist strongholds such as Djidjelli [modern Jijel] in the traditionalist Constantine department regularly the setting for football-related public disorder. In this way, Algerian stadiums became microcosms of the colonial encounter, encouraging the emergence of a revolutionary national consciousness through the playing out, both on and off the pitch, of the confrontation between coloniser and colonised (Fates 1994, pp. 30–31). The governor-general's reassertion in 1936 of the administrative requirement that all football teams should include at least three European players was, once again, widely flouted.

For his part, the young Ahmed Ben Bella was to combine a playing career that included a brief stint at the celebrated Olympique de Marseille with political engagement as one of the revolution's historic leaders and independent Algeria's first president. Commenting on Algerian football in the 1930s, Ben Bella states that he had played as a schoolboy in racially integrated teams in his home village. However, he discovered a very different side to the game as one of the few indigenous children to have been given the opportunity to go on to secondary education:

> For at Tlemcen, unlike what happened at Marnia, segregation had even penetrated the world of sport. There were two teams, one of Algerians, and

one of *colons*. . . . It was at this period that I made contact with Nationalist groups.

(Merle 1967, pp. 44–45)

Not coincidentally, the Marseille club drew at this time, and subsequently, on the city's demographic diversity as France's principal colonial port, remaining a symbol of ethnic pluralism to this day. Moreover, Ben Bella was following in the footsteps of Moroccan trailblazer Larbi Ben Barek, the so-called Black Pearl, who played for the club in two spells between 1938 and 1955, either side of a successful stay at Atlético Madrid. Ben Barek also amassed 17 international caps for France over this same extended period. Other imports to Marseille at this time included the Algerian Abdelkader Ben Bouali, whose single international appearance in 1937 made him the first North African to play for France. Ben Bella's own playing career was cut short by the onset of the Second World War, during which he was one of the many nationalists to serve with distinction in the French Army, in the belief that such engagement would help the Algerian cause once peace had been restored. As would be made clear by the ferocious military suppression of nationalist demonstrations in and around Sétif, in the Constantine department, on VE Day, 8 May 1945, this faith in the restored republic was tragically misplaced. Yet it would take another decade of missed French opportunities to bring Algeria to the inter-communal savagery of the 1954–1962 war of independence.

The Algerian war began on 1 November 1954, with a series of isolated attacks across the vast territory and, in its early stages, continued to be characterised by such sporadic violence. However, at Philippeville [modern Skikda] in the Constantine department, on 20 August 1955, an appalling massacre of local Europeans – men, women and children – together with Algerians loyal to France, marked a watershed in the hitherto limited conflict. French government responses sought to combine repression and reform, but typically prioritised troop deployments, sending not only battle-hardened professionals but also conscripts, numbering well over two million by the time a ceasefire was declared on 17 March 1962. Having fought and lost its war of attempted reconquest in what was then known as French Indochina between 1946 and 1954, France would thus become embroiled in a second colonial conflict destined to end in defeat and ignominious withdrawal. Moreover, the Algerian conflict caused political division that led in 1958 to the collapse of the Fourth Republic and the return to power of the country's wartime 'saviour,' General Charles de Gaulle, as the only alternative to the combined threats of civil war and a military coup.

Remarkably, football would be utilised even more creatively by Algerian revolutionaries during the armed struggle for independence. The continuation and intensification of pre-war crowd disturbances was underscored in 1955, when a riot occurred in Algiers following the match between the nationalist Mouloudia Club Algérois and the *Pied-Noir* Association Sportive de Saint-Eugène. Such incidents explain the authorities' intervention in the 1956 North Africa Cup, a tournament that brought together leading Algerian sides and those from French-administered Morocco and Tunisia. That year's final was due to be played by two teams from the same town, additionally the home base of the Foreign Legion: namely, the *Pied-Noir* Sporting Club Bel-Abbès and the nationalist Union Sportive Musulmane Bel-Abbès. The colonial administration's fear of public disorder resulted in the cancellation of the match, which in turn prompted the FLN to call on indigenous clubs to withdraw from all competitions, a move that was widely backed by sporting nationalists (Dine and Rey 2012, pp. 29–30).

Meanwhile, settler-supported clubs not only continued to play but also to attract substantial crowds, which were targeted by coordinated FLN bomb attacks on 10 February 1957, as part of the pivotal, and reciprocally vicious, Battle of Algiers of 1956–1957. Taking the struggle to the French 'mainland' on 26 May 1957, an FLN gunman killed a leading loyalist politician, the Bachaga Ali Chekkal, as he watched the French Cup final at the Colombes stadium. The nationalists thus deftly brought together the assassin and his target in the highly symbolic location, together with an extensive supporting cast of players, managers and team fans, in a forceful proclamation of Algerian independence (Amar 1987, p. 194). Such was the affective charge of this incident that it would subsequently be celebrated by Rachid Boudjedra in his novel *Le Vainqueur de coupe* [The Cup Winner] (1981). On the day, the political symbolism of the assassination was effectively underlined by the outcome of the match, as Toulouse defeated Angers 6–3, a result that included goals from both of the club's Algerian stars, Abdelhamid Bouchouk and Saïd Brahimi. Moreover, in the earlier rounds of this same tournament, the mighty Stade de Reims club had been knocked out by the lowly Sporting Club Union from El Biar in the suburbs of Algiers. As the SCU's home ground had previously been the target of FLN bomb attacks, the match was played at a neutral venue in Toulouse in early February 1957. There, the Algerian amateurs stunned French football with a 2–0 victory over a side that had just a few months before been runners-up in the inaugural European Cup competition (Marseille 2002, p. 227).

In April 1958, the Toulouse players Bouchouk and Brahimi would be among the ten French-based professionals who responded to the FLN's appeal to show solidarity with the cause of independence by leaving France to establish a national side in exile in Tunis. Others who heeded the call included two who had already played for France, Mustapha Zitouni (of Cannes and Monaco), and the group's leading figure, Rachid Mekhloufi (of Saint-Étienne), who would become known as 'the footballer of the Revolution.' Initially reported in *L'Équipe*, France's leading sports daily, the shock move also made the front page of *Le Monde*, the national journal of record and, as an editorialist remarked, is likely to have had a far greater impact on popular perceptions of the Algerian conflict than any number of anti-war petitions, marches and newspaper articles (Lanfranchi 1994, p. 72). The FLN team would also be commemorated as the primary manifestation in the cultural sphere of the Algerian people's commitment to independence (Abderrahim 2008; Nait-Challal 2008; Yahi 2010). In response, the colonial authorities organised matches in Algiers and Oran by leading French sides, as part of a broader demonstration of sporting continuity in *Algérie française* (Amar 1987, pp. 193–194). These games notably included the encounter in Oran on 8 May 1958 between Stade de Reims and Real Madrid, two sides that had previously met as finalists in the first ever European Cup final in 1956.

The Algerian Revolution's footballing ambassadors played 57 matches between 1958 and 1962, winning 43 times and scoring 244 goals. These games were played against future allies of the Algerian Republic, including the Soviet Union, China, North Vietnam and various Arab nations. The response of the world governing body, the Fédération Internationale de Football Association, which had been established in Paris in 1904, was to ban the Algerian players themselves, together with any national federation that played against them. This included Algeria's neighbour Morocco, whose expulsion was successfully demanded by the Fédération Française de Football after the Moroccan national side played a friendly against the FLN team in 1958 (Lanfranchi 1994, p. 71). However, the rebel footballers' effectiveness as symbols of Algerian popular aspirations was only underlined by such outrage on the part of the colonial power.

Paradoxically, the heroic image of Rachid Mekhloufi, *le footballeur de la révolution*, conceals a more complex reality, as part of the almost uninterrupted flow of Algerian professional players to France from the 1950s to the 1980s (Frenkiel and Bancel 2008). Unlike most of the other members of the FLN side, Mekhloufi returned to France in 1962, picking up where he had left off with Saint-Etienne before finishing his career as a player-coach at Bastia, in Corsica. Returning definitively to Algeria in 1970, he became the trainer of the national side, which had been internationally recognised since the country's independence in 1962, in line with the Algerian football federation's admittance by FIFA. However, neither Mekhloufi's links with France nor his background in professional football made it easy for him to be accepted by the revolutionary socialist administration in Algeria. Unforgiven by many former French fans for what they saw as his act of betrayal in 1958, Mekhloufi was tainted by colonial association at home, where he was perceived as technically competent but incapable of fully appreciating Algeria's sporting specificity (Lanfranchi 1994, pp. 70–71).

Nation-building and soft power: Algerian football on the world stage

With Ahmed Ben Bella as its first president, independent Algeria embarked on a programme of state management of football intended to promote unity at home and prestige abroad. Under the former Olympique de Marseille player, and then Colonel Houari Boumediene, who ousted Ben Bella in a military coup in 1965, the country's leading clubs were reorganised and renamed, being formally associated from 1977 onwards with state-run companies, led by the nationalised oil and gas industries (Fates 2009, p. 39; Amara 2012b, p. 38). This Soviet-style model of centralised control was accompanied by significant support throughout the 1960s and 1970s, both technical and financial, which would be rewarded by a series of notable performances by the national side. The first of these came at the 1975 Mediterranean Games, hosted by Algeria, when the home team beat France 3–2 in the final of the football competition. Although the French representatives did not constitute their country's full professional team, the symbolism of the victory was not lost on Algeria's rulers nor on the 70,000 local spectators who filled the national stadium. *Les Verts* [The Greens] went on to win the 1978 African Games and to perform with distinction at the 1979 Mediterranean Games, the 1980 (Moscow) Olympics and the 1982 African Nations Cup, hosted by neighbouring Libya.

Algeria would also qualify for the World Cup for the first time in 1982, when the tournament was hosted by Spain. In a memorable opening group match, the team defeated the mighty West Germany 2–1. A highly suspicious result in the group's final round between the Germans and their neighbours Austria saw Algeria knocked out of the competition. The resulting scandal led FIFA to reorganise the scheduling of the final round of group games in subsequent World Cups so that all such games kick off simultaneously (Doyle 2010; Goldblatt 2006, p. 654). Nevertheless, the remarkable achievements of the Algerian side ensured the state's continued investment in its footballing representatives, even in what were difficult times for the country's economy (Amara 2014). This success also encouraged a new flexibility on the part of the national selectors, who had previously prioritised Algerian-based players. Henceforth, the international stage would be open not only to foreign-based players but also to French-born professionals whose family connections made them eligible to play for *Les Verts* (Scagnetti 2008, p. 56).

These two varieties of recruitment are exemplified respectively by the 1982 team's outstanding forward, Rabah Madjer, who had opened the scoring against West Germany, and its imposing central defender, Nordine Kourichi. Thus, Madjer's professional itinerary took him from his home club of Nasr Athlétique de Hussein Dey in the suburbs of Algiers to the Paris-based Racing Club de France in 1983. Joining FC Porto in 1985, he played a key role in the Portuguese champions' triumph in the 1987 European Cup final against Bayern Munich, scoring one goal and laying on another. Crowned that year's African Footballer of the Year, Madjer would also be named Player of the Tournament at the 1990 African Cup of Nations, which Algeria both hosted and won for the first time. Having been runners-up in 1980, Algeria's next triumph in the competition would not come until 2019, in a competition hosted by Egypt, the country's bitter rivals for North African footballing supremacy. On his retirement as a player in 1992, Madjer became manager of the Algerian side, continuing in that role on an on-off basis between 1993 and 2018.

Born in 1952, Nordine Kourichi owed his eligibility to play for Algeria to the wave of North African migration prompted by post-1945 reconstruction in France. In fact, such population flows had begun in the wake of the First World War and would be maintained through the inter-war years, peaking during the so-called *Trente Glorieuses* (1945–1975). During these 'thirty glorious years,' the French economy saw sustained economic growth, with inward migration actively encouraged by the state. The new arrivals came not only from the Maghreb, but also from France's sub-Saharan territories, as well as from less economically prosperous European countries, notably Portugal, all of which would, in due course, be reflected in the composition of French national football teams. Kourichi's family settled in the northern footballing hotbed of the Lille conurbation, and the player's professional career would include lengthy stays at the local Valenciennes and Lille clubs, either side of a season with Bordeaux. This extensive experience underpinned Kourichi's 30 international appearances for Algeria between 1980 and 1986 (Yahi 2010). Following his retirement as a player, Kourichi's involvement as a coach in the French lower divisions led to his appointment as the Algerian team's assistant manager from 2011 to 2014. The northward player migration that had seen talented Algerians cross the Mediterranean since the 1930s was thus accompanied from the 1980s onwards by an accompanying phenomenon of reverse migration, as pioneered by Nordine Kourichi as a player and then utilised by him as a manager.

Following Algerian football's dramatic entrance onto the world stage in 1982, hopes were high when the national side qualified for the 1986 World Cup, hosted by Mexico. However, with a difficult draw, Algeria recorded disappointing performances against Northern Ireland, Brazil and Spain, meaning that *Les Verts* were eliminated at the group stage once again. In 1990, Algeria would just miss out on qualification for the finals in Italy. However, sporting developments at this time were overshadowed by the onset of the country's civil war, marking the beginning of a 'black decade,' which would pit the FLN state against Islamist insurgents in a conflict every bit as brutal as the 1954–1962 war of independence. The resulting devastation was to affect every aspect of life in Algeria, including football. The assassination of prominent figures became commonplace during this period and included club presidents and even, in 1995, Rachid Haraigue, the president of the Algerian Football Federation (Amara 2012a, p. 47). That same year, and at the other end of the country's footballing spectrum, the murder of totemic Algiers super-supporter Dehimi Hocine, better known as 'Yamaha,' was commemorated by fellow fans and, once again, by novelist Rachid Boudjedra. In *La Vie à l'endroit* [Life the Right Way Up] (1997), a semi-autobiographical account of his experience of living under an Islamist *fatwa*, the writer highlighted Yamaha's symbolic value as an incarnation of football's mobilisation by Algerian youth as an expression of its resilience and resistance against both sides in the civil war.

Since the gradual restoration of something approaching normality from 2002 onwards, football has continued to serve as a tribune for popular protest in Algeria, especially on the part of alienated youth, much as it did in the colonial period (Dorsey 2014, 2016). On the pitch, the turbulence of the civil war period and the multiple uncertainties that followed would for many years prevent the competitive promise of the national side in the 1980s from being brought to fruition. It was consequently only with Algeria's qualification for the 2010 (South Africa) and 2014 (Brazil) World Cup tournaments that a new footballing generation would make its presence felt in the world game. In contrast, in the intervening decades, French-born players of Algerian heritage would bring an unprecedented visibility to the Franco-Algerian sporting connection.

Algeria in France, France in Algeria: mobilising the diaspora

There can be few football fans who are not familiar with Zinedine Zidane, whether as an outstanding player (1989–2006) or more recently as a manager at Real Madrid (2014–present). In addition to a stellar career at club level, Zidane made 108 appearances for France, scoring 31 times, not least the decisive first two goals at the Stade de France in the country's 3–0 victory over Brazil in the 1998 World Cup final. Perceived at the time and since as an exemplar of successful integration on the republican model, this son of Algerian immigrants was easily the most lauded member of the country's so-called *Black-Blanc-Beur* [Black-White-Arab] football team.[2] World Cup success in 1998 came in a competition that the French not only hosted, but could also legitimately claim to have invented, thanks to the farsightedness in 1930 of the then FIFA president, Jules Rimet. The victory gave rise to spontaneous celebrations on a scale unseen since the Liberation, together with extensive appropriation of the event by politicians and the media, as well as by academic and artistic commentators. In the warm glow of victory, it appeared to many observers that the country's multicultural football team offered a new and more inclusive vision of French identity. This was all the more welcome given the challenging economic and political circumstances, which included the rise of the far-right and specifically anti-immigrant *Front National*, led by a veteran of the Algerian war, Jean-Marie Le Pen.

Although this optimism was widely shared, it would ultimately evaporate in the face of the continuation of structural disparities in the housing, employment, health and educational circumstances of communities of ethnic minority origin. Discussion of these issues has tended to focus on the frequently troubled *banlieue* [suburbs], the high-density housing schemes ringing major French cities that are typically home to populations of migrant family origin. This was the prevailing background of Algerian supporters who, on 6 October 2001, and back at the Stade de France, targeted the first match between the full teams of the two countries in order to highlight the alienation of young French citizens of Maghrebi heritage. Beginning by booing *La Marseillaise*, these French-born fans then systematically barracked the home side – with the general exception of the great Zidane – before bringing the encounter to a premature end with a non-violent but nevertheless effective pitch invasion. With both the Prime Minister and the Minister of Sport in attendance, the reaction of the French authorities was predictably outraged, while the bemused Algerian delegation, led by former star Rabah Madjer, responded with a mixture of incomprehension and embarrassment. For the self-aware and even consciously carnivalesque supporters themselves, the match provided

> an occasion for the Algerian community in France to celebrate their own double sense of belonging to a 'hybrid' identity . . . an amalgam of some aspects of both Algerian culture and French citizenship, neither expressed in terms of fully belonging to 'French culture' or that of (Algerian) 'culture of origin.'
>
> (Amara 2006, pp. 221–222)

Characteristically, Zidane himself refrained from comment on the outcome of this first and supposedly 'friendly' encounter between the former colonial adversaries, which came a full four decades on from Algerian independence. However, he did speak out in 2002, urging French voters to reject the extreme right, when Jean-Marie Le Pen was involved in a presidential run-off against the incumbent, Jacques Chirac, who went on to win by a landslide. 'Zizou,' as he is still popularly known in France, intervened similarly in 2017, by which time the former paratrooper's estranged daughter Marine Le Pen had replaced her father as the presidential candidate of the xenophobic Front National and was herself duly defeated by a wide margin by Emmanuel Macron. At other times, Zidane has generally maintained a detached reserve that has served him well in public life, being voted the nation's favourite figure [*la personnalité préférée des Français*] no less than six times in an opinion poll conducted annually by the Institut français d'opinion publique (IFOP) and the *Journal du Dimanche* newspaper. In the process, the star's media persona has served as a screen onto which competing constructions of the French and Algerian nations may be projected.

Zidane has accordingly been acclaimed not only as an incarnation of French universalist inclusivity but also as a talisman of Algerian specificity on both sides of the Mediterranean (Dauncey and Morrey 2008, pp. 303–306). Indeed, his characteristic inscrutability has rendered the megastar as suitable for appropriation by advertisers for everything from mineral water to eyeglasses as well as by French presidents and their Algerian counterparts. Thus, following the spectacular conclusion to his international career, Zidane was lauded by Jacques Chirac, who had also been on hand to join in the World Cup celebrations in 1998. Having been awarded the *Légion d'Honneur* by the French state following that 1998 triumph, Zidane was hailed by the President of the Republic at a reception in July 2006 at the Élysée Palace. While the whole French squad was praised, Zidane was singled out both for his technical skills and for his moral qualities, which Chirac brought together in a concluding declaration of national appreciation and affection: 'And that is why France admires you and loves you' ['Et c'est pour cela que la France vous admire et vous aime'] (Agence France-Presse 2006).

In December of that same year, Zidane would be similarly honoured by the president of the Algerian Republic, Abdelaziz Bouteflika. The player's trip to

Algeria was primarily intended to allow his parents to visit their family home in the Béjaia [formerly Bougie] region of Kayblia, while Zidane himself engaged in charity work. In the event, the visit took on the character of a state mission, both in terms of the hugely enthusiastic public response and the extensive security apparatus deployed (Gastaut 2008). The visit culminated in Bouteflika's ceremonial presentation to Zidane of the *Al-Athir* medal, a particularly prestigious award in the Algerian order of merit more typically granted to visiting dignitaries – although not, significantly, to Jacques Chirac during his own historic visit in 2003. That trip was not only the first by a French president since Algerian independence, but also marked Chirac's return to the site of his service as a conscripted lieutenant during the 1954–1962 liberation war. While the French Head of State was warmly received by the Algerian public, his official visit may thus be fruitfully contrasted with the triumphal 'homecoming' of the most celebrated son of the Algerian diaspora.

As regards his development as a player, Zidane had started as a junior with the Cannes club before embarking on a senior career with Bordeaux, which would take him in turn to Juventus and Real Madrid, as well as the French national side. However, it is as a product of the Mediterranean port city of Marseille that the intersection of his personal itinerary and public persona may best be appreciated. For Zidane grew up among the tower blocks of La Castellane, a high-density housing scheme in the northern suburbs of what is still France's most obviously migrant-influenced city. Built in the 1960s, this project's concrete brutalism hints both at the architectural fashions of the day and the speed of its construction, which was a response by city planners to the continuing influx of arrivals from the former French colonies. These population flows included the estimated 700,000 French citizens who were 'repatriated' from Algeria in 1962, some 450,000 of whom disembarked in Marseille, with 120,000 becoming permanent residents of the city. In 1971, the municipality erected a monument to this very particular group of *Marseillais* on the city's Corniche (*L'Obs* 2012). This seafront location would also attract the attention of Adidas, the global sportswear giant, which in 1998 erected an enormous billboard image of Zidane with the slogan 'Made in Marseille.' Although the player had never worn the sky-blue-and-white strip of the local Olympique de Marseille club, he did powerfully embody the port city's long tradition of diversity and inclusion. Such was the appeal of the billboard that it became a tourist attraction in its own right, remaining in place between 1998 and 2007 (*Le Monde* 2013).

This striking visual encapsulation of local rootedness, migrant relatedness and player mobility, not forgetting multinational corporate image-making, highlights the enduring dependence of professional football in France on demographic flows that began in the colonial period and continue to shape the lives of both individuals and communities. More specifically, today's Franco-Algerian sporting relationship typically exploits such ongoing population movements to the advantage of the former colonial power but may also, through the phenomenon of reverse migration, enable the ex-colony to enhance its competitive profile on the international stage. Whether parasitic or symbiotic, such interactions between the French football federation and its Algerian counterpart have been most noticeable in the constitution of their respective national sides. As part of the broader movement of both North and sub-Saharan African footballers to France (and also to neighbouring Belgium), this phenomenon underlines the continued importance of established patterns of player recruitment alongside the new mobilities associated with globalisation (Poli 2010, pp. 1005–1006).

Against this backdrop, Zinedine Zidane's family connections with Marseille may usefully be compared with those of a number of leading French and Algerian international players based in Lyon, France's second city. One indicator of the conurbation's Franco-Algerian specificity is the existence of the Association Sportive Algérienne de Villeurbanne, an amateur club founded in 1979 and located in the city's northeastern suburbs. This thriving and self-consciously 'national' sports association came to the attention of the wider sporting public in the 2002–2003 season, when it reached the last 32 of the French Cup (Gastaut 2003; Hernandez 2016). At the international level, Lyon-born players to have appeared in the colours of Algeria range from Fathi Chebel's single cap against Ireland in 1982 to Carl Medjani's 62 caps between 2010 and 2018. On the French side, the career paths of leading players from the locality have highlighted the personal and professional choices required of emerging talent. Thus, two outstanding products of the Olympique Lyonnais youth academy who were to opt for *Les Bleus* rather than *Les Verts*, Karim Benzema in 2007 and Nabil Fékir in 2015, have recognised that career considerations usually outweigh family affinities (Bouchafra-Hennequin 2008, p. 25). The fact that both players also left their home club to pursue careers in Spain, with Real Madrid and Real Betis respectively, further underlines the globalised character of the contemporary Franco-Algerian sportscape.

It follows from the above that those dual-qualified professionals who do opt to play for Algeria are generally drawn from less prestigious leagues and clubs. This was certainly true of the Algerian squad that travelled to the 2010 World Cup in South Africa, which included players from middle-ranking French clubs as well as representatives of the less fashionable European sides. However, a goalless draw against England more than made up for 1–0 defeats against Slovenia and the United States, enabling supporters of *Les Verts* to celebrate on both sides of the Mediterranean. In contrast, a much more strongly fancied French side opened with a goalless draw against Uruguay and then lost to both Mexico and hosts South Africa, with this unexpected expulsion at the group stage compounded by serious disputes between players and management that led to one of the team's stars being sent home and others responding with a training strike.

Algeria's commendable return to top-flight competition in South Africa would lay the ground for an even more impressive performance in Brazil four years later. Having made history by progressing from the group stage for the first time, the Algerian side came close to producing a shock to compare with that of 1982, moreover against the same opposition. On this occasion, they were knocked out after extra time by Germany, who would go on to defeat France in the quarter-finals, on the way to a fourth World Cup triumph. As at the previous competition, the 2014 Algerian squad drew on a number of the more modest French sides, as well as middle-ranking clubs from right across Europe. However, *Les Verts* could also now count on players attached to some of the continent's more prestigious clubs, such as Inter Milan and Tottenham Hostpur, as well as rising stars such as Riyad Mahrez, then attached to Leicester City. In 2018, this player was transferred to Manchester City, the Abu Dhabi-financed English champions, for 60 million pounds, a record for both clubs and the highest ever paid for an African footballer, in what was a striking illustration of the transnational marketability of Algeria-qualified professionals. In this case, the player was born in the northern Paris suburb of Sarcelles and played for his local youth side, moving on to Quimper and then Le Havre, both in the French lower divisions, before being spotted by Leicester City. While the player's high value may be exceptional, his accession to the Algerian international side in 2014 was typical of the reverse migration that characterised both the 2010 and 2014 World Cup squads. On both occasions, over two-thirds of the Algerian players were born in France, giving some observers the impression of their constituting a second French side, not least because several members of the team had been capped by France at youth level. In 2010, these players included Mourad Meghni (from the Lazio club in Rome) and Hassan Yebda (one of two Portsmouth representatives), both of whom had been in the French team that won the FIFA Under-17 World Cup in 2001 (Kessous 2010).

Conclusion

Since a French expeditionary force landed on the beach at Sidi Ferruch [modern Sidi Fredj] in 1830, Algeria has regularly dominated French politics and not infrequently haunted French dreams. Located just across the Mediterranean, a sea that since antiquity has linked as much as it has divided, the territory became home to a million European settlers, until the war of independence prompted the *Pied-Noir* community's exile in a France which few of its members regarded as their native land. In addition, a century-long pattern of indigenous Algerian migration was not only maintained throughout the 1954–1962 conflict but actually intensified over the decade that followed. These and subsequent population flows have been accompanied by the ever-increasing mobility of money, information and ideas between the two countries, which has only intensified under the impact of new technologies and globalised markets. Football, for its part, remains the most visible signifier of the continuing co-dependence of the former coloniser and colonised, a love-hate relationship rooted in mutual self-interest that finds diverse expression in the economic, political and cultural spheres. The game's long-standing contribution to the sporting and societal connectedness of the two countries was again foregrounded in 2018, when France won a second World Cup, this time in Russia. The undoubted star of the multicultural French side on this occasion was Kylian Mbappé, born in Paris and attached to the Qatari-owned Paris Saint-Germain club. Of mixed Algerian and Cameroonian heritage, Mbappé was voted the event's outstanding young player, suggesting the continuing reliance, by turns symbiotic and parasitic, of French football on its former colonies.

Notes

1 The origins of this term remain obscure. It may refer to the boots worn by invading French troops or to the fact that settlers had their feet tanned by the African sun.
2 The term *Beur* is not unproblematic but was widely used in the 1980s and 1990s to refer to French citizens from Maghrebi family backgrounds. The word itself originates in the *Verlan* back-slang version of the word *Arabe*, reversing its consonants.

References

Abderrahim, K. (2008) *L'indépendance comme seul but*, Paris: Paris-Méditerranée.

Agence France-Presse (no author named) (2006) 'Les bleus reçus à l'Elysée', *La Croix*, 10 July.

Amar, M. (1987) *Nés pour courir: La Quatrième République face au sport*, Grenoble: Presses Universitaires de Grenoble.

Amara, M. (2006) 'Soccer, Post-Colonial and Post-Conflict Discourses in Algeria: Algérie-France, 6 Octobre 2001, "ce n'était pas un simple match de foot"', *International Review of Modern Sociology*, 32 (2), 217–239.

Amara, M. (2012a) 'Football Sub-Culture and Youth Politics in Algeria', *Mediterranean Politics*, 17 (1), 41–58.

Amara, M. (2012b) *Sport, Politics and Society in the Arab World*, London: Palgrave Macmillan.

Amara, M. (2014) 'Sport and Political Leaders in the Arab World', *Histoire@Politique*, 2 (23), 142–153.

Bouandel, Y. and Amara, M. (2019) 'Moments and Memories: Football and State Narratives in Algeria', *Soccer & Society*, 20 (7–8), 1084–1094.

Bouchafra-Hennequin, I. (2008) 'Le choix de la nationalité sportive', *Migrance*, 29, 25–26.

Boudjedra, R. (1981) *Le Vainqueur de Coupe*, Paris: Denoël.

Boudjedra, R. (1997) *La Vie à l'endroit*, Paris: Grasset.

Camus, A. (2008) 'Pourquoi je fais du théâtre?', in *Œuvres complètes (1957–1959)*, Bibliothèque de la Pléiade IV, Paris: Gallimard.

CAOM (1931–1941) AOM, ALG/GGA/Affaires Indigènes / 9H Surveillance politique des indigènes, 9H39 Sociétés sportives musulmanes (1931–1941). Archive holdings at the Centre des Archives d'Outre-Mer, Aix-en-Provence.

Dauncey, H. and Morrey, D. (2008) 'Quiet Contradictions of Celebrity: Zinedine Zidane, Image, Sound, Silence and Fury', *International Journal of Cultural Studies*, 11 (3), 301–320.

Dine, P. and Rey, D. (2012) 'Le football en guerre d'Algérie', *Matériaux pour l'Histoire de Notre Temps*, 2 (106), 27–32.

Dorsey, J. (2014) 'Rooted in History: Politics, Identity and Ultras in North African Soccer', in Onwumechili, C. and Akindes, G. (eds.), *Identity and Nation in African Football: Fans, Community and Clubs*, London: Palgrave Macmillan, 50–66.

Dorsey, J. (2016) *The Turbulent World of Middle East Soccer*, London: Hurst.
Doyle, P. (2010) 'The Day in 1982 When the World Wept for Algeria', *The Guardian*, 13 June.
Fates, Y. (1994) *Sport et Tiers-Monde*, Paris: Presses Universitaires de France.
Fates, Y. (2009) *Sport et politique en Algérie*, Paris: L'Harmattan.
Frenkiel, S. and Bancel, N. (2008) 'The Migration of Professional Algerian Footballers to the French Championship, 1956–82: The "Desire for France" and the Prevailing National Contexts', *International Journal of the History of Sport*, 25 (8), 1031–1050.
Gastaut, Y. (2003) 'AS Algérienne de Villeurbanne', *Migrance*, 22, 48–49.
Gastaut, Y. (2008) 'Le "voyage officiel" de Zinedine Zidane en Algérie ou le retour du fils prodige', *Migrance*, 29, 60–72.
Goldblatt, D. (2006) *The Ball is Round: A Global History of Football*, London: Penguin.
Hernandez, A. (2016) 'A l'Algérienne de Villeurbanne, le football rend hommage aux anciens', *Le Monde*, 4 November.
Kessous, M. (2010) 'L'Algérie, l'autre équipe de France', *Le Monde*, 18 June.
Lanfranchi, P. (1994) 'Mekloufi, un footballeur français dans la guerre d'Algérie', *Actes de la Recherche en Sciences Sociales*, 103, 70–74.
Le Monde (no author named) (2013) 'Tête d'Affiche: À Marseille, une belle anonyme sur le "mur Zidane"', 12 July.
L'Obs [*Le Nouvel Observateur*] (no author named) (2012) 'Marseille, 1962: le cauchemar des rapatriés d'Algérie', 6 July.
Marseille, J. (ed.) (2002) 'Du paradis à l'enfer', in *France et Algérie: Journal d'une passion*, Paris: Larousse/Vuef, 227.
Merle, R. (1967) *Ahmed Ben Bella*, London: Michael Joseph. Translation by Camilla Sykes.
Nait-Challal, M. (2008) *Dribbleurs de l'indépendance: L'incroyable histoire de l'équipe de football du FLN algérien*, Paris: Éditions Prolongations.
Poli, R. (2010) 'African Migrants in Asian and European football: Hopes and Realities', *Sport in Society*, 13 (6), 1001–1011.
Scagnetti, J.-C. (2008) 'Coupe du monde 1982: les internationaux algériens et leur équipe nationale', *Migrance*, 29, 45–58.
Wahl, A. (1992) 'Football et jeux de ballon', in Hick, D. (ed.), *L'Empire du sport: Les sports dans les anciennes colonies françaises*, Aix-en-Provence: Centre des Archives d'Outre-mer, 44–45.
Yahi, N. (2010) 'Nordine Kourichi, international algérien', in Boli, C., Gastaut, Y. and Grognet, F. (eds), *Allez la France: Football et Immigration*, Paris: Gallimard/Cité Nationale de l'Histoire de l'Immigration/Musée National du Sport, 109.

Chapter 6

Enduring passions

Football, Peronism and the politics of national identity in Argentina

Jim O'Brien

The roots of football culture in Argentina

The rise of Peronism as a defining force in Argentinian politics stems from the authoritarian populism of the government of President Juan Perón between 1946 and 1955, and briefly again after his return from exile from 1973 to 1974. Although he was elected to office, his military background and ruthless hold on power gave his regime dictatorial tendencies. A mixture of strong leadership, charisma, working-class populism and the cause of social justice helped spawn the complex mass movement of Peronism. During the long period of his exile and since his death, political culture in Argentina has largely been framed in terms of either Peronism or anti-Peronism. Even in the 21st century, the spectre of Peronism casts a lasting shadow over Argentinian political identity.

This chapter explains the enduring legacy of the political and cultural phenomena of Peronism and its relationship to football. The dribbling skills of Messi, the devilish charm of Maradona, the gangster-like presence of Simeone all create potent images of Argentinian football. For those with longer memories, the towering figure of Rattín leaving the Wembley pitch in 1966 or the protracted battle between FC Barcelona and Real Madrid for Di Stefano's signature reflect the historic global culture of the Argentinian game. Its folklore both predates and postdates the Peronist era and is rich in the heroes, antiheroes and villains that have fashioned the game's societal and political culture.

Football grew out of Europe, its genesis and development stemming from British immigrants to Argentina in the 1860s and 1870s (Goldblatt 2006; Campomar 2014). By the 1920s and 1930s, the growth of professionalism, passionate club rivalry with a volatile fanbase and the evolution of a particular style of play stressing individual passion, flair and dribbling ability (Nadel 2014) had merged with the interlocking synthesis between football, politics and the representation of identities (Wilson 2016). Within the Argentinian state and nation, these forces gave rise to the seminal notions of *Argentinidad*, the sense of being Argentinian as a distinctive cultural identity, and *La Nuestra*, the free-flowing way of playing the game. The roots of the former can be traced back to Argentinian independence in 1810, providing a catalyst for the historic break with Spanish colonial rule. Impetus was given to the concept of this sentiment of being Argentinian or *Argentinidad*, following the influx of European immigration in the late 19th century, which created an ethnically diverse society. Fashioning a sense of national identity in an attempt to create cultural and political cohesion in a fragmented population became a key governmental objective. The start of Argentinian football's first boom period in the 1920s as a consequence of urbanisation and industrialisation (Wilson 2016) dovetailed perfectly with the growth of international competition in the shape of *La Copa América*, so that pride in *La Nuestra*, especially when channelled through the national team, became a major factor in the shaping of *Argentinidad* or Argentine identity (Giulianotti 2000; Wilson 2016). The nexus between football and politics is crucial to a critical understanding of the historical and cultural development of the Argentinian game (Goldblatt 2006), and by the time Perón came to power, football already had a distinctive Argentinian identity.

This chapter considers the relationship between football and Peronism in Argentina, both in respect of Peron's first period in power, from 1946 to 1955, and with regard to his return from exile in 1973–1974. The study has four main themes. First, it examines the game's symbolic representation of the Perón regime, with all its ambiguities and contradictions, contextualised within the seminal cultural values of *La Nuestra*. Second, it considers the demise of the idealised concept of the Argentinian game in the post-Peronist phase of the late 1950s and 1960s. It then evaluates the relationship between football and Peronism during his brief return from exile during the 1970s, before reflecting upon the legacy of Perón in the construction of nation and identity within the contemporary Argentinian game. As the cohesive links between the regime and football became embedded in Argentinian society, the shadow of Peronism was only partially eclipsed by the nation's World Cup victories in 1978 and 1986 (Wilson 2016).

Football has played a key role in defining the shifting mores of Argentinian national identity; the game's mass popular appeal has made it a potent vehicle for political exploitation and manipulation through its capacity to reflect and articulate collective populist sentiments (Goldblatt 2006). The game's foundation and subsequent growth in the late 19th and early 20th centuries was inextricably interlinked with the demographic changes, urbanisation and industrialisation that defined the social and economic developments underpinning the rise of nationalist sentiments (Hedges 2014; Wagg 1995). Football became a focal point in the emergence of class-centred politics in the 1910s and 1920s (Munck 2012), serving as a means to incorporate migrant workers, particularly from Southern Europe, within the sprawling urban communities of the game's heartland, particularly in Buenos Aires. This also fractured the middle- and upper-class elitism that had been central to football's British roots in Argentina (Goldblatt 2006). These roots had stressed football's amateur traditions and harked back to an earlier epoch of innocence (Giulianotti and Williams 1994). With the rise of organised nation-centred politics after the First World War, the game became an increasingly significant cultural and social force in defining Argentine identity, not only representing the break with Europe but also in framing distinguishing features of the sport as part of the struggle to define the Argentine nation, first expressed in the rivalry with Uruguay (Campomar 2014). Indeed, when the first World Cup final was played in Montevideo in July 1930, it reflected divergent constructions of contrasting Latin American ethnicities on either side of the River Plate (Glanville 2014).

By this time, the folkloric mores of Argentinian football were located as a cohesive set of values to bind the male urban working class together within the densely populated 'barrios' or neighbourhoods of Buenos Aires and Rosario, tapping into a complex mosaic of local, class-orientated and regional rivalries resonating in the boom of club football in Argentina from the 1920s to the early 1950s, with surging attendances and extensive media coverage (Wilson 2016). Within this lexicon, the iconography of *El Pibe*, ('The working-class kid'), *El Potrero*, ('The urban wasteland'), *El Criollo*, ('Native boy born in Argentina') and *El Crack* ('The star') (Galeano 2013; Sibaja and Parrish 2014) became identified with the emergence of a distinctive way of playing the game. It established the special characteristics of *La Nuestra*, which celebrated individualism, culturally rooted in the romantic escape of the poor boy, crafting the art of the Argentinian style of play in the urban wastelands of his local neighbourhood before escaping to enthral the crowds by becoming a star (Nadel 2014).

This image of the game rejected the dour tactics and the organisational strengths of the European game (Campomar 2014), underpinning the ideals governing the formation of the Argentinian Football Association in 1931, which was a highly politicised structure of governance from its inception, overseeing important cultural shifts such as the adoption of Spanish, replacing English as the game's linguistic modus operandi in 1934. This was part of a raft of developments during the 1930s, leading to the subsequent professionalisation of the Argentine Game (Giulianotti and Williams 1994), fashioning a hybrid mix of bohemian idealism and practical realism as the backdrop to Peron's emergence from the ranks of the military. The national team was the embodiment of the cherished values of *La Nuestra*, a potent symbol of national pride, a cultural representation of the nation, cast in the same vein as the tango in its manifestation of bravado, masculinity and panache (Archetti 1999; Giulianotti 2000).

The actual history of Argentinian football's cultural traditions was more fluid than these sacred myths suggest, with several ethnicities and identities shaping its origins and tactical diversity, including English and Scottish influences among others (Wagg 1995). However, the distinctive sense of national identity was significant in legitimising football as a central tenet of Argentinian statehood. By the early 1940s, at the start of Peron's gradual rise to power, football had already carved a niche within the political and cultural fabric of Argentinian society. The hierarchical nature of the Argentinian Football Association, allied to the cohesive structure of club football, based on member associations, became fused with its capacity to express mass populism. Perón was able to exploit and manipulate these factors for political purposes (Wilson 2016).

Football, Peronism and the politics of national identity 1946–1955

Peron's rise to power in the early 1940s is well documented (Bolton 2014). The evolution of the paradoxes of Peronism as a force for both inspirational unity and violent division in Argentinian society is profoundly etched within the political culture of the country (Hedges 2014). Moreover, the cult of personality around both Perón himself and the international profile and publicity surrounding his relationship with Eva Perón Duarte engendered a plethora of aspirations, policy achievements and myths during his first presidency, which have endured to fashion the most potent cluster of idealised images and symbols within the vortex of the nation's political history and cultural identity (Rock 1986). For all its contradictions and ambivalences, Peronism shaped the development of contemporary Argentina, embracing the revolution of October 1945, *El Caudillo's* two-term presidency and his fall from grace in 1955, followed by the mystique and drama of his exile and his brief return to power in the 1970s (Bolton 2014). The factionalism and violence that permeated the Peronist/anti-Peronist dichotomy defined both the internal dynamics of Argentine society and its international image and reputation for over 30 years and left a lasting imprint on the juxtaposition of militarism and democracy, which defined politics in the post-Peron era (Hedges 2014).

While there is some evidence to suggest that Perón preferred hunting and fishing (Wilson 2016), there was a close association between football and the regime. He was adored by the fans of Boca Juniors, and his government exploited the exposure and publicity of this association. In common with Mussolini's affinity with Lazio in Italy, and Franco's adoption of Real Madrid in Spain, Perón was quick to perceive the potential of sport in general, and football in particular as a potent political weapon, within the axis of class identity, mass populism and popular culture (Campomar 2014). Within the emergent quasi ideology and doctrine of Peronism in the late 1940s, the game's secure place within the cultural and sporting mores of a maturing sense of national identity suggested that it could serve the aims of the regime well as a focal point of cohesion between the diverse elements of Argentinian society while encouraging patriotism, pride and loyalty in the 'new' Argentina (Wilson 2016). The complexity of Peronism as a force of social and cultural change made use of football in four seminal ways.

First, it utilised the game's latent power to promote the objectives of *Justicialismo* or social justice as a mode of social inclusion and citizenship in the sprawling communities of what had become a predominantly urban society (Bolton 2014). Second, Peron's power base within the burgeoning power of the trade unions exploited the potential of football to permeate working-class populism in Buenos Aires and other cities where support for the game was passionate and loyal (Wilson 2016). Furthermore, Peron's rise to power and his first period in office coincided with a 'Golden Age' of Argentinian football, at both club and international levels (Campomar 2014). This enabled the regime to maximise the game's popularity and success as vehicles for political legitimacy, containment and distraction in domestic economics and politics, as achievements, both real and imagined, were used in a censored sporting and non-sporting media to project positive coverage around both Perón himself and significantly on the personality of his wife Evita (Bolton 2014; Wilson 2016). Finally, the national team was used to project and legitimise Perón and Peronism internationally, being represented as a reflection not only of the special characteristics of *La Nuestra* but also as indicative of the Peronist doctrine of the 'Third Way' as a key dynamic in the new post-war order of international politics (Bolton 2014; Hedges 2014). This 'Third Way,' neither overtly Marxist nor capitalist, sought to harness the divergent elements of Argentinian society within a nationalist agenda promoting patriotism and unity. The national pride engendered by *La Nuestra* suited this objective perfectly.

The relationship between football and politics under Peronism in the period 1946–1955 illustrates a scenario in which the fortunes of the game and of the regime itself reveal close parallels. Football mirrors many of the ambivalences, contradictions, successes and failures of Peronism itself, while Peronism inculcates many of the illusions, folkloric myths and ultimate disappointments of the Argentinian game into its manufacture of cohesion and consent within a complex and politically volatile society. The fusion of football and Peronism was emotionally charged. Passion, rivalry, patriotism and idealism provide the coherent threads linking the game with the contemporary politics of the period. The exploitation of *La Nuestra* and other potent representations of football in the first Peronist period demonstrate the interdependence between the game, nation and political culture.

The volatile politics and mass organised protest that culminated in Peron's ascent to power coincided with a 'Golden Age' for Argentinian football at both club and national level in the 1940s and 1950s, in which the principles and values underpinning *La Nuestra* were critical in defining the concept of *Argentinidad* (Campomar 2014; Wilson 2016). The great River Plate team of the 1940s, famous for '*La Maquina*' ('the machine') of its forward line (Muñoz, Moreno, Pedernera, Labruna and Loustau) immortalised the beauty and flair of the Argentinian game. While the team did not always sweep everything before it on the field, given the intense competition within the domestic game at the time, the side's attacking football and charismatic players cemented its niche in the folklore of the nation's sporting heritage (Galeano 2013). The emergence of Racing Club and the achievements of the national side gave full rein to the sacred precepts of *El Pibe* and *El Potrero*, releasing *Los Cracks* to exhibit the distinctive skills of *Los Criollos*, the native sons of Argentina playing the beautiful game with panache and style (Sibaja and Parrish 2014). These values incorporated the aspirational nature of sport, idealistically allowing the underdog to escape from urban poverty to become a star within the collective power of football's mass populism. During the 1940s, a close symmetry existed between the game's continued boom and the organised street politics of '*Los Descamisados*,' or the 'shirtless ones,' a working-class movement of the forgotten underclass and unrepresented groups in Argentinian society, which enshrined the dual objectives of social justice and reform so central to Peronist doctrine and its popular appeal (Wilson 2016) This found subsequent expression in the activities of the Eva Perón Foundation (Bolton 2014; Hedges 2014). By the late 1940s, aided by the increased mediatisation of the game through the radio coverage, which reinforced the mass circulation of the sporting press, particularly in respect of the newspaper *El Grafico* (Wilson 2016), football became increasingly perceived as a means of projecting national cohesion and identity within the traditional framework of local club rivalries. The regime was adept at implementing the twin strategies of direct involvement in the administration and structure of the domestic game, while carefully exploiting the values of nationalism and patriotism around the national team. The political patronage underscoring Peronism's links with the game found expression in the development of infrastructure during the period, with funding and subsidy provided for stadium construction in return for compliance and support for the wider political aims of the Peronist doctrine. This close association between football and the state fuelled allegations of corruption and financial irregularities, which subsequently became such a defining feature of the nation's football (Nadel 2014). Moreover, the high public and media profile during the game's boom period secured both legitimacy and publicity for Perón and Evita and allowed the regime to at least partially paper over the deep divisions and splits in Argentinian society.

The most direct link between football and Peronism was reflected by the setting up of the Evita Championship in 1949 (Campomar 2014; Wilson 2016). Perón himself had allegedly remarked that he had risen to power on the back of male support, that his second term would be based on the female vote and that a third term would be founded on children. In this way, primarily with football but also embracing other sports, the Eva Perón Foundation made use of the competition to promote the political goals of citizenship, patriotism and social inclusion for girls (Goldblatt 2006). Above all, the prominent media coverage of the annual event provided the regime with a cluster of images of Evita as mother and saviour of the nation and attempted to inculcate and legitimise Peronism as the nation's future.

While the cultural heritage of football was exploited by Peronism to manufacture an idealised sense of nationalism, the reality of the game's development in the Perón era revealed ambivalences and contradictions. The battle for professionalism had largely been fought during the 1930s, but the consequences spilled over into the Peronist years. The fluid nature of *Argentinidad* rooted in immigrant stock had already witnessed the Italian ancestry of three stars of the game in the 1930s, Monti, Guaita and Orsi, all of whom had played for Argentina in the 1930 World Cup Final before representing the Mussolini regime's World Cup winning side of 1934, with Monti playing in the final itself. (Glanville 2014; Wilson 2016). Even in the pioneering days of the international game, nationality and cultural identity was fluid, with football being exploited to legitimise fascism in the fashioning of Italy's successful, winning national team. This established a pattern that was repeated by the loss of star players to Italy and Spain in the post-war years and by the further exile of the so-called deadly trio of Maschio, Angelillo and Sivori to play for Italy in the 1950s (Wilson 2016). This player exodus reduced the potency of *La Nuestra* as a sporting and cultural force and was exacerbated by the frequent disputes around unionisation and player power in the late 1940s, underscoring a wider political turbulence. This was most clearly expressed with the poaching of star players by the incipient commercialism of *Los Millonarios*, Bogota, which paid huge salaries to lure a cluster of star players, including Di Stéfano and Rossi from the Argentinian game (Goldblatt 2006).

The multiple associations of football under Perón manufactured images and illusions of cohesion and certainty while the reality was more indicative of factionalism and protectionism within a culture of insularity and defensive paternalism. The aura of invincibility, the mystique of *La Nuestra* is especially apparent in the fortunes of the national team at the zenith of the golden age for the nation's football. By the late 1940s, Brazil had replaced Uruguay as the archenemy, the eulogised victory over three turbulent matches in 1946 coinciding not only with Peron's first election success, but seeping into the myths of folkloric representations of identity (Hedges 2014; Wilson 2016). This pinpointed a less parochial and provincial attitude in the new international order of the post-war world, in which Argentina and Brazil would be in the vanguard of development and economic growth. The intensity of the football rivalry between the two nations gave contested cultural and sporting power a new edge and kudos. Yet for all the rhetoric surrounding the national team, its prowess was rarely tested outside South America. This demonstrated the pragmatic paradox between internationalism and insularity at the heart of the Peronist doctrine, in which the protective shield of isolation masked fragility and weakness within the nation's football. On the one hand, the heroic and noble defeat of the national team by England at Wembley in 1951 and the subsequent defeat of the supposed masters of the game in Buenos Aires in 1953 (Clack 2011; Wilson 2016) were portrayed in the Argentinian media as evidence of the new, confident, successful Argentina, displaying the skills of *La Nuestra* on the international stage, a fitting testimony to the third way of stable governance and a coherent political ideology (Bolton 2014). Yet underlying this bravado, the insecurity of potential failure lay deep within the Argentine psyche. As a result, the national team did not participate in either the 1950 Brazil World Cup or in Switzerland 1954. A mixture of disputes with the AFA and FIFA, coupled with Peron's pragmatism, survival instincts and paranoia suggested that the political risks were too great, that the enormous political and cultural capital of victory were offset by the passions unleashed by potential failure (Campomar 2014; Nadel 2014). Beneath the swagger and confidence of *La Nuestra,* lurked the fear that the tactical and organisational shortcomings of the game would be exposed, most of all in Brazil's hosting of the World Cup.

These paradoxes meant that football was largely cocooned within the bubble of hyperbole encompassing Peronism (Taylor 1999). It served the key purposes of juxtaposing authoritarianism, autocracy and populism to present a positive sense of cultural coherence in the Perón years. It left the potent legacy of romanticism, idealism and hope. The fragility of these notions was cruelly exposed in the period following *El Caudillo's* fall from power in 1955, when they were eventually reduced to nostalgic memories of a glorious past.

The life and death of Eva Perón was soon immortalised in a pastiche of myths, symbols and representations within the nation's cultural folklore, while Juan Peron's many years of exile, mostly in Franco's Spain, kept the idealised flame of Peronism alive, serving as a reference point for both his supporters and detractors to reflect the deep political divisions within the frequently violent and repressive fabric of the Argentinian nation and state (Bolton 2014; Hedges 2014). Consequently, shortly after *El Caudillo's* overthrow in a military coup in 1955, it proved impossible to suppress the ideas Perón represented. Political battle lines were largely drawn along the lines of a Peronist and anti-Peronist dichotomy for the following 20 years. A powerful mixture of an idealised revisionism of the Perón regime, focusing on its achievements but oblivious to its many darker elements, together with its overt or thinly disguised survival, remained as important elements within the Argentinian state. Furthermore, the reassertion of those powerful factions in Argentinian society, which had been eclipsed by years of Peronism, ushered in a lengthy period characterised by class-centred political factionalism, unstable governments and the increased involvement of the police and the military in civil society (Hedges 2014; Munck 2012). The cultural cleavages unleashed by this instability impacted both on the fragile nature of Argentine identity and frequently exploded into mass political protest quelled by the reactive forces of repression and violence, underpinned by an economic slowdown culminating in the hyper-inflation of the early 1970s. Within the volatile politics of the 1960s, the nostalgic iconography surrounding Evita and the clandestine activities of the Peronists plotting the return of *El Caudillo* as the nation's saviour meant that Peronism itself remained the defining reference point in Argentine politics, culture and society. The cultural and political significance of football allowed it to continue to be a metaphor for wider societal issues in the post-Peron era because the game had become inextricably bound up in the historic constructions of nation and identity and had been a barometer of the mass populism of Peronism. It mirrored many of the cultural divisions of post-Peron Argentina, while paradoxically acting as a fragile point of unity and cohesion within Argentine society.

The myths and illusions surrounding the fabled properties of *La Nuestra* were cruelly exposed when the national team emerged from isolation to participate in the 1958 World Cup in Sweden. In contrast to the vibrant success of archrival Brazil, with a youthful and effervescent Pele as the new international star, Argentina performed abysmally in the tournament, culminating with a 6–1 defeat to Czechoslovakia, the worst debacle in the nation's football history (Wilson 2016). The success of the side in the South American Championship in 1957, based on individual flair, only masked the internal conflicts around coaching and tactics within the Argentinian Football Association and the lawless factionalism of post-Peron Argentina. The team's displays in Sweden, followed by poor performances in the Chile World Cup 1962, presaged not only criticism of adherence to the vaunted values of *La Nuestra*, which had produced a generation of tactically naive, poorly organised and indulgent, even lazy players, it also led to more protracted debates within the football authorities and the sporting media surrounding the future direction of Argentinian football (Campomar 2014). The insularity of the game in its supposed golden era suggested that the protectionism of Peronism and its rhetoric of superiority had concealed the underlying weaknesses of *La Nuestra* when opposed by the tactical acumen of European football.

The failures of 1958 and 1962 punctured national pride and challenged many of the cultural certainties around the Argentinian way of playing the game. It seemed to produce talented individuals who could become stars in the richer arenas of Europe, but it also resulted in failure. The ideals and values encompassing *La Nuestra* mirrored the idealistic assertions of Peronism itself. With *El Caudillo* in exile, the divided sensibility emerged, which was to fracture the Argentinian game until the World Cup victory of 1978 and beyond, whether to protect the traditional, pure values of *La Nuestra*, even if this resulted in heroic failure, or to adopt a more pragmatic, tactically astute and well-organised perspective that would project winning as the main objective. This gave rise to the growth of anti-football during the 1960s and 1970s, when winning became the defining motive at club and national levels (Campomar 2014; Wilson 2016). This schism within Argentine football echoed the paradoxes of Peronism; the idealism and the violence going hand in glove. It also produced distinctive representations of the game in post-Peron Argentina during the 1960s and early 1970s, as it articulated and mirrored the escalating violence of Argentine society in the period and projected repeated negative imagery surrounding the nation's football to intense international media scrutiny, particularly in respect of television coverage (Archetti 1999). The resort to the gamesmanship, sporadic violence and spoiling rationale of anti-football failed to produce a successful formula for the national team, when the raw promise of the side's performance in the 1964 tournament, which saw Brazil beaten in a style reminiscent of *La Nuestra* in its pomp, was abandoned in favour of a more cynical, negative approach. The side's performance in the 1966 World Cup in England, when the technical ability of the team was sacrificed in favour of an ultra- defensive professionalism in the match against West Germany, and the expulsion of team captain Antonio Rattín from the Wembley quarterfinal against England suggested the demise of *La Nuestra* (Clack 2011; Wilson 2016). For all the furore surrounding the allegations of conspiratorial refereeing against the South American sides, and the portrayal of the side as the victims and moral victors upon their return to Buenos Aires, the team's display matched the darker elements of lawlessness within the volatile politics of Argentinian society at that time (Hedges 2014).

The impact of anti-football at club level was more brutal and successful. The explosive violence that lay beneath the idealist protestations of Peronism found its most vibrant articulation in the participation of Racing Club and Estudiantes in both the Libertadores and the Inter-Continental Cup competitions. International television and press coverage of these harsh, violent encounters reinforced the images of Argentinian football from the 1966 World Cup and pointed at a moral and political societal decline (Glanville 2014; Goldblatt 2006). The brutality of the three matches in the Inter-Continental Cup between Racing Club and Celtic in 1967 was a bleak indicator of what was to come in the shape of Zubeldia's coaching of the Estudiantes side, which won three successive Libertadores Cups and overcame both Manchester United and AC Milan in the Inter-Continental Cup in the late 1960s and early 1970s. Zubeldia became recognised as the high priest of anti-football, in which every type of provocation and intimidation was exploited to gain advantage in the ruthless pursuit of winning (Campomar 2014; Wilson 2016) The Estudiantes side was tactically astute with a group of talented players; it broke the stranglehold that River Plate, Boca Juniors and the bigger clubs traditionally held over the domestic game, but at the cost of adding to the damaged reputation of Argentinian football. Few tears were shed outside the country when the national side failed to qualify for the Mexico World Cup in 1970, beaten by a resurgent Peru (Campomar 2014). Both the nation and football were in a state of crisis, the one feeding off the other in a cauldron of instability and doubt. Within the game, the furore and internal debate surrounding its image and performance led to calls for a return to its more traditional values; within the political arena the clamour intensified for the return of Perón.

The massacre that marked Peron's arrival at Buenos Aire's Ezeiza Airport in July 1973 dramatically symbolised Argentina's descent into political chaos and economic crisis. His brief third period in power before his death in June 1974 coincided with the national team's preparation for and participation in the West Germany World Cup. The build up to the tournament reflected the internal struggles for control and direction within the Argentinian game, as the Football Association, the clubs and a succession of coaches remained torn between the traditional values of *La Nuestra* and the aftermath of the success generated by the rationale of anti-football. The team's performance in failing to emerge from a group including Italy and Poland illustrated this ambivalence, in which a group of talented individuals once again flattered to deceive. Moreover, the side's failure was indicative of the undercurrents of political tensions, which even the mass popular appeal of the game was unable to disguise. The rising tide of repression, torture and kidnapping increasingly came to characterise the crisis of the Argentinian state during the 1970s. Cast in this light, the halcyon days of the 1940s and 1950s, when the cult of Peronism brought the panache of *La Nuestra* and the working-class attachment to football fully into the political orbit of the regime, became couched in the folkloric politics of nostalgia. The death of Perón left the power vacuum of a deeply divided society, with football reduced to mirroring these divisions in both on the field and off the field violence, particularly in the activities of the *Barras Bravas*, Argentina's Ultras, which suggested the degeneration of the game into the lawlessness permeating the state itself, although hooliganism had been a traditional feature within the patchwork nature of the local and regional rivalry of Argentinian football (Giulianotti 2000; Paradiso 2009). It came as little surprise when the coup of April 1976 ushered in an era of military rule and an attempt to banish the spectre of Peronism from the political landscape, when the idealism of the Perón doctrine was replaced by the brutal authoritarianism of a police state (Hedges 2014).

The Hand of God – the enduring legacies of Perón and Peronism

The ticker-tape iconography of Argentina's hosting of the 1978 World Cup and ultimate triumph of the host nation in winning the trophy took place against the backdrop of torture, disappearance, state censorship and the denial of fundamental human and political rights (Galeano 2013). While FIFA's decision to award the tournament to Argentina paid homage to the nation's rich football heritage, within the interwoven tapestry of football and politics, it seemed to offer succour to a failed state and was subsequently exploited and manipulated by the governing military junta to legitimise an oppressive regime in a panoply of mass distraction and patriotic fervour (Glanville 2014; Wilson 2016). While concentration camps silenced and tortured within earshot of the celebrations of victory, the success of Menotti's team suggested at least a partial return and adherence to the traditional values of *La Nuestra*. The rejection of anti-football in favour of the fluent, organised team play of Kempes, Ardilles, Pasarella and Luque paradoxically restored some of the international prestige of the Argentinian game and re -awakened the spirit of Peronism in the fusion between the vaunted values of *La Nuestra* and national pride. Nevertheless, the victory was both tainted by its political and cultural context and by the allegations of corruption, which tarnished the achievement of Menotti's side. The remarkable 6–0 victory in the decisive match against Peru, which denied Brazil a place in the final, was accompanied by accusations of bribery and match-fixing, with the dark hand of *La Junta* said to be directly involved in securing the right outcome for the regime (Nadel 2014; Wilson 2016). Furthermore, the 1978 success continued to embellish the paradoxes and ambivalences underscoring the football-politics synthesis within the Argentinian game. It reinforced the Peronist impulses of populism, patriotism and mass cultural identity within the framework of an autocratic military dictatorship, registering a pattern of similarity and divergence with the past (Goldblatt 2006).

The impact of Perón, Evita and the myriad implications of the Peronist/anti-Peronist dichotomy still casts a shadow over political and cultural life in Argentina more than 60 years after his fall from power and over 40 years after his death. The debate surrounding football's politicisation and the schisms that have characterised the game post-Peron has continued (Taylor 1999). The victory of Bilardo's team in the Mexico World Cup of 1986 constituted a return to a more pragmatic approach in which the dazzling individual skills of Maradona were harnessed to a tactically astute and organised team ethos, which was not averse to resorting to some of the questionable gamesmanship and unsporting play, evoking memories of the anti-football dialectic (Campomar 2014; Wilson 2016). The team's cynical defence of the trophy in Italy 1990, illuminated only occasionally by Maradona's brilliance suggested that the values of *La Nuestra* had been almost completely abandoned (Glanville 2014).

During the 1990s when the neoliberalism of the Menem government struggled to contain mass protest and dissent, the social drug of football seemed to be the only form of cultural cohesion, constituting the counterbalancing safety valve of banal nationalism (Billig 1995). By this time, the continued exodus of star players to the elite European leagues, coupled with the violent image and reputation of much of the domestic game, resulted in a pattern of falling attendances for club football, as commercially driven mediatisation located the game within the fulcrum of mass popular entertainment (Wilson 2016). The nascent globalisation of the 1980s and 1990s catapulted Argentinian football into the postmodern era of commodification and consumption, so that the traditional mores of the relationship between *La Nuestra* and Argentine identity became culturally blurred in the global marketplace of contemporary sport. The most direct manifestations of political protests in a democratic Argentina surfaced in 2001, coinciding with the national team's qualification and preparation for the Korea/ Japan World Cup in 2002 (Goldblatt 2006). In the tournament itself, defeat by England and failure to get beyond the group stage came to define many of the national team's performances of failure and underachievement in post-millennium international competition. In spite of his key role in getting Argentina to the 2014 final, Messi's failure to achieve the crowning glory of winning the world cup both signposted his inability thus far to emulate Maradona's success and echoed the pattern of earlier disappointments for the national side (Campomar 2014; Wilson 2016). The Perón years explicitly legitimised the indelible link between football, politics and cultural identity. This legacy is articulated in the contrasting cultural imagery associated with the two main stars, Maradona and Messi, who have dominated the export of the heroes, antiheroes and villains of the Argentinian game to a global audience. Their contrasting stories shed light on the folkloric heritage and traditions of Argentinian football.

The mercurial life of Diego Maradona chronicled the rise of the poor working-class street urchin from the wrong side of the tracks, perfecting his skills in the roughly hewn urban wasteland on the outskirts of his impoverished barrio, rising from nothing to become a star on the global stage, dazzling millions with his skills. He is the personification of *El Pibe* (Nadel 2014). His story is that of the underdog, the rebel, the irrepressible individual whose rise to the top and fall from grace captures the very essence of *La Nuestra*, *El Criollo* and all the folkloric values endemic to the romanticised idealism of the Argentinian game (Galeano 2013). His pivotal role in the defeat of England in the Mexico World Cup of 1986 captures these elements perfectly. The iconic 'Hand of God' goal, in which gamesmanship or even cheating is reconstructed as the morally justified revenge of the patriot defending the nation's honour after the abyss of the conflict over Las Malvinas is quickly followed by the brilliance of his second stunning individual goal (Campomar 2014; Wilson 2016). The multi-layered complexities of Argentine identity are confirmed by Maradona's place in the nation's cultural iconography. The case of Lionel Messi, however, is more complex (Nadel 2014). His lower-middle-class roots in Rosario, coupled with his departure from Argentina at an early age to be incorporated into the academy of FC Barcelona, has raised questions around his patriotism and his attachment to the country of his birth. This has created a paradox in which his sublime talent is commensurate with the values of *La Nuestra*, while his presumed cultural conformity prevents him from having the wider cultural authenticity associated with Maradona (Nadel 2014; Wilson 2016). These cultural mores around the game are rooted in the fusion of football and identity, which remains at the heart of the Peronist legacy.

This legacy found a contemporary expression with Christina Kirchner's reintroduction of the Evita Championships (Wilson 2016). Not only did the democratic structure of the contemporary state tap into the politics of nostalgia emanating from the Perón years in a rather slick public relations exercise, the enduring mass populism of football, for all its paradoxes and contradictions, was exploited as a means of nation-building and the promotion of citizenship while confirming its function as a distraction from economic and political problems (Hedges 2014; Wilson 2016). Some 60 years after her death, the mystique of Evita and the pastiche of cultural references surrounding Perón and Peronism were still being juxtaposed with the native hue of the Argentinian game in an attempt to foster national cohesion and unity.

The myths of Argentina's glorious past and the eulogising of the nation's footballing heritage and traditions are a lasting testimony to the powerful association between football, politics and national identity during the Peronist years. The first presidency in particular secured the cultural heritage of Peronism, which shaped the nation's political identity for at least a couple of political generations. The reality of much of football's development both during *El Caudillo's* exile and after his brief return and death in the 1970s are often at sharp odds with the soaring rhetoric of its mythologised heritage. Violence, corruption, gamesmanship and failure have frequently been at the core of the game at both domestic and international levels. Yet still the myths, the nostalgia, the symbols and images of Peronism resonate powerfully within the cultural representations of Argentinian football in the vortex of national identity.

The contemporary game is torn between the stifling pull of history and tradition and the impulses of reform, with financial problems, images of violence and the burgeoning relationship between the clubs and television being in the vanguard of potential change. The ugly clashes between fans of River Plate and Boca Juniors prior to the 2018 final of *La Copa Libertadores* in Buenos Aires demonstrated that the controversy, passion and rivalry at the core of the club game continues to resonate powerfully. After much rancour and furore that further worsened the tarnished reputation of Argentinian football, the deciding match saw River Plate emerge victorious 3–1 at the Bernebeu Stadium in Madrid, bringing to a close a dramatic chapter in the history of these folkloric enemies. This high-profile spectacle sat alongside the failure of the national team at the 2018 Russia World Cup, the abject defeat by Croatia, coupled with the forlorn, disconsolate images of Messi, both during and after the match seemingly defining a deeper malaise at the heart of the Argentinian game.

The attempts to address this malaise came with the bloated restructuring of *La Superliga Argentina* in the wake of the power vacuum arising out of the 2017 scandal within the Argentinian Football Association. The new format would embrace 26 clubs, with an end of season *Copa Superliga* representing the first hesitant steps in this process of reform. Decisions such as the appointment of former international Juan Sebastián Verón as Head of Youth Development indicate more strategic and coherent planning for stability after years of chaotic infighting, which not only seemed to mirror the country's economic and political turmoil, but squandered the talents of a generation of outstanding players on the international stage. In spite of these reasons for guarded optimism, the entrenched nature of the juxtaposition between football, politics and culture in Argentina might suggest that change and reform are doomed to fail, as the legacies of Peronism resurface to frustrate reformist initiatives. While the folkloric traditions of *La Nuestra* and *Argentinidad* will still produce urban working-class boys to become stars to dazzle and captivate within the elite clubs of the game's global audience, the indelible fusion between ideology, the state and football will continue to carve a distinctive symmetry around constructions and representations of national identity in Argentina.

References

Archetti, E (1999). *Masculinities: Football, Polo, and The Tango in Argentina.* London: Berg Global Issues Series.

Billig, M (1995). *Banal Nationalism.* London: Sage.

Bolton, K (2014). *Perón and Peronism.* London: Black House Publishing.

Campomar, A (2014). *Golazo! A History of Latin American Football.* London: Quercus.

Clack, N (2011). *Animals! The Story of England v Argentina.* Brighton: Pitch Publishing.

Galeano, E (2013). *Soccer in Sun and Shadow.* London: Fourth Estate.

Giulianotti, R (2000). *Football; A Sociology of the Global Game.* London: Polity Press.

Giulianotti, R and Williams, J eds (1994). *Game without Frontiers; Football, Identity and Modernity.* London: Routledge.

Glanville, B (2014). *The Story of the World Cup, Second Edition* London: Faber and Faber.

Goldblatt, D (2006). *The Ball is Round; A Global History of Soccer.* London: Viking.

Hedges, J (2014). *Argentina; A Modern History.* London: I.B. Tauris.

Munck, R (2012). *Contemporary Latin America,* Third Edition. London: Palgrave Macmillan.

Nadel, J (2014). *Futbol! Why Soccer Matters in Latin America.* Miami: University Press of Florida.

Paradiso, E (2009) "The Social, Political and Economic Causes of Violence in Argentine Soccer." *Nexus: The Canadian Journal of Anthropology,* Volume 24, pp 65–79.

Rock, D. (1986). *Argentina 1516–1982*. London: Tauris IB.
Sibaja, R and Parrish, C (2014). "Pibes, Cracks and Caudillos; Argentina, The World Cup and Identity Politics." *Soccer and Society*, Volume 15, Issue 5, pp 655–670.
Taylor, C (1999). *The Beautiful Game; A Journey Through Latin American Football*. London: Phoenix.
Wagg, S (1995). *Giving the Game Away; Football Across Five Continents*. Leicester: Leicester University Press.
Wilson, J (2016). *Angels with Dirty Faces; The Footballing History of Argentina*. London: Orion Books.

Chapter 7

'Defenders of European culture' – 'refugee crisis,'[1] football hooliganism and the right-wing shift in Europe[2]

Pavel Brunssen, Robert Claus and Peter Römer

A new transnational racism developed during the so-called refugee crisis with its peak in 2015. Far-right protagonists are drawing a threatening scenario of a Muslim migration that will replace a supposedly all-white and all-Christian European culture. Far-right European ultras and hooligans claim to be the 'defenders' of this right-wing cultural idea. In and around European stadiums, right-wing slogans increased during the peak of the discourse on refugees between 2014 and 2016. They are well organised. Their protest has influenced national policies, and their violence is well trained in combat sports, as many national and regional examples – for instance, from Poland, Hungary, the Czech Republic and Germany – display.

The smoke of pyrotechnics is in the air. People chant and wave flags. These descriptions could evoke images of a football derby, but instead, they are scenes from Poland's National Independence Day, where tens of thousands march through the streets of Warsaw each year on the 11th of November. Among them are hundreds of nationalistic ultras and hooligans. In contrast to a football derby, the hardcore fans of rivalry clubs march side by side. For them, the nation is bigger than the club. For years on this day, these fan groups have been provoking clashes with anti-racist counter-protesters and the police, but no more. In 2015, the atmosphere at the Poland Independence Day demonstrations changed. Although hardly any clashes have taken place since then, the ultras and hooligans are still marching in significant numbers. They chant 'God, honor, homeland!' or 'We will kill communists' (DeutscheWelle, 2019).

What made the Polish ultras and hooligans stop provoking clashes in 2015? If we aim to understand contemporary right-wing politics, we must understand their triple strategy. Right-wing ultras and hooligans, as well as neo-Nazis and far-right politicians, aim to spread their ideas, gain representation in parliaments and obtain physical superiority over antifascist groups. Already in 1997, the chairman of the far-right 'Nationaldemokratische Partei Deutschlands' ('National Democratic Party of Germany,' NPD) proclaimed a new strategy: He declared the struggle for the minds, the parliaments and the street, thereby providing us also with a framework to analyse right-wing movements (Brandstetter, 2006).

The anti-refugee campaigns in Europe are, we argue, best understood as part of larger political practices by the far-right. We show in this chapter that football fans played a crucial role in this process between 2014 and 2016. Ultras and hooligans did not only display their worldview in the stadiums, they also gathered for the fight on the streets, thereby allowing right-wing politicians to enter public spaces that otherwise would not have been available or at least would have been more contested, for instance, by counter-demonstrators. In Poland, the clashes on the Independence Day stopped because of the election of the right-wing populist political party Law and Order (PiS). In 2016, the Independence Day demonstration was named 'Poland, the Bastion of Europe' in line with the political ideology of the Polish government (Zeit Online, 2016).

Ultras and hooligans opened space for right-wing politicians in several European countries. These fans keep counter-demonstrators away from right-wing demonstrations. One example are the demonstrations of 'Patriotische Europäer gegen die Islamisierung des Abendlandes' ('Patriotic Europeans Against the Islamization of the Occident,' Pegida) in Dresden, Germany. Here, the 'front men' of the movements speak to the crowd, while hooligans stand as guards at the edges of the public places of right-wing gatherings.[3] The struggles for the minds, the parliaments and the streets are conflated in these public spaces. This happened, as we will show in this chapter, simultaneously in various countries, enforced by the international networks between these groups.

In this chapter, we will focus on the time between October 2014, when the 'Hooligans gegen Salafismus' ('Hooligans against Salafism,' HogeSa) marched through Cologne, and the EURO 2016 tournament in France. We argue that right-wing fans, ultras and hooligans in Europe reacted, participated in and sometimes even initiated racist discourses about refugees. They did so on several levels. First, they displayed their racist worldview publicly and symbolically at the stadiums. Second, they took their campaigns to the streets, where they not only marched against but also attacked migrants, counter-demonstrators and journalists. Third, they reinforced old networks or initiated new ones in online chat groups during combat-sport events, concerts and demonstrations.

We are focusing in this chapter on a variety of groups and movements that differ in terms of their self-definition as fans, ultras or hooligans, in their regional contexts, and in other aspects. Despite their differences, these groups share their engagement in far-right activities during the 'refugee crisis.' In order to discuss these activities from a variety of places together, we necessarily have to simplify and generalise to some degree by speaking of 'ultras and hooligans' in a broader sense. We acknowledge that these fan cultures differ from country to country, from club to club and from group to group. Still, it is possible to define the transnational characteristics of these fan cultures. Ultras differ in their political attitudes and their range of activities. All ultras share that they are mainly concerned with the auditive and visual support of the respective clubs in the stadiums.[4] Hooligans, in contrast, focus mainly on violent clashes.[5] In some cases, both fan cultures merge or act together; in others, they don't.

Racism and anti-racism in football fan cultures have been the subject of academic inquiry in various cases (Burdsey, 2011; Cashmore and Cleland, 2014; Doidge, 2015; Endemann et al., 2015; Garland and Rowe, 2001; Gebhardt, 2017; Hodges, 2019; King, 2004; Millward, 2008). We agree with Doidge et al. (2020) that 'politics in the stadium does not automatically translate as a clear expression of ideology' because the 'use of symbols and political terminology can help reinforce a sense of collective identity without necessarily constituting instrumental political action' (Doidge et al., 2020, p. 6f.). In the case of the groups and actors we are concerned with in this chapter, the racist performances are also acts of intentional racism, performed with the goal of spreading and manifesting anti-Muslim and anti-refugee racism across Europe. Ultras and hooligans are diverse fan cultures, but racist ideologists with clear political goals and strategies are influential in some of them. These circles were at the peak of their public outreach during the 'refugee crisis' and the EURO 2016.

While some anti-refugee incidents in and outside the stadiums of national leagues preceding the EURO 2016 remained almost unnoticed, racist actions and clashes at the EURO 2016 in France were a shock for the public and therefore widely discussed in the media. Videos that circulated online show how English fans humiliated Roma children and derogated Islam (Vice Sports, 2016). Hungarian ultras displayed rune symbols, which are a symbol for nationalist ideology. Ukrainian fans showed the red-and-black flag of the nationalist and antisemitic Ukrainian Insurgent Army. German hooligans showed the German Reich flag and chanted 'We have marched in again' (Tagesspiegel, 2016). International tournaments are also media spectacles, dominating the news coverage in most parts of Europe. These tournaments thus also come with more attention to the fans' actions than usual.

One month before the kickoff in Saint-Denis, scholars and journalists from all over Europe travelled to the Anne Frank House in Amsterdam, with the aim to discuss how European football fans react to the discourse on refugees. Dario Brentin, who co-organised the workshop, said: 'It is troubling how well and structurally profound the far-right has re-established itself in European football fan scenes, to a degree that we haven't had since the late 1980s and this in both Eastern and Western Europe' (Brunssen and Römer, 2017). While the idea for the workshop at the Anne Frank House had been around for a long time, it became an urgent task considering the abundance of the fans' reactions to the 'refugee crisis,' Brentin said.

While many European countries are ruled by centrist parties, many events have erupted on the political landscape: Brexit, the refugee debate with its peak in summer 2015, the election of or growing success of right-wing parties in countries like Poland, Germany, Hungary or Italy.

These events polarised the organised fans in Europe. Many fan groups supported refugees, inviting them to the games or collecting clothes and food for them, especially many ultra groups in Germany, even those considering themselves to be non-political like in Dortmund or Cologne.

On the other hand, all over Europe, right-wing politics became part of the mainstream discourse. Hooligans and ultras supported this development. For instance, the globally recognised clashes in the East-German town Chemnitz in summer 2018 were initiated by local hooligans mobilising many neo-Nazis who then marched in the streets led by key figures of the 'Alternative für Deutschland.' Again, the struggle for the minds and the parliaments merged on the streets (Claus n.d.).

The case of Hungary – right-wing extremism in the parliament and on the terraces

The similarity of right-wing politics in the parliament and at the stadiums became probably most visible during the games of the Hungarian national team at the EURO 2016. While the Hungarian prime minister Viktor Orbán (Fidesz), who is transforming Hungary according to his nationalist and racist ideas, was present in the grandstand, the Hungarian fan section was dominated by men in black T-shirts. This group of fans calls itself 'Carpathian Brigade' and is known to be 'a paramilitary group consisting of neo-Nazis,' as described by Bálint Josá, founder of the organisation Subjective Values Foundation (Niessen, 2016). This non-governmental organisation is committed to fighting discrimination and neo-Nazism in Hungarian football. Josá explained in an interview that the 'Carpathian Brigade' is the most violent and influential group in the stands, and, as the name suggests, their aim is to restore the old territories and borders of Greater Hungary.

Ultras of various Hungarian football teams are coming together in the 'Carpathian Brigade,' thereby leaving rivalries aside: 'The history of Hungary has shown time and time again, if there is an enemy, the Hungarian people unite. It's the same with the national team,' said Josá. Ties between ultras and the far-right exist, although the relationship between ultras and politicians and political parties is not without conflicts: 'Orbán is a big football fan, he let many stadiums be built and is a close friend of the national football association. The ultras like Orbán's politics, but their political party is – if at all – the ultra-right Jobbik party.' 'The situation got worse in light of the refugee situation,' Josá says. Furthermore, 'politics brought a more general form of xenophobia to society and football through campaigns against refugees. For example, the largest Hungarian ultra-website, "Ultras Liberi", called for a distribution of poisoned food to refugees.'

A nationalist cooperation between Slovak and Czech hooligans

Just a few miles northwest of Hungary, several thousand people gathered in the Slovakian capital Bratislava for a right-wing demonstration on 20 June 2015. Among the demonstrators were hundreds of football fans from the Czech Republic and Slovakia. Ultras from Slovan Bratislava had mobilised. Adam Lupták from

Oxford University reported at the workshop in Amsterdam how actors from the far-right spoke on stage, while the counter-demonstration was hailed by the demonstrators with the football chant 'Vy kurvy, co vás tak málo?' ('You whores, why so few?') and how the demonstration was followed by clashes between fan groups and the police. To Lupták, the participation of fans was not surprising: 'Many of the football fans come from the far-right,' he said.

Ultras from the Czech Republic not only attended this demonstration in Bratislava, they also displayed many banners against refugees at the stadia. Mirek (name changed), an ultra from the Czech Republic, told us about the numerous banners and right-wing actions that accompanied the discourse on refugees. Ultras of Viktoria Pilsen showed, for instance, a huge choreography displaying a muscular white man standing over a falling person depicted as a Muslim. The white man holds an axe in his hands and is ready to strike immediately. The choreography is accompanied by a banner that says 'Europe wake up.' Similar actions have taken place at the stadiums of FK Jablonec, Banik Ostrava, Sparta Prague and others.

'The general mood in the Czech Republic is rather unfriendly towards refugees,' Mirek told us. All major parliamentary parties in the Czech Republic are against the immigration of refugees. 'The right-wing fans feel that this topic can also gain greater "acceptance for themselves and their ideas,"' said Mirek. Right-wing fans also aim to gain hegemony through violence. The 'Barflies,' a Bohemians Prague fan group, posed with the statement 'Refugees Welcome' and published a photo of this on social media (Barflies United, 2015). Soon after, the group was attacked by right-wing hooligans from Bohemians. During the attack, the 'Barflies' banner was stolen, and the group has not been present at the stadium since. The struggle for the streets thus becomes also a struggle for the stadiums.

As part of their struggle for a right-wing political hegemony in the stadiums, Czech Ultras did not only take part in demonstrations, show banners and attack anti-racist fans; some groups also took part in anti-refugee campaigns in an international context: ultras from Sparta Prague and Viktoria Pilsen boycotted Europa League games in September 2015, when one euro of every ticket of a team's first home game in the Champions or Europa League was donated to refugees as part of the 'European Club Association' initiative '90 minutes for hope.' Only the third Czech representative in the group stage, Slovan Liberec, did not participate in the boycott.

Poland – anti-Muslim racism and a nationalist history policy leads to actions

Boycotts did not take place only in the Czech Republic; Polish fans and ultras boycotted games too. Before the boycott, in August 2015, the away sector of FC Basel's 'St. Jakob-Park' was sold out by Lech Posen's fans who travelled from Poland to Basel for a Champions League qualification game. Local spectators later spoke of the most impressive support for a visiting team in 'St. Jakob-Park' ever. Only eight weeks later, the two teams met again in Basel. This time the away sector remained practically empty – Poznan's fans did not want to participate in the '90 minutes for hope' initiative. They had already boycotted Poznan's home game against Belenenses Lisbon. The organised Lech fans did not want to support 'the flood of Muslim immigrants to Europe,' they wrote on Facebook (Gisi, 2018). They refused the idea to donate one euro per ticket, and finally not even 8,000 fans made it to the stadium. The home game against AC Florence, for which no euro was paid in favour of refugees, attracted over 22,000 fans. Legia Warsaw supporters also drew attention before the home game against Zagłębie Lubin with banners such as 'We want home comers, not illegal immigrants' and 'Welcome to hell, wandering sheep.' The display of crossed-out mosques and crescents underlined the anti-Muslim tenor of their statements. In contrast, as the people in charge of the capital city club subsequently campaigned to donate the money from the initiative to Polish-born refugees who had fled Eastern Ukraine, the Legia stadium was crowded against SSC Napoli.

Their nationalist and racist rhetoric was echoed in many Polish stadiums. In the fall of 2015, Slask Wroclaw's ultras showed a crusader who, by means of a sword, prevented three refugee boats from reaching mainland Europe. 'If Europe is flooded by the Islamic plague, let's defend Christianity,' said the choreography. At the EURO 2016, Polish fans travelled in large numbers to see their national team play Ukraine in Marseille. On their way to the stadium, they carried the banner 'Defenders of European Culture.' Later, they also displayed the banner at the stadium, and thus in front of all of Europe. The choreographies, actions and banners of the largest Polish fan groups illustrate what their vision of Europe is: Christian, racist, and hostile towards refugees.

All these events at and around stadiums led simultaneously to street politics and violence: in September 2015, Legia fans attacked 20 refugees from Syria in the proximity of an asylum centre. Five of them were seriously injured (Faith Matters, 2015). Legia fans had already sent a clear signal two weeks earlier: fans of both Lechia Gdansk and Legia Warsaw had advertised demonstrations in Gdansk and Warsaw calling for a stop to immigration. At the Legia stadium, a banner was presented, saying, 'All of Warsaw is shouting out loud – No to the Islamic hordes. Everybody to the march on September 12.' Their call was heard by 5,000–7,000 demonstrators in Warsaw and several thousand in Gdansk, among them many fans, who demanded 'No to the Islamization of Poland,' although only about 200 people are granted the right of asylum every year in a country with 38.5 million inhabitants.

Refugees in Poland are mostly perceived as a risk rather than victims or people who flee from violence and war to come from another country to live in Poland. After the election in 2015, Law and Justice has tightened its refugee policies. Muslim refugees from the Middle East are no longer accepted, and agreements with the EU on the acceptance of 7,000 refugees from Italy and Greece, which had been negotiated under the previous government, were cancelled and money for civil society institutions was cut. Thus, the policies from the parliament seem in line with the demands raised by right-wing ultras, hooligans and neo-Nazis in the stadium and on the streets. Although numerous initiatives have been developed in larger Polish cities to oppose the racist anti-refugee discourse, Polish football fans have, in most cases, taken a firm stand against them.

The Polish government met the demands for a Poland without Muslim refugees, by rejecting asylum seekers in 2015 – even at the price of breaking European laws. This issue is thus polarising in a country deeply divided between modernisation and traditionalism, which often considers itself a victim of foreign influence. A central historical-political event in the collective Polish memory is the Warsaw Uprising of 1944, in which the Polish Army 'Armia Krajowa,' supported by a large part of Polish civil society, tried to revolt without a chance against the German occupation, while the Red Army stood just outside the city before marching into Warsaw itself. To this day, football fans commemorate the event on every match day around the anniversary of the uprising. We argue that the anti-refugee actions by Polish football fans align with their nationalistic interpretation of the Warsaw Uprising: Poland defends itself against invaders who want to subjugate the country. Thus, in many of the anti-refugee protests in the streets, the symbol of the Warsaw Uprising was worn by the hooligans. It is a historical construction from WWII to the refugee debate today. A nationalist perspective on WWII emphasises that Poland has been suppressed first by the national socialists, then by communists – and is still fighting for its own historical narrative to be heard by the world. Any intervention from outside of Poland is therefore seen very skeptically, and the Islamic background of many refugees has led the Christianity of nationalist Poles to be shown and shouted by hooligans.

'For the homeland – ready!' – the former Yugoslavia

Banners like 'Defenders of European Culture,' which Polish ultras and hooligans showed in Marseille 2016, have long been seen at the stadiums of the former Yugoslavia. For example, fans of Vardar Skopje (now the capital of North Macedonia) presented the banner 'Stop Islamization of Balkans' when conflicts between Orthodox Macedonians and Muslim Albanians escalated in spring 2012. Right-wing organisations and groups throughout the region are pursuing a strategy of expanding their influence in the fan scenes (Raschke, 2015). By spreading right-wing attitudes, the fans provide extreme right-wing groups with a permanent constituency, according to Holger Raschke. 'Even though many fans often refuse to take a direct part in the protest, they are irreplaceable for mobilizing to street protests' (Raschke, 2015, p. 302). Especially in the nationalistic mood in the successor states of Yugoslavia, the fan groups represent an attractive offer for young people. They usually grow up with a feeling of insecurity; the fan groups can offer a feeling of security – here young people find a firm affiliation and identity. These can be charged with rejection and hatred of the alleged other(s). Nationalism, homophobia, antigypsyism or anti-Muslim racism are common phenomena. According to Raschke,

> Many fan scenes describe themselves as apolitical. This seems paradoxical, because what began insidiously in some fan groups in the 1980s and escalated in the 1990s has survived to this day: many fan groups reproduce and embody in an almost ideal-typical way the aggressive, nationalistic and extreme right-wing attitude patterns that had established and intensified in the course of the conflicts and wars.
>
> (Raschke, 2015, p. 290)

There are hardly any countermovements. The fan group 'White Angels Zagreb' from the NK Zagreb (now Croatia), which openly positions itself against right-wing groups, is an absolute exception.

At the EURO 2016 in France, Croatian fans were once again in the public eye: due to a conflict with the Croatian Football Association (the association is accused of corruption), they interrupted a game in the match against the Czech Republic by throwing flares and firecrackers. However, Croatian fans often attract attention with right-wing chants and actions, and this also applies to individual players: in 2013, the Croatian national player Josip Šimunić celebrated Croatia's successful World Cup qualification with an antiphonal song with the fans, which he sang over the stadium microphone: 'Za dom – Spremni' ('For the homeland – Ready') – the slogan of the fascist 'Ustaša'; FIFA subsequently banned him for ten games. At the EURO 2016 in France, Šimunić was a 'national motivator' as part of the coaching staff. This is one example among many of the right-wing tendencies of football in the states of the former Yugoslavia, which can also be traced back to the central role of football fans already during the nationalist struggles over the dissolution of Yugoslavia.[6] The incidents during the EURO 2016 in France had precursors in the stadiums across Europe.

A Western European issue as well

Anti-Muslim racism and hatred against refugees are not only propagated by East Central European football fans. In Germany, the 'Hooligans gegen Salafismus' was a kind of Europe-wide pioneer, when approximately 5,000 hooligans and neo-Nazis marched through Cologne in Germany in October 2014. In Belgium, the authorities were surprised when 450 hooligans suddenly disrupted the commemoration ceremonies after Islamist attacks in Brussels. They chanted 'Belgian Hooligans. We are at home here' and 'All together against the Islamic State.' Local media also reported racist slogans and sporadic Hitler salutes. Hooligans from different clubs travelled together to Antwerp, leaving rivalries aside for common political goals – a pattern that runs through the whole of Europe when it comes to racist mobilisation: together against the supposed enemy. This continued on New Year's Eve: in Antwerp, hooligans from various clubs had come together to 'defend the city against terrorists.' It is unknown whether the meeting finally took place, but it is known that notorious nationalist hooligans had made announcements in advance (Die Presse, 2016).

In France too, right-wing actors took advantage of the racist mood in the run-up to the EURO 2016. The martial arts brand 'Pride France' produced a T-shirt with the inscription 'Turkey – not welcome.' For weeks, fans from Eastern and Western Europe posed with this motif on the brand's own Facebook page (Claus, 2016). The slogan goes back to the right-wing ultra-group 'Kop of Boulogne' from the French capital city club Paris St. Germain, which had already chosen Turkey as the enemy of the EURO 2016 in November 2015, when they posed with an identical banner in front of their home stadium and thus drew a lot of attention. The clothing brand 'Pride France' advertised the slogan and was just as successful among football fans in Europe as the 'ultras-tifo.net' platform, which is popular across the continent and which came up with 'FCK ISIS' ('Fuck ISIS') T-shirts in the run-up to the EURO 2016. This was also taken up at the EURO by English fans who provoked in the multicultural city of Marseille with 'ISIS, where are you?' chants. Their provocations resulted in clashes with local Arabic-born youngsters. The democratic attitude against ISIS was instrumentalised by right-wing fans in order to create a general mood against Muslims and Arabs.

In Austria, hooligans from clubs which are usually known as rivals acted together as well. Hooligans of the derby rivals Rapid and Austria Vienna organised carpools for the 'Hooligans gegen Salafisten' demonstration 2014 in Cologne. Two years later, they participated in a march of the 'Identitarian Movement.' 'The defining bracket for all these activities is the mobilization against refugees which has brought a new generation of extreme right-wing activists,' according to the Austrian journalist Michael Bonvalot (Bonvalot, 2016, p. 21). The hooligans of Austria Vienna call themselves 'Unsterblich' ('Immortal'). Their banner is made in the style of the neo-Nazi network 'Blood & Honour.' The group is encouraged by Austria's leading ultra-group 'Fanatics.' Bonvalot describes an event from September 2011, which illustrates the acceptance of the group and its proximity to the radical right-wing milieu:

> One of the 'Unsterblich' comrades, Uwe B., committed suicide. During the match against Metalist Kharkiv, a collective 'mourning phase' of 15 minutes was declared for the entire stand. Those who did not want to take part were attacked by members of the groups 'Unsterblich' and 'Fanatics'. At the same time, a funeral march of several dozen people took place in the stand, during which the Hitler salute was shown and in which leaders of the Austrian neo-Nazi scene participated.
>
> (Bonvalot, 2016, p. 24)

The connections between 'Unsterblich' and neo-Nazis are one example among many, illustrating close ties between right-wing hooligans and neo-Nazis. Furthermore, 'Unsterblich' has friendships with other right-wing ultra and hooligan groups throughout Europe: the 'Ultras Sur' of Real Madrid, the 'Kop of Boulogne' from Paris and supporters of Lokomotive Leipzig are among them.

The club has forbidden symbols of 'Unsterblich,' but the problem is by no means solved. 'Younger fan groups are joining in,' writes Bonvalot.

> From outside the stadium, the 'Identitarian Movement' also seems to seek influence. One indication of this is that last October a banner with the words 'Islamists not welcome Europe awake' was shown for a few minutes in the stand. Shortly after, the banner was shown in the stadium, a picture of it was distributed via the 'Twitter' accounts of IB cadres. The blurred milieu between the 'Identitarian Movement', German-national fraternities and the FPÖ is quite identical to the milieu in which extreme right-wing fans of Austria (and Rapid) also navigate.
>
> (Bonvalot, 2016, p. 25)

Although right-wing groups are currently unable to appear in the stadium of Rapid Vienna, the right-wing activities from the Rapid fan scene increased, says Bonvalot. There were also numerous pro-refugee activities by fans in Austria in 2016, and some clubs, including Austria and Rapid Vienna, invited refugees to home matches in their stadiums. The clubs tried to send a signal to their own fans. The attitude of the clubs, however, was often half-hearted, criticizes Bonvalot: 'The principle of "no politics" is repeatedly referred to instead of taking a clear position against racism, sexism and homophobia' (Bonvalot, 2016, p. 21).

In the Spanish capital of Madrid, Atlético and Real, two of Europe's best teams, are both supported by far-right fan groups – 'Frente' (Atletico) and 'Ultras Sur' (Real). Despite repeated bans, both groups are still active. Members of both groups participate in the extreme right movement 'Hogar Social' ('Social Home'). When Real Madrid played Deportivo La Coruna in December 2016, 'Hogar Social' and 'Ultras Sur' organised a fund-raising campaign for the poor. However, only people with Spanish passports could benefit (Hidalgo, 2016). The name 'Hogar Social' goes back to a squatted house.[7] Here, food is only distributed after a passport control. 'Hogar Social' has repeatedly organised anti-refugee demonstrations; the 'Ultras Sur' and 'Frente Atletico' always participated (Bock, 2016). Personal overlaps, networks and collaborations between football fans and neo-Nazis bring a fourth strategy to the surface. So far, we have argued that the strategies of far-right actors can be categorised as the struggle for the mind, the parliaments and the streets. In 2004, the National Democratic Party of Germany (NPD) added a fourth strategy – the fight for the organised will. The intention for making the triple strategy a quadruple strategy was to unify the far-right. Although this unification was successful only to some degree (there is still scepticism and distance between political parties and right-wing fans), anti-Muslim and anti-refugee racism became a content-bracket for these groups. The time between 2014 and 2016 was a boost for far-right networks, with football being at the centre of their activities.

From Cottbus to Europe – an international network of far-right combat sport and music

These developments of active, violent networks can also be plastically shown in Eastern Germany, where the hooligans from Energie Cottbus have tight relations to those in Eastern Europe as a part of far-right militant scenes. In April 2019 German authorities from the district of Brandenburg searched 22 objects in Eastern Germany – most of them in Cottbus, close to the polish border – with the aim of gaining information and secure evidence for the existence of a far-right so-called schnelle Eingreiftruppe (rapid deployment force). The approximately 25 members were suspected of having founded a same-named messenger group with the purpose of quickly mobilizing far-right fighters in case of urgent conflicts with either local Hell's Angels – which they often do business with – political opponents, or migrants. The organisation's aim was to gain physical supremacy over others.

Most of the members are part of Cottbus' far-right hooligan scene, which is well connected to all kinds of far-right groups in Germany. Therefore, the retained objects of the search have not been surprising: swastikas; weapons and propaganda material from the 'Identitarian Movement'; and different kinds of clothing labelled by the hooligan group 'Inferno Cottbus,' 'Label 23 – Boxing Connection'– which sponsored the international homepage www.hooligans.tv in 2016 – 'Kickboxteam Cottbus' and the far-right brand 'Black Legion.' The far-right hooligan scene in Cottbus belongs to the best organised and most violent far-right groups in Germany.

For decades, the region of Cottbus has been a hotspot of far-right violence. The refugee Farid Guendoul was hunted to death by neo-Nazis in Guben in February 1999. The far-right comradeship 'Spreelichter' has been forbidden since 2012. Especially since 2015 – the year the number of asylum seekers rapidly increased – the list of far-right attacks and hate crimes has exploded: the 'Opferperspektive Brandenburg' counted 174 cases of far-right violence in the state of Brandenburg in 2017, 35 of them in the region of Cottbus (Opferperspektive Brandenburg, 2020). It is the highest number of all districts.

This racist violence is supported by parts of the population. For instance, the club 'Zukunft Heimat' ('Future Homeland'), founded in August 2015, organises racist demonstrations and rallies in Cottbus. 'Zukunft Heimat' is closely linked to the far-right 'Identitarian Movement' and the party 'Alternative für Deutschland'; 300 to 400 people often join the events, when speakers hatefully address the so-called 'destruction of the homeland' and 'the extinction of the German people' by immigrants and non-European refugees (Aktionsbündnis Brandenburg, 2018). These demonstrations are guarded by far-right hooligans,[8] who operate as non-official security.

The hooligans are also connected to far-right circles of combat sports, who organise the annual event 'Kampf der Nibelungen.' The 'Kampf der Nibelungen' – It was named 'Ring der Nibelungen' for the first two years – and has been deeply entrenched in militant German neo-Nazi structures from its first day onwards in 2013. The event quickly developed from a small but dangerous and secret fight night in North-Rhein Westphalia and Hessen to a major event. In 2017, the label was officially registered. In the same year more than 500 people attended the event. Due to this high number, it could no longer be organised secretly. In 2018, the event moved to Ostritz in Saxony, where the well-organised structures of militant fascists in the region were helpful. Three events took place – two of them as part of the fascist music event 'Schild und Schwert' ('shield and sword'). Over 800 people attended the main event of the 'Kampf der Nibelungen.' As in the years before, far-right combat athletes and hooligans came from all over Germany – from Dortmund to Cottbus – and from throughout Europe; from France to Ukraine; from Russia, Italy, the Czech Republic and Sweden (Claus, 2017; Runter von der Matte, 2018).

This development did not occur by accident. On the one hand, violence is a fundamental element of far-right ideology. Neo-Nazis and far-right hooligans have always trained in how to fight. On the other hand, the market of fitness and combat sports has grown – not only in Germany – over the past decade under the influence of globalisation and neoliberal health policies.

In the 2000s a central reform of the German health system has dominated the political discussion. In the end, major parts of the public health sector have been privatised – accompanied by the call for responsible self-care to everyone. Memberships in fitness studios have partially been paid for by health insurance companies. Since then, advertisement slogans such as 'Make yourself true' are setting the tone of the fitness business. At the same time the combat sport market has grown globally: the 'Ultime Fighting Championship' (UFC) has become the biggest promotion in mixed martial arts. It was founded in California at the beginning of the 1990s and nowadays presents fight nights all over the world.

Far-right organisations adapted to these developments by investing in their own structures in the field of combat sports: 'It should be a matter of course to limber up. Combat sport is predestinated for this, here body control, discipline and concentration are taught. Moreover, combat sport bolsters up feistiness,' say the promoters of the far-right combat sport event 'TIWAZ – Combat of the freemen' from Saxony in an interview with the magazine *N.S. heute* ('Der Kampf der freien Männer. Im Gespräch mit TIWAZ,' 2019). Moreover, the main slogan of the far-right 'Kampf der Nibelungen' is 'will, discipline and effort' – and not 'fight for your race,' although their racist bias remains – and they use the hashtag #UFC quite often on Instagram.

German Russian hooligan and leading figure of the far-right combat sport brand 'White Rex' (founded in 2008) Denis 'Nikitin' Kapustin said in an interview with the Ukrainian hooligan website www.troublemakers.com in 2017, 'My task is global, I have to cover all parts of life of a modern human. White Rex is an alternative attitude to life, which I want to create hundred percent. With clothing, tournaments, nutrition and fitness studios' ('www.troublemakers.com,' 2017). Far-right agents want to make money with the general fitness boom (Claus, n.d.).

Therefore, far-right hooligans from Cottbus did create fashion labels and a company that sells nutrition supplies and outdoor survival trips. In Germany and Europe, Kapustin was a key figure in the development of the 'Kampf der Nibelungen' – until German authorities forbade him from entering the Schengen area for ten years in February 2019 (Flade and Pinkert, 2020).

The far-right network can be illustrated by looking at the far-right combat sport merchandise homepage '2yt4u.' This is the acronym for the racist slogan 'Too White for You.' On this homepage, a broad range of brands from the European far-right offer their combat sport gear and casual clothing. Among them are 'White Rex,' 'Black Legion' from Cottbus (founded in 2016), 'Greifvogel' from Germany (2014), 'Pride France' (2013), 'Sva Stone' from Ukraine (2010) and 'Rodobran' from Bulgaria (2018). Their symbolism moves between supposedly harmless animal motifs, martial and warlike pictures, NS symbols, and alleged German or Slavic runes (Claus, 2018). By this less theoretic but rather violent focus on physical action as well as on business networks, German and Eastern European neo-Nazis seem to be able to overcome racist and nationalist conflicts from earlier decades among themselves. They have internationalised their networks.

These networks also operate as sponsors of 'Kampf der Nibelungen' and similar far-right fight nights in France, Ukraine, Italy, Bulgaria and Greece. Some also run far-right music concerts and festivals. In May 2020, the brand 'Sva Stone' organised the festival 'Fortress Europe' in the 'Bingo Club' in Kiev. The club is part of the network belonging to the far-right Asow regiment, which operated as an independent battalion in the recent war against Russia in Donbass. They announced that the bands 'Bronson' from Italy, 'Kratky process' from Slovakia, and 'Frontalkraft' from Cottbus were playing at the festival. 'Frontalkraft' is one of the oldest far-right bands in Germany. The band played at almost every birthday party of the far-right hooligan group 'Inferno' from Cottbus. Their aim is to 'convey nationalist messages and thoughts to the people' as they put it in an interview with the far-right zine 'Blood & Honour.' In that same 'Bingo Club,' the far-right combat sport event 'Fight Kingz' took place in 2019. Other far-right musical festivals like 'Asgardsrei' even had public combat sport presentations. Combat sports and music are closely linked in the far-right militant scene. Together with football, they are fundamental parts of fascist youth culture.

The promoters of 'Kampf der Niebelungen' have never hidden their disgust for the liberal democracy in Germany; they call it a 'rotten political system' on their homepage (www.kampf-der-nibelungen.com, 2020). A seminar in March 2019 has been advertised as 'Street Fight.' The network and agents consider themselves to be the elite of white European political fighters and are aiming to recruit people from the hooligan scene to whom they offer action, masculinity, political hatred and racial boundaries. They have created an event culture that connects the practice of political violence with modern event management (Claus, 2017).

To analyse far-right violence, Gideon Botsch proposed two axes. One axis is *spontaneity – preparation*. The other one is *threat – heavy political violence*, even terror (Botsch, 2019). On these axes, combat sport among the far-right has to be located at the two ends: neo-Nazis and far-right hooligans prepare themselves in (semi) professional tactical training for different kinds of political violence. Right-wing hooligans have developed from a culture of street riots to an internationally organised, professionalised network of combat sport and business. Their training has mostly one purpose: it is seen as preparation for political violence and terror on the so-called Day X, the day they take power and destroy democracy in order to establish a fascist regime.

The quality of networks and mobilisation of right-wing football fans are the basis of the increase of banners, demonstrations and attacks during the so-called refugee debate. At the same time, right-wing parties like the German 'Alternative für Deutschland' are succeeding in the parliaments. Political work in the parliaments and attacks in the streets condition each other. The so-called refugee debate in summer 2015 has led to a mighty increase of xenophobic tendencies. Dario Brentin said,

> We are dealing with an increase of right-wing and propagandistic operating football fans, as it hasn't been for many years. This goes along with a political shift to the right in entire Europe and a generally poisoned social atmosphere, which aggressively polarizes and opens spaces, in which racist and discriminating content can be articulated.

Although not all hooligans share right-wing attitudes, personal connections and networks between neo-Nazis and hooligans exist across Europe. The political leaders can attach themselves to joint moral concepts of hegemonial masculinity and the mystification of a diffuse tradition. The hooligan band 'Kategorie C' from Germany connects hooligans and neo-Nazis by using those aspects. Until 2019, the band played at far-right music festivals all over Europe. Their concerts have been meeting points for leaders of the extreme right, right-wing youngsters and far-right hooligans. The band also uses its fame for far-right mobilisations. In November 2014 – one month after the 'Hooligans against Salafism' demonstration in Cologne, the 'wonder of cologne,' as hooligans called it, was supposed to be exported: The concert of 'Kategorie C,' planned for 15 November in and around Basel, should have been the start of a similar movement in Switzerland (Eberhard, 2014). However, local authorities forbade the concert and, in consequence, HogeSa has not been founded there. Nonetheless, this plan underscores that the band is aware of its role and wants to use it.

Conclusion: a European movement?

While racism is a problem of European fan cultures, hundreds of fan initiatives against racism exist as well. Those fans developed strong European networks around organisations such as 'Football Supporters Europe,' 'Alerta Network,' the 'Mondiali Antirazzisti' in Italy and the 'Antira-Turnier' (an anti-racist tournament initiated by ultras and fans of FC St. Pauli). These fan groups, many of them ultras, started various projects to integrate refugees, often supported by the respective football clubs. While these initiatives may be highly praised by football associations in many countries, many of them are also under attack by right-wing fan groups – often, by fans of the same club.

Fans in Eastern Central Europe have displayed their racist banners more openly in the stadiums than their counterparts in Western Europe. Here, the fans focused more on particularly political occasions in the streets. Despite these differences, many ultras and hooligans across Europe share similar ideas and have shown the ability to mobilise large crowds. Between 2014 and 2016, right-wing fans expressed their nationalistic and racist ideas with more self-confidence and more publicly than in the years before.

Ultras and hooligans mobilised through their international networks to travel to the EURO 2016 in France and bring their strategy of the struggle for minds, parliaments, streets and organised will with them. These fans would not only support their respective national teams but also express their nationalist and racist ideas. Ultras and hooligans positioned themselves against 'foreign infiltration,' refugees and ISIS, thereby conflating these three and thus defaming all refugees as hostile and dangerous terrorists. These ultras and hooligans portray themselves as 'Defenders of European Culture.' What became visible to a broader public at the EURO 2016 resulted from the atmosphere in stadiums, parliaments and streets across Europe.

The debates around the 'refugee crisis' in 2014–2016 have shown that right-wing ultras and hooligans are well organised and violent. They can mobilise hundreds, even thousands, of people to participate in racist demonstrations. It is striking that football fans whom we often think of as hostile and irreconcilable enemies march side by side for their racist cause. Anti-Muslim and anti-refugee racism became a content bracket for fans who claim to 'defend the occident.' They construct their collective identities around what they understand as Western Christian civilization; they are an international movement of nationalists.

Notes

1 We use this term in quotes only, since the phrase indicates that the number of refugees in Europe was the *real* problem, and that the responsibility for the development was caused by refugees themselves and not by political push-factors. Thus, it became a term used by major parts of European society.
2 This chapter is partly based on the article 'Fußballfans gegen ein buntes Europa' that was written by Pavel Brunssen and Peter Römer and published in the 18th volume of *Transparent Magazin* in 2016 (Brunssen and Römer, 2016).
3 This became evident when we observed Pegida-demonstrations in Dresden: small groups of 10–15 hooligans each stood guard at the edges of the gathering. Similarly, during a demonstration of Legida (as Pegida in Leipzig is called) in Leipzig, the hooligans were addressed from the stage directly: 'Nun ein Wort an euch Hools, die ihr heute Abend wieder hier seid, weil ihr versprochen habt, das Volk vor der Antifa zu schützen' ['Now a word to the hooligans, who are among us again, because you have promised to protect the Volk from the Antifa.'] (Sundermeier, 2015).

4 One of the most recent attempts to define ultras claims the following: 'Across the globe, one particular group has taken a leading role in creating these highly passionate atmospheres: the ultras. They produce choreographies (also known as "tifos" or "choreos") that regularly involve collective chanting, flags, banners, clothing and pyrotechnics. . . . Ultras are one of the only groups displaying collective behaviour that pride themselves on having a shared, coherent sense of identity based on an act of consumption: that of football' (Doidge et al., 2020, p. 2).
5 Ramón Spaaij (2006) distinguishes football hooliganism from spectator violence, whereby he defines football hooliganism as 'the competitive violence of socially organized fan groups in football, principally directed against opposing fan groups' (Spaaij, 2006, p. 11). We argue in this chapter that some hooligans (and ultras) also use their high level of organisation for political purposes.
6 By the end of the 1980s, against the background of Yugoslavia's severe economic and social crisis, the stadiums had already developed into a place of political-nationalist demonstrations. To this day, there is a plaque at the Maksimir Stadium of the Croatian capital club Dinamo Zagreb commemorating the members of the 'Bad Blue Boys' who died in the war. Many fans had gone to war as volunteers, and some had even formed their own units. So 'Arkan,' leader of the fan scene of Red Star Belgrade, even founded his own paramilitary unit with the 'Serbian Volunteer Guard' ('Arkan's Tiger'). The massive riots in the context of the never-kicked-off game between Dinamo Zagreb and Red Star Belgrade on 13 May 1990 are still considered a decisive event with great symbolic power for the breakup of Yugoslavia (Raschke, 2015).
7 Illegally occupied property.
8 This article deals with far-right hooligans in Germany and Europe. For completeness it has to be mentioned that, at least in Germany, not all hooligans are neo-Nazis, although their violence always had big attraction for the far-right. Nonetheless, the most agile and threatening developments have always taken part at the far-right end of the scene.

Bibliography

Aktionsbündnis Brandenburg. 2018. "Zukunft Heimat." www.aktionsbuendnis-brandenburg.de/zukunft-heimat/.

Barflies United. 2015. "Facebook." 4 August 2015. www.facebook.com/barfliesunited/photos/a.10153219936504024/10153219981529024/?type=1&theater.

Bock, Andreas. 2016. "Rechtskurve – Neonazis bei Real und Atletico Madrid." 11FREUNDE. 27 May 2016. https://11freunde.de/artikel/rechtskurve/508303.

Bonvalot, Michael. 2016. "Ein 'Judenverein' und seine Neonazis." *Transparent – Magazin für Fußball und Fankultur* 18: 20–25.

Botsch, Gideon. 2019. "Was ist Rechtsterrorismus?" *Aus Politik und Zeitgeschichte* 69: 49–50.

Brandstetter, Marc. 2006. "Die vier Säulen der NPD." *Blätter für deutsche und internationale Politik*, September 2006: 1029–1031.

Brunssen, Pavel, and Peter Römer. 2016. "Fußballfans gegen ein buntes Europa." *Transparent – Magazin für Fußball und Fankultur* 18: 12–16.

———. 2017. "'Verteidiger der Europäischen Kultur – Hooligans und der Rechtsruck in Europa." In *Fäuste, Fahnen, Fankulturen. Die Rückkehr der Hooligans auf der Straße und im Stadion*, 48–71. Köln: PappyRossa.

Burdsey, Daniel, ed. 2011. *Race, Ethnicity, and Football: Persisting Debates and Emergent Issues*. Routledge Research in Sport, Culture and Society 6. New York: Routledge.

Cashmore, Ellis, and Jamie Cleland. 2014. *Football's Dark Side: Corruption, Homophobia, Violence and Racism in the Beautiful Game*. Basingstoke: Palgrave Macmillan.

Claus, Robert. 2016. "'Pride France'. Rassismus mit Mundschutz." *Transparent – Magazin für Fußball und Fankultur* 17: 28–29.

———. 2017. *Hooligans: Eine Welt zwischen Fussball, Gewalt und Politik*. Göttingen: Die Werkstatt.

———. 2018. "Der extrem rechte Kampfsportboom." bpb.de. 5 November 2018. www.bpb.de/politik/extremismus/rechtsextremismus/279552/der-extrem-rechte-kampfsportboom.

———. n.d. "Wehrhaftigkeit und Selbstoptimierung: Kampfsport in der extremen Rechten." Das Versteckspiel. Accessed 13 January 2020. https://dasversteckspiel.de/hintergruende/wehrhaftigkeit-und-selbstoptimierung-kampfsport-in-der-extremen-rechten-330.html?more=true.

DeutscheWelle. 2019. "Polen: Zehntausende bei Rechtsextremem Marsch." 11 November 2019. www.dw.com/de/polen-zehntausende-bei-rechtsextremem-marsch/a-51205901.

Die Presse. 2016. "Belgien: Hooligans als Schutzengel?" Die Presse. 27 December 2016. www.diepresse.com/5139771/belgien-hooligans-als-schutzengel.

Doidge, Mark. 2015. "'If You Jump Up and Down, Balotelli Dies': Racism and Player Abuse in Italian Football." *International Review for the Sociology of Sport* 50 (3): 249–264. https://doi.org/10.1177/1012690213480354.

Doidge, Mark, Radosław Kossakowski, and Svenja Mintert. 2020. *Ultras: The Passion and Performance of Contemporary Football Fandom*. Manchester: Manchester University Press.

Eberhard, Fabian. 2014. "Rechtsextreme Hooligans formieren sich in der Schweiz." Störungsmelder. 7 November 2014. https://blog.zeit.de/stoerungsmelder/2014/11/07/rechtsextreme-hooligans-formieren-sich-in-der-schweiz_17483.

Endemann, Martin, Robert Claus, Gerd Dembowski, and Jonas Gabler, eds. 2015. *Zurück am Tatort Stadion: Diskriminierung und Antidiskriminierung in Fussball-Fankulturen*. Göttingen: Die Werkstatt.

Faith Matters. 2015. "Legia Warsaw Fans Attack and Brutally Beat up 20 Syrian Muslim Refugees." Faith Matters. 24 September 2015. www.faith-matters.org/2015/09/24/legia-warsaw-fans-attack-and-brutally-beat-up-20-syrian-muslim-refugees/.

Flade, Florian, and Reiko Pinkert. 2020. "Einreiseverbot für rechtsextremen Kampfsportler 'Nikitin.'" tagesschau.de. 13 January 2020. www.tagesschau.de/investigativ/ndr-wdr/nikitin-einreiseverbot-101.html.

Garland, Jon, and Michael Rowe. 2001. *Racism and Anti-Racism in Football*. London: Palgrave Macmillan UK. https://doi.org/10.1057/9780230502529.

Gebhardt, Richard, ed. 2017. *Fäuste, Fahnen, Fankulturen*. Cologne: PappyRossa.

Gisi, Emanuel. 2018. "Wegen FCB-Spende für Flüchtlinge: Posen-Hooligans wollen Spiel boykottieren." 30 September 2018. www.blick.ch/sport/fussball/europaleague/wegen-fcb-spende-fuer-fluechtlinge-posen-hooligans-wollen-spiel-boykottieren-id4219485.html.

Hidalgo, Carlos. 2016. "Los Ultras Sur y los neonazis del Hogar Social se unen en la recogida de comida 'solo para españoles.'" abc. 14 December 2016. www.abc.es/espana/madrid/abci-ultras-y-neonazis-hogar-social-unen-recogida-comida-solo-para-espanoles-201612140125_noticia.html.

Hodges, Andrew. 2019. *Fan Activism, Protest and Politics: Ultras in Post-Socialist Croatia*. London, New York: Routledge. https://doi.org/10.4324/9781351118866.

King, Colin. 2004. *Offside Racism: Playing the White Man*. Oxford; New York: Berg.
Millward, Peter. 2008. "Rivalries and Racisms: 'Closed' and 'Open' Islamophobic Dispositions Amongst Football Supporters." *Sociological Research Online* 13 (6). https://doi.org/10.5153/sro.1816.
Niessen, Benedikt. 2016. "Wer ist die 'Carpathian Brigade', Ungarns Neonazi-Ultragruppe?" 22 June 2016. www.vice.com/de/article/ezynwa/wer-ist-die-carpathian-brigade-ungarns-neonazi-ultragruppe.
N.S. *Heute*. 2019. "Der Kampf der freien Männer. Im Gespräch mit TIWAZ." 14 edition.
Opferperspektive Brandenburg. 2020. "Statistik rechter Gewalttaten in Brandenburg 2017." 13 January 2020. www.opferperspektive.de/rechte-angriffe/statistik-brandenburg/statistik-rechter-gewalttaten-in-brandenburg.
Raschke, Holger. 2015. "Football with a Lot of Politics. Die Fankultur im ehemaligen Jugoslawien." In *Zurück am Tatort Stadion: Diskriminierung und Antidiskriminierung in Fussball-Fankulturen*, edited by Martin Endemann, Robert Claus, Gerd Dembowski, and Jonas Gabler, 286–304. Göttingen: Die Werkstatt.
Runter von der Matte. 2018. "Der Kampf der Nibelungen 2018 – Eine erste Auswertung." www.runtervondermatte.noblogs.org/der-kampf-der-nibelungen-2018-eine-erste-auswertung.
Spaaij, Ramón. 2006. *Understanding Football Hooliganism : A Comparison of Six Western European Football Clubs*. Amsterdam: Amsterdam University Press. https://doi.org/10.5117/9789056294458.
Sundermeier, Olaf. 2015. "Pegida und der Fußball: Hooligans als Schutztruppe." Frankfurter Allgemeine Zeitung. 2 February 2015. www.faz.net/1.3403341.
Tagesspiegel. 2016. "Die Gegenwart der Gewalt." 13 June 2016. www.tagesspiegel.de/sport/deutsche-hooligans-bei-der-em-in-lille-die-gegenwart-der-gewalt/13724238.html.
Vice Sports. 2016. "Undercover-Video filmt englische Fans bei Pädophilensprüchen gegen Roma-Kinder." 29 June 2016. www.vice.com/de/article/jp79xy/undercover-video-filmt-englische-fans-bei-widerlichen-paedophilenspruechen-71.
www.kampf-der-nibelungen.com. 2020. www.kampf-der-nibelungen.com.
www.troublemakers.com. 2017. www.troublemakers.com.
Zeit Online. 2016. "Zehntausende Demonstranten marschieren durch Warschau." 11 November 2016. www.zeit.de/politik/ausland/2016-11/polen-warschau-marsch-unabhaengigkeitstag-nationalisten.

Chapter 8

Ehhhhh pu! . . . what?

A critical conversation about Mexican football fandom and the word at the centre of a homophobic chant

Melissa Mora Hidalgo and Giovanni Hortua Vargas

Introduction

La Selección de *fútbol* de México, or the Mexican national football team, known by their fans as El Tri, defeated defending champion Germany in its first match of the 2018 World Cup. Amid the post-game reports of this historic victory for México – especially symbolic at the time considering the racist anti-Mexican rhetoric and policies promoted by the Trump presidency – there remained the nagging news that FIFA once again will 'investigate' Mexico fans for their use of a controversial and homophobic term as part of a chant during matches (*BBC.com* 2018). It ended with FIFA's crackdown on the usage of the chant through a fine of 10,000 US dollars on the Mexican Football Federation after its opening match against Germany (*ESPN.com* 2018).

During the 2014 World Cup, international media outlets including the National Public Radio (NPR) and *Sports Illustrated* magazine in the United States started running stories about FIFA's investigations into the Mexican team fans' use of a 'homophobic slur' as a chant (Kahn 2014). In 2017, FIFA reported that Brazil, Argentina and Mexico were among the teams sanctioned for fans' 'discriminatory' conduct, including 'homophobic chants,' during the 2018 World Cup qualifying matches (*FIFA.com* 2017).

To be sure, Mexican football fans are not unique in their use of offensive words as chants during matches. Fans' racist slurs, actions and expressions aimed at black players in particular have been widely documented at the national and club team levels from the United Kingdom and all over Europe to Latin America. However, the controversy over this particular '*ehhhh . . . puto!*' chant favoured by Mexican football fans is the word '*puto*' itself.[1]

Mexican *fútbol* fans do not reserve this chant solely for the World Cup and other big international champion cup tournaments where Mexico's national team plays. The chant's origins, and the use of this term in particular, go back to the early 2000s with fans at the Mexican club-team level, specifically the supporters of Club Atlas FC in Guadalajara. Most recently, the chant appeared on 28 September 2019, when Mexican soccer league team Las Chivas de Guadalajara faced off on their home turf against their *clásico* super-rivals, Club América.[2] At other club matches in the nation's first division league, known as Liga MX, or at any given match played in any division in the Mexican Soccer Federation (FMF), fans taunt the opposing goalie with the offensive chant: pointedly, it surfaces only at particular moments in the match when the opposing team's goalie kicks the ball during a goal kick.[3] What began as localised fan practice aimed at one player has since morphed into a controversial expression of fandom on the Mexican national-team level and, thus, the global stage.

As two US-based scholars, educators and *fútbol* fans of Latin American[4] descent based in Los Angeles – and who watch and cheer for Team México – we critique the persistent use of this homophobic and misogynist term by Mexican fans during national and club matches on both sides of the US-Mexico border. In this chapter, we aim to unpack the controversial chant starting with these questions: why this specific word? Why *fútbol*? And why these particular fans?

We organise the chapter in two parts. Part 1 provides some key historical and cultural contexts for understanding the power of this particular word as a homophobic fan chant that is rooted in misogynist, masculinist and mythical narratives of Mexican nationalism. Starting with the established club-team origin story of the chant, an early 2000s trade of a goalie from his 'home team' to one of its historic rivals, we link the usage of this term by Mexican fans during a game-specific moment and aimed only at a specific position player – the goalie on the opposing team – to another, more ancient era: the downfall of the Aztec Empire via the colonisation of the 'New World' by Spanish *Conquistadores* in the 1520s.

More specifically, we trace the root of this term and the purpose of its use in a football stadium chant to the founding Mexican nationalist myth of *La Malinche*, the ultimate '*puta*' – a misogynist term[5] for a female prostitute – and sexual traitor whose story of betrayal has been used to in part characterise the origins of Mexico. Our analysis of the term and the chant draws from an interdisciplinary combination of humanist and cultural studies fields and methods, including Latin American history, Chicano/a/x literature and cultural studies, linguistics, gender and sexuality studies and media studies. Part 1 provides an overview of some key contexts and frameworks for the questions we address in our conversation that follows in Part 2.

Part 2 is fashioned as a dialogue between the authors, a critical conversation between fans about the violent impact of the term inside and outside of the soccer stadium as well as its cultural circulation outside of soccer. We exchange thoughts on the nationalist dimensions of fandom and why Mexico fans insist on using this word, even after repeated requests by the Mexican federation for fans to stop – albeit as part of a public relations campaign. We also consider other fans' thoughts and inputs about the chant, which remains a subject of debate among those who wax and wane between using it anyway as their own special expression of Team México support and banning the chant completely.

We model our chapter on critical race and feminist scholarly conversations that are exchanged among academics, thinkers and writers such as Cornel West, bell hooks and Cherríe Moraga. They and many other public-facing scholars in the US have published their dialogic exchanges in which they actively and collaboratively produce knowledge. This method acknowledges the living languages we explore, the shifting terrains on which we practice fan culture and the ongoing discussions about the use of our term with each new football season.

Part I: some historical, cultural and social contexts of a homophobic term turned soccer chant

It starts with a goalie in Guadalajara

The most common story of the chant's origins starts with Liga MX and national team goalie, Oswaldo Sánchez. Sánchez played on four Liga MX teams – Atlas, Club América, Chivas de Guadalajara and Santos Laguna – and in three World Cups as the goalie for the Mexican national team. In 2000, Sánchez left América to come home to Guadalajara, only to play for his former team's fierce rival, Las Chivas. Sources say that Atlas fans started the chant at the 2003 Clásico Tapatío (Guadalajara derby) when they aimed the homophobic expletive at Sánchez, whom they saw as a traitor playing goalie for the hated Chivas (*Mediotiempo* 2016). 'Atlas fans will say Oswaldo Sánchez "sold out,"' said Alexander Aviña, associate professor of Latin American history at Arizona State University and *fútbol* fan in a telephone interview. 'The homophobic insult likely started with the Atlas ultras who wanted the worst thing you could possibly say to [Sánchez], to break him down,' Aviña explained. The notion of 'selling out' falls in line with the literal meaning of the feminine (-a ending) version of our term, which means 'whore' or 'prostitute,' and the added element of 'traitor' resonates with the myth of La Malinche.

As Liga MX and Santos Laguna fan Felipe de la Rosa described in a telephone conversation with the authors,

> [Sánchez] leaving America to join Chivas . . . added more fuel to the already heated rivalry between Atlas and Chivas. The Atlas fans first started that infamous chant for Oswaldo Sánchez because they hated him for going to Chivas, and Atlas and Chivas are city rivals. So the only way to get back at him was by coming up with that chant and saying that word to him at every one of his goal-kicks.

To 'get back at' Sánchez, the Atlas fans reverted to the basest of insults one could hurl at a hegemonically masculine figure – the male national *fútbol* player.

The word and its meanings in transnational Mexican and Mexican American/Chicano (US) culture

As in most languages around the world, Spanish spoken in the Americas contains a host of words whose meanings are largely regionally determined.[6] A word like '*niño*' (boy) and '*niña*' (girl) signals gender difference with the masculine -o and feminine -a endings of the same base of the word, '*niñ-*.' The term at the centre of the Mexican fan chant, 'puto' is both gendered and sexualised. Here, the -o ending of the word signifies a masculine treatment of the feminine -a ending word, 'puta.' Fans' use of the masculine -o ending of this term as a taunting chant serves a dual purpose – to feminise *and* queer the goalie, taking him to the 'lowest of the low' (Aviña int.) from the fans' perspective by calling him a male prostitute and by extension, a submissive feminised 'bottom' or 'sodomite,' a synonym of our term as included by the *Real Academia de Español* (*RAE*) dictionary.[7]

Many different news sources, artists, scholars, writers and others have attempted to define this complicated and controversial word. Because of its literal meaning as a 'male whore' or 'male prostitute,' most Spanish speakers commonly understand our term as deriving from its feminine form. However, in her essay, 'Origen de la palabra "puta,"' Argentine literature professor Nora Buich argues that the feminine form actually originates from the masculine word 'puto,' which she found appears in the 1st century when the term originally meant *jovencito* ('young man') (Buich 2016). She argues that from that point on, the word switched to its feminine form. Furthermore,

> [b]y 1611, Sebastian Covarrubais' Castellano Spanish dictionary definition of *puta* became a woman who is 'almost rotten, who is always in heat and with bad odor,' likely taken from the Latin 'putta' for 'chica de calle'/girl or woman of the street.
>
> (Buich 2016)

Following this meaning of the term, Spanish newspaper *El País* reported in 2018 that 'puta,' usually defined as a 'public woman,' also functions as a euphemism for *muchacha* ('gal') (Grijelmo 2018). However, in Latin American contexts, the feminine -a version of the word remains mired in malintent, with definitions that include the epithets 'slut,' 'bitch' and 'whore.' Fans of the Netflix show *Narcos*, for example, know the word well, used throughout the series to mean the above and as a synonym for 'motherfucker,' as translated in subtitles. The show's executive producer, Eric Newman, calls the word 'one of those sort of catch-all insults' (Miller 2017). Of course, demonising women and denigrating men by feminising them is nothing new. The feminine ending of the term helps explain the most accepted meaning of the masculine -o ending of 'p . . .' as a vulgar word for a male prostitute. The *Guardian* describes it as 'homophobic slang for a male sex worker' (Balta 2018), while *Vice* calls it a word that 'in its crudest' form refers to a 'male prostitute' or as 'slang for "fag,"' the queer implications clear (Castillo and Noel 2014).

Other sources provide definitions of the term that attempt to distinguish it from these commonly held meanings. According to the *Washington Post*, 'p . . .' can be defined as a 'derogatory slang term referring to a homosexual man' (Payne 2017), while *GQ Mexico* states that the *RAE* considered the word is 'not an insult . . . if it is used as an intensifier prefix that should be used to indicate something is bigger or more intense' (González 2019). In other words, the *RAE* as the authoritative dictionary of the Spanish language supports public usage as long as the word accentuates a situation and is not directed at an individual, as in '*que puto calor*' (what incredible heat). In popular music, the Mexican band Molotov (Molotov 1997) released a song called "Puto," which the singer Tito Fuentes defends as not homophobic at all, but rather a word for 'a bad person' (Planas 2013). The 'Puto' in the song is the one who steals food from people's mouths ('El que nos quita la papa') or who trusts the mainstream news ('El que creyó lo del informe'). For Molotov, the song addresses the evident corruption and social inequalities in Mexican society.

In contemporary US/Mexico borderland culture, we can look to theatre and the stage for more critical meanings of the term. For example, queer Chicano activist and playwright Ricardo Abreu Bracho's 2011 play *Puto* is billed as a 'sexy sci-fi' that 'confronts some of California's most pressing social concerns: prisons, immigration, industrial farming and the failing economy within the context of queer Latina/o militant activism, romance and art practice.'[8] Bracho, who identifies as a Marxist, wrote his protagonist and title character as 'a photographer, a player, a counterfeiter, [and] a currency trader on the brown market' (Bracho 2011).[9] For director Mark David Pinate, who helmed a production of Bracho's play at DePaul University, a large Catholic institution in Chicago, Bracho's unassuming hero represents a critique of a rampant capitalist system that demands 'people become whores to [it].' In an interview with *Remezcla*, Pinate says, 'I definitely think Bracho, the playwright, is making a pretty big statement by naming the play and the protagonist, PUTO. The word itself has several meanings – all of them negative – like: whore, slut, fag, fucked' (Gallardo 2011). In these usages, the word 'quivers like a sharp weapon' (Paz 1961, p. 74), whose purpose is to harm.

These negative meanings are amplified in the context of the hyper-capitalist billion-dollar global world of football team ownership. World football is a male-dominated corporate globalised industry whose profit-oriented goals demand a traffic in men who must necessarily sell their body and labour to the highest team bidder and become essentially 'whores' of the capitalist system, to echo Pinate about Bracho's Marxist protagonist.

When aimed at the goalie, who got 'scored on' and let the other team in, the homophobic intentions of the term become ever clear. As Juliana Jiménez Jaramilla writes in *Slate*, 'You see where this is going: The embarrassment of allowing a goal in your net is akin to being on the receiving end of anal sex – you know, like a gay guy' (Jaramillo 2014). Furthermore, '[n]o one can defend the word itself as *never* homophobic,' writes Jennifer Doyle, professor of English at the University of California at Riverside, and author of the football blog *From a Left Wing* (2007–2013). 'Behind that word are quite specific histories of violence, aimed at quite specific people' (Doyle 2014). The choice of this particular word by Mexican fans reveals such deep histories of misogynistic violence that originate with the ultimate myth of betrayal and birth – the original 'puta' in Mexican lore, La Malinche.

Misogyny, masculinity and the mythology of Mexican nationalism

Depending on whose gendered perspective from which we see her, La Malinche, also known as Malintzin or Doña Marina in Mexican national mytho-history, was either a slave sold to her Spanish conquering master, Hernán Cortés; his translator, whose command of language helped the Spaniards and facilitated the conquest of what we now call Mexico City; or the 'Mexican Eve' (Castillo 1995) or the 'violated mother' (Paz 1961, p. 86) of the new Mexican race. Along with the Catholic Virgen de Guadalupe and Aztec plumed serpent god Quetzalcoátl, La Malinche – who stands in contrast to the Virgin Mother as the 'whore' in the impossible binary of femininity – completes a trinity of founding figures central to the imagination of the origins of the Mexican nation.

Mexican writer Octavio Paz has written perhaps the most well-known literary rendering of the national mytho-history of La Malinche as the original *chingada* ('fucked' or 'violated one') in his 1950 work, *The Labyrinth of Solitude*.[10] In chapter 4, 'The Sons of La Malinche,' Paz writes,

> If the Chingada is a representation of the violated Mother, it is appropriate to associate her with the Conquest, which was also a violation, not only in the historical sense but also in the very flesh of Indian women. The symbol of this violation is doña Malinche, the mistress of Cortés. . . . The Mexican people have not forgiven La Malinche for her betrayal.
>
> (Paz 1961, pp. 86–87)

La Malinche's 'betrayal' of her people by sleeping with the conqueror results in the birth of 'Viva México, hijos de la chingada!' Paz describes this phrase as Mexicans' 'peculiar battle cry' of independence from Spain, at once an affirmation of Mexican identity 'against and in spite of the others.' 'Who are the "others,"' asks Paz, but 'strangers, bad Mexicans, our enemies, our rivals. And these "others" are not defined except as the sons of a mother as vague and indeterminate as themselves' (Paz 1961, p. 75). The 'othering' mechanism aimed at 'rivals' is already inherent in the phrase 'hijos de la chingada' ('sons of the violated/fucked mother'), according to Paz, and neatly translates to a national sporting context.

Some 40 years after Paz published his classic tome on Mexico, Chicana[11] feminists writing in the US began to reassess and reclaim the figure of La Malinche, while challenging the biblical 'Eve' story to which La Malinche is often compared. In her chapter 'In the beginning, there was Eva,' Xicana[12] novelist and writer Ana Castillo reminds us that Eve's mythology, which 'has affected civilization in the last four to five thousand years, was created out of the imaginations of men' (Castillo 1995, p. 106). Therefore, the idea of La Malinche as the reason for the 'fall' of Mexican (men) is a biblical story that predates the conquest, according to Castillo.

The history of Mexico, and of most nations, are also written by and 'created out of the imaginations of men' (Castillo 1995, p. 106), including Paz. Chicana feminist theorist Norma Alarcón acknowledges that Paz, 'whose implied audience is male,' may have very well been the first writer to discursively 'advance forcefully the metonymic relations between three terms – Malintzin, La Chingada, and rape'; the 'so-called rape is largely figurative [for men], a sign of their emasculating loss' (Alarcón 1989, pp. 82–83). Here, Alarcón makes a critical link between sexual violation and gender: the 'emasculating loss' that Paz's male audience and, by extension, the men of the nation suffer as being 'hijos de la chingada,' born already-defeated due to 'Cortés's whore' (Alarcón 1989, p. 58). This Malinche-chingada-puta origin story, when mapped onto national football contexts, serves as a way to frame the goalie as the 'Malinche,' an emasculated *vendido* ('sell-out') who, when he fails at his job and lets the opposition score on him, becomes the 'chingada-puta' and the symbol of Mexico's loss.

Alarcón and other Chicana feminists have taught us that gender orders in Mexican and Chicano culture remain informed by the Catholic Church and ideologies of nationalism. Accordingly, as the Mexican sociologist Gutiérrez Chong writes, '[n]ation, like gender, is a social construct' and famously an 'imagined community' (Gutiérrez Chong 2006, p. 340). In Mexico, anti-female and pro-masculine rhetoric was evident during the 19th century, during both the Enlightenment and the rise of liberalism[13] and the nation's independence movement. Mexico's 'founding fathers,' Miguel Hidalgo y Costilla and José María Morelos, interjected with their own vision of a gendered nationalism for an emerging Mexico. Hidalgo stated in the declaration of independence from Spain in 1821 that he would march 'on the front line of men who appreciate being free' (Hidalgo 1810), while ironically employing the banner of the Virgin of Guadalupe to the nationalist cause. Undoubtedly, the 'Mexican woman exists in a double bind as a female in a patriarchal society formed as part of the European colonialist empire' (Cypess 1989, p. 340).

When General Porfirio Díaz controversially took control of Mexico in 1876, he created an ambitious and strong-arm presidential government that ultimately sought to preserve his form of peace (*Paz Porfiriana*). Peacekeeping for Díaz meant inviting foreign investment from nations such as the United States, France and England; preserving the peace with the Catholic Church by not enforcing Mexico's anti-clerical laws; improving the national economy; and modernising (eg build railroads, bridges, monuments) Mexico's major political centres. As Irwin reminds us, the *Porfiriato* was also known for gendering the modernisation project in Mexico (Irwin 2003, p. 50). During this era, 'gender was represented in an absolute binary model of masculine or feminine with no other options' and 'when the meaning of masculinity was never questioned' (Irwin 2003, p. 50).

In the midst of this political upheaval, the Cornish community, practicing soccer in the Real del Monte, founded the first Mexican soccer club team in 1901: the Real del Monte Pachuca Athletic Club. One year later, the first organised soccer tournament included Real Union Pachuca, Real Union Orizaba and Mexico DF Club de *Fútbol*. On 19 July 1907, the Mexican First Division was created, with Pachuca serving as a major organiser and participant.

While *fútbol* in Mexico was underway, the ideals of gender were also pronounced during the course of the Mexican Revolution. While 'notions of masculinity and male sexuality would fall into major crisis' (Irwin 2003, p. 50) at the turn of the 20th century, a 'masculinist nationalist ideology' that 'identifi[ed] heterosexual masculinity with political authority and national identity' (Macías-González and Rubenstein 2012, pp. 19–20) remained a powerfully pervasive ideology in the post–Mexican Revolutionary era 1910 and well throughout the course of the 20th century.

The Mexican Revolution of 1910 was sparked by the severe socio-economic inequalities exacerbated by the incredible land grants given to foreign investors (eg the British), mixed in with the *Porfiriato*'s brutal repression of the lower classes, and the rule of Mexico by Porfirio Díaz for over 30 years. The Mexican Revolution created different opportunities for women on different sides of the war. Ana Macías and Stephanie Smith each describe the influential political positions that women, pro- or anti-Mexican government, held during the revolution. For Macias, women in the revolution were teachers, journalists, poets, spies, soldiers and activists, veering away from the 'myth of Mexican women as weak, inert, passive, and dependent human beings' (Macias 1980). At the same time, Smith also warned Mexican revolution enthusiasts by asserting that the 'cultural climate and revolutionary personnel generally upheld men's patriarchal claims to power and opposed women's rights' (Smith 2009).

While women were memorialised in patriarchal *corridos*,[14] women were written out from inheriting property thanks to an addition to the Constitution of 1927, where Article 27 stipulated that women peasants would be restricted to own communal land (known as *ejido*) unless they were 'the sole support of a family unit [which would qualify them] for ejido membership.'[15] Cypess states, 'The Mexican woman exists in a double bind as a female in a patriarchal society formed as part of the European colonialist enterprise. She becomes further colonized within the gender hierarchy of her own culture' (Cypess 1989, p. 492). With masculinity at the centre of the post-revolutionary Mexican state, the world of *fútbol* would make its return with the establishment of the Mexican Football Federation in 1929, two decades after the Cornish founded the club in Pachuca.

In the world of professional soccer, whether at the local or national team level, the '*ehhhhh puto*' chant persists in Mexico's soccer league, we argue, due largely to normative notions of masculinity and femininity that run deep through the discourses of Mexican nationalism. It will be interesting to see whether or not FIFA and Qatar Football Association will voice their opposition in the upcoming 2022 World Cup in Qatar to the Mexican Soccer Federation and fans as much as their opposition to racism in the stands, in-and-out of stadium soccer violence and acts of sexism that exclude women from playing a more significant role during major football tournaments. We turn now to Part 2 and our conversation.

Part 2: a critical conversation about football fandom and Mexico fans' controversial chant

The following conversation is based on a recorded phone call between the authors, which took place in Southern California in December 2019. We have edited it for clarity.

MELISSA HIDALGO (MH): Let's start with how this term moves from the regional Mexican football club scene to becoming the centre of a national chant. How do you think fans brought '*ehhhh p . . . !*' from a localised practice to the Mexican national and international stage?

GIOVANNI HORTUA (GH): A lot of it has to do with televised coverage. Liga MX is popular in Mexico and as a recognised professional league, it gets incredible amounts of press coverage, from television and newspapers, to fanzines. You also can't rule out fandom and the influence of what Europe labels as *ultra-fans*. On TV, you see where they sit and hear the songs they chant, see the size of their banners. Those ultra-fans in Liga MX are the backbone of the support of all the club teams. Whether América de México or Las Chivas de Guadalajara, each club has their own *porra* or *barra*, or 'ultra-fans.'

MH: The role of super-fans, these *ultras* or *porras* as they are called in Mexico and throughout Latin America is to grow and solidify fandom at the national team level [because] presumably, these are a lot of the same club players and therefore fans.

GH: When it comes to national team competition, some fans watching their club team player will put the club rivalry on pause for about 90 minutes. Everyone takes on this new homogenous identity defined by nationalism. It's not about the rivalry momentarily, but collaborating for the national cause.

MH: The national cause. And this particular chant has roots in a very particular nationalist, masculinist expression of Mexican football fandom. But the first time I experienced that chant was at an LA Galaxy game on 'Pride Night' a few seasons ago. I was already vaguely aware of the chant because I had heard it on television during the Mexico vs Brazil game in the 2014 World Cup. I didn't expect to hear it at an LA Galaxy Pride match, of all places. 'P . . .' does not stay inside the stadium or at Mexican club *fútbol* games anymore. This word is violent. There are actual consequences outside the stadium. And the only reason to use it is to express violence or hatred, whether against the other team's goalie or fans or the ref who just made a bad call against your team.

GH: No question. Watching the Mexican national team in Los Angeles, specifically after 2010s, I remember hearing the chant in the stands in games against Argentina, Colombia, El Salvador. It was something to expect when watching the Mexican national team. This chant reminds me how the term *'puto'* itself circulates around Latin America. A lot of fans may or may not be thinking of the goalie's sexual preferences or activity. They're thinking, 'I'm going to do the worst thing I can do to insult this player to emasculate him to the point where he's going to make errors while launching the ball back into play.'

MH: That's key, especially when we know that there is ongoing violence against women everywhere in the world. In Mexico, they take the form of femicides as in the Juárez *maquiladora* murders in the 1990s and early 2000s.[16] Femicides and misogyny translates to violence against queer and gay men, the 'joto,' 'maricón,' or other synonyms for our derogatory word. This language doesn't just stay in Mexico because fan practices migrate. We're geographically and culturally close to each other. There are plenty of Team Mexico fans in the US. Here in Los Angeles, this chant is an unmistakable expression of Mexican national support for the team on either side of the border.

GH: This has become a transnational cheer, right?

MH: Absolutely. There are ways that this fan chant travels across borders, just like homophobia and misogyny, racism. Once I start to hear this stuff at Galaxy matches, the chant is no longer about the Mexican national team anymore, but about something else.

GH: The fact of the matter is that the supporters use this language to reject femininity. Full rejection! Unless it can be sexualised. In Latin American soccer, where exactly do women play a role? Cheerleading.

MH: The only type of femininity allowed is when it's hypersexualised, usually in the form of busty big-haired cheerleaders, and presumably for the men playing the game and watching it, not for the women who may be watching the game. It's a very heteronormative framework.

GH: In the Women's World Cup, you are not going to see any of the sexualisation of women's bodies you see in men's soccer. You're not going to hear homophobic and misogynist chants. The Women's World Cup is not about demeaning anyone.

MH: And there is a difference, right?

GH: An extreme difference! One of the arguments we were trying to make in our presentation[17] was that the only accepted homosexual is the one you could pick out publicly. This is the effeminate homosexual that's not threatening to masculinity in Latin America. This is the one that society has accepted as 'okay' if you're a male. The idea of female homosexuality or anything other than the expected norm for women is made invisible. There's countless room to understand that when we go to a stadium, whether in England, Mexico or Argentina, it's a boys' club. And it's been that way for a very long time. Any woman who disagrees is immediately ostracised. Anyone who doesn't want to partake in the chants is not man enough. This is the idea, right?

Alienation plays a huge part in the world of football. In other words, if you're not with it, you're against it.

MH: It's going back to militarism and nationalism, right? Inclusion-exclusion.

GH: All the national symbols are there: a flag you have to defend, a jersey or uniform that identifies your allegiance to the nation. A lot of this gets inculcated at a very young age. Families that embrace soccer tend to rally around a particular team. This team is drilled into the child not just as a sport to enjoy, but as what the family specifically supports. The choosing of a team is very paternal and patriarchal. If you don't choose your father's team, then did you choose your grandfather's team? Family plays a huge role in team loyalty. You see it here in the US with Raider Nation[18] and the Dodgers, and it's very intense.

MH: The idea of a family team is very familiar to me. My dad bleeds Dodger Blue, and my sisters and I get our Dodger fandom from him, who got it from his father.

GH: Some families are more intense about this than others. Again, it really becomes a moment where we've taken the tenets of nationalism and applied them to sport. I think it's important to recognise that placing national teams against each other is no different than the Olympics. There's a lot to say by the press and the population if Mexico doesn't destroy Jamaica or beat Trinidad and Tobago 15 to 0, then the nationalism is in crisis. And so perhaps they're not 'man enough' for the task.

MH: The nation is in crisis because they didn't step up as men on the field. There's the militarism element, too, the idea of 'dying on a battlefield for your country.'

GH: I've heard this commentary from one of the most passionate coaches I've ever seen in my life: Miguel Herrera. Maradona and Herrera both had very similar comments when they said you have to, in a nutshell, 'play with balls' (*jugar con huevos*). You have to put your *huevos* on the line. If you don't do that, then you should not be playing. None of this is surprising if we look at the history of organised sports. Sports expresses idealised masculinity, and the players show us what it has to look like. If it's not the expressions of toxic masculinity we're familiar with, then it's not a strong nation.

MH: There it is, equating the nation with the masculine body. And if masculinity fails, then the nation fails. We can't get any clearer than that in soccer or anywhere sports and nationalism converge. And that this particular chant has come to represent Mexican soccer fans beyond Mexico again is the big convergence here. I'm thinking of Alex Aviña,[19] one of the fans I spoke to, who called the chant 'cringeworthy' and suggested that the Mexican federation bear some responsibility for 'allowing it to become a chant.' He also made an important point about how the chant builds fan community, but in negative and violent ways. There are other, better, more positive and clever things that El Tri fans can come up with, and there are models of that everywhere. What about some of the fans you spoke to? What did they think about the chant, and why hold on to it, even though FIFA and the Mexican Football Federation have done this lip service through legislation and campaigning to stop using it?

GH: When I talked to fans, I noticed that people didn't want the chant, and some people were completely in favour. Some of the fans interviewed identified as Mexican, Mexican American, Salvadoran, and what I found was folks who did not want this chant had a lot to do with what they considered appropriate behaviour at a stadium. They felt going to the stadium is a family event. This concept veers away from the boys' club nationalism and actually encompasses another vision of nationalism: the family-oriented nationalism. It's not about having respect for women. We're still going to hold up men on the field as champions, but I don't have to put up with this!

MH: Did anyone identify as queer?

GH: Nobody identified as queer. I have a feeling even if they wanted to, they were in a situation and scenario where they were not allowed to. I visited soccer stores, soccer training and tournament facilities. I suspect that even if they had the space to divulge, it most likely would not have occurred. In fact, some of the interviewees commented, when asked about gender, 'What do you mean by that?' The older community would just remark 'Well, look at me!'

MH: The people you interviewed were more against the chant because it was inappropriate for families and less about a concern for the misogyny and homophobia. But those who want to hold on to it, what's their rationale?

GH: There was one young man who mentioned that asking about gender was irrelevant to the questionnaire, that his family are huge soccer fans and he's participated in football his entire life. For him, '*puto*' means '*güey*.' The term '*güey*' in Mexico is situational, and for him it meant 'asshole' versus another definition, which translates güey to 'bro' or 'dude.' For him, it is not a derogatory term at all. He says he's been participating in it and that he's 'going with the flow.' He thinks the only reason FIFA is cracking down is to make money. It is not a moral issue, but rather a way for FIFA to get more money from the Mexican Football Federation.

MH: I think it also has to do with where the recent World Cups were and will be played, in Russia 2018 and Qatar 2022, where homosexuality is illegal, so FIFA takes this public stance against these chants. FIFA might say 'We're not going to let this happen' and look how we're taking a stance against this discrimination by fining these countries for fans' inappropriate behaviour. But somehow Mexico gets singled out because of this chant, which is offensive under FIFA's rules. You're saying that there are fans who don't see the offense.

GH: They see the chant as part of the game and to quote one of the interviewees, 'It's only to antagonize opponents.' He wasn't the only one who felt this way. Another young man mentioned that '*puto*' means '*bitch*.' For him, he feels that FIFA sanctioning Mexico is an 'approach driven by monetary reasons,' but the fines won't affect fans much.

MH: Do you think the fans are interested in stopping this chant? Gustavo Arellano, the Orange County-born Mexican journalist, has said that the chant 'will never go away. It's Mexico's Confederate flag – a nasty part of our supposed heritage that no outsider can ever tell us is wrong, and that we grip onto even tighter when they tell us it is. And that stubborn pride will deservedly screw us in the end' (Arellano 2017).

GH: Completely. I think it's about holding on to something that has no real tradition, but rather expresses a sense of privilege.

MH: As a queer fan, I don't necessarily want to go see the Mexican national team at the Rose Bowl because of this fan environment. I don't want to be subjected to this word, the violence behind it. What are the alternatives? I'd go to the women's games if LA had an NWSL team. What are your thoughts about those fans who don't want to participate in or take part in this type of practice?

GH: People who want to get away from this, at least in the US context, fortunately there are sanctions against offensive chants at some MSL teams, like at the LAFC stadium. A fan's choice to support or not becomes a very politicised decision, and choosing to boycott the Mexican national team until they clean this out is one way to go. We need grassroots campaigning to ban the 'ehhhh p . . .' chant, not just hashtags, but boycotting the game, whether at the LA Coliseum or the Rose Bowl, the Estadio Azteca in Mexico City, especially during a big game like Mexico vs USA where it will be packed. Football is a juggernaut. It's FIFA, the Mexican Federation, it's the culture, and this is what we're up against. We're up against a very developed system of cultural violence.

MH: Your point is well taken. Homophobia, misogyny and racism will always be a part of the soccer game as long as it's tied to the nation. It is systemic. And yet to reimagine another kind of fan space and practice really does require, on the one hand, maybe separating the nationalism from the sport, like now you're rooting for LAFC or the Colorado Rapids or one of the NWSL teams, and fandom becomes about that team, those players. I see it in the WNBA, where the league, the teams and the fans build another kind of community that may not immediately be about the nation. But as long as we have to play the damn national anthem in every arena or stadium before every single sporting event, men or women, at every level, escaping nationalism in sports seems impossible, right? There are other models, but it almost seems like if you're going to root for the national team, then this is what we have to put up with, no matter what.

GH: There's no solution any time soon. It's such a multifaceted issue that it takes organisers, coaches, players, families, children to step back and ask, what is it that we want to instil for the future?

GH: It's a good chance for all fans, for all players, to reflect: what are we doing? What are we supporting?

MH: It's a chance for us to reflect on our fan practices and the kind of cultures we want to create. There's nothing coded into cheering for a team that requires you to be racist or homophobic or misogynist. There are other ways to be a fan. We don't have to come down to the most base attacks. We can't just blame the culture. We are the culture; the fans create the culture and the practices, so we can create something new if people really want to. The Mexican national team at least made that part clear in their Twitter promo video[20] about the chant.

GH: And it's not just what are we doing, but why are we doing this? What do we want to represent as fans?

Notes

1 We do not wish to reproduce the violence of this term by writing it repeatedly. From this point on in our chapter, we will refer to the fan practice as 'the chant' and to the term itself by other means, including 'p . . . .' We will only reproduce the term when necessary in quotes from other sources.
2 Both teams have a historic rivalry that goes back to 1944, when Club América defeated Chivas by the score 7–2. The rivalry was initially based on economic disparities where Club América is considered as the 'wealthy' team sponsored by Mexico's largest television conglomerate *Televisa*, while Chivas is considered the 'people's' team for preserving Mexican-style football and not allowing international players to partake in their team. See González (2018).
3 Also sometimes when the goalie is kicking off around his area when a foul is committed in his team's favour.
4 Hidalgo is a queer US-born Chicana/Mexican American feminist writer, scholar, teacher and novice *fútbol* fan. Hortua Vargas is a Colombian-born, US-based heterosexual male historian, teacher, father and longtime *fútbol* fan, player and coach. Both teach at college and university campuses across the Los Angeles and Orange County region of Southern California.
5 We maintain the same position as in note 1 above regarding the term and its feminised, -a ending form. We will reproduce this word only when necessary for clarification and when part of quoted text from other sources.
6 It is important to remember that the 'creolisation' of the Spanish language in Latin America and parts of the United States testifies to the complexities of considering any language as static and not consistently evolving.
7 The *Real Academia Española* is considered to be the authoritative dictionary of the Spanish language, akin to the *OED*.
8 We want to note that one of the co-authors, Dr Melissa Mora Hidalgo, read two parts in this staged reading on 20 April 2011. Quotes from the play are taken directly from Hidalgo's personal copy of the 2011 Company of Angels script.
9 Bracho is currently the Abrams Artist-in-Residence in the Alice Paul Center for Research on Gender, Sexuality, and Women. He also developed the 'La Malinche' character in Cherríe Moraga's 2017 play, *The Mathematics of Love*, which premiered at Brava Theater Center in San Francisco, California.
10 We cite from the Grove Press (New York) edition, 1961.
11 'Chicana' (feminised form of 'Chicano') refers to a person of Mexican descent born and/or raised on the US side of the US-Mexico border. The term came to mean a politicised Mexican American after the Chicano-era civil rights movements of the late 1960s and early 1970s around the US Southwest and borderland region. Several Chicana writers, poets and artists have reclaimed and embraced La Malinche as a feminist figure. See the works of Cherríe Moraga, Gloria E. Anzaldúa, Lorna D. Cervantes, Ana Castillo, Lucha Corpi and Norma Alarcón.

12 Castillo uses the term 'Xicanisma' to 'refer to the concept of Chicana feminism' (1995, p. 11). The 'X'-spelling of 'Chicana' honours the indigenous spelling and language use of 'x' in place of the Spanish sound for 'ch.' See also Moraga (2011), *A Xicana Codex of Changing Consciousness: Writings, 2000–2010* (Durham: Duke UP).

13 This era also coincided with the rise of liberalism in and out of Mexico. The rise of liberalism in Latin America (and other parts of the American continent), during the Enlightenment, exhibited a shift in social policies regarding citizenship (eg John Locke) and land ownership. One of the tenets of liberalism was that citizenship and owning land rested in the hands of the elite (creole) class of Latin America; this political ideology signified that the political process rested solely in the power of men, thereby excluding women, the indigenous population and (of course) black slaves.

14 In Mexican culture, the *corrido*, or folk song, plays a vital role in immortalising revered and heroic figures like Mexican Revolution leaders such as Emiliano Zapata and Pancho Villa. Women who are memorialised through the *corrido*, 'Adelita' and 'Valentina,' are objectified versus emphasis on their roles as front-line soldiers.

15 Albeit many restrictions, women in Mexico were also able to access divorce under special circumstances by 1914, a right afforded in a region ahead of many parts of the continent.

16 We refer to the so-called Juarez 'femicides' during the late 20th and early 21st century, which witnessed the rape, torture and beatings of over a thousand young women going to and coming back from working in *maquiladoras* or factory sweatshops. For more on this subject, see Alicia Gaspar de Alba and Georgina Guzmán *Making a Killing: Femicide, Free Trade, and La Frontera*. Austin: University of Texas Press, 2010 and the 2001 documentary film by Lourdes Portillo, *Señorita Extraviada (Missing Young Woman)*.

17 Melissa Mora Hidalgo and Giovanni Hortua, "Ehhhhh pu! . . . what? Mexican Soccer Fandom, Hegemonic Masculinity, and the Controversial *Puto* Chant," Football Collective 2017 Conference, University of Limerick.

18 In order to create a fanbase, the former coach Al Davis promoted the idea of 'nationalising' the Raider experience as *Raider Nation*, especially after returning to Oakland from Los Angeles. See the 2012 KTLA Channel 5 news segment, 'We are the Raider Nation,' linked in References.

19 Arizona State University professor and fan quoted in Part 1.

20 On 11 October 2019, the official Spanish and English language Twitter accounts for the Mexican national team posted a video to campaign for their #FueraJuega, or 'out of the game,' campaign. They implored fans to stop the chant or else face FIFA's punishment of being thrown 'out of the game.' Spanish: @miseleccionmx. English: @miseleccionmxEN. Pinned tweet with video remained during the writing of this draft in November–December 2019.

References

Alarcón, N. (1989) 'Traddutora, Traditora: A Paradigmatic Figure of Chicana Feminism,' *Cultural Critique*, 13, 57–87.

Arellano, G. (2017) 'Mexico's "Puto" Chant Won't Ever Go Away, No Matter What FIFA Does,' *Remezcla.com*, 09 Nov., available: https://remezcla.com/features/sports/mexico-puto-chant-fifa/ [Accessed 13 Dec. 2019].

Balta, V. (2018) '"Homophobic and Not Very Clever": Why Puto Chants Haunt Mexican Football,' *The Guardian*, 18 June, available: www.theguardian.com/football/2018/jun/18/puto- chants-mexico-football-world-cup [Accessed 11 Dec. 2019].

BBC.com. (2018) 'World Cup 2018: FIFA Investigates "Homophobic Chanting" by Mexico Fans,' *BBC.com*, 18 June, available: www.bbc.com/sport/football/44525523 [Accessed 03 May 2019].

Bracho, R. (2011) *Puto*, Unpublished script.

Buich, N. (2016) 'Origen de la Palabra "Puta": De Diccionarios, Acepciones, Etimologías e Idiologías,' *La Izquierda Diario*, 21 Aug., available: www.laizquierdadiario.com/ Origen-de-la-palabra-puta [Accessed 11 Dec. 2019].

Castillo, A. (1995) *Massacre of the Dreamers: Essays on Xicanisma*. New York: Plume.

Castillo, R. and Noel, A. (2014) 'Mexico Soccer Fans Debate Use of Controversial "Puto" Chant,' *VICE.com*, 26 June, available: www.vice.com/en_us/article/nemkxw/mexico- soccer-fans-debate-use-of-controversial-puto-chant [Accessed 10 Nov. 2019].

Cypess, S. M. (1989) 'From Colonial Constructs to Feminist Figures: Re/visions by Mexican Women Dramatists,' *Theater Journal*, 41(4), 492–504.

Doyle, J. (2014) 'Mexican Gothic (It IS a Curse!),' *The Sport Spectacle*, 29 June, available: https://thesportspectacle.com/2014/06/29/mexican-gothic/ [Accessed 09 Dec. 2019].

ESPN. (2018) 'FIFA Fines Mexico Federation $10K for Chants in Germany Match,' *ESPN.com*, 20 June, available: www.espn.com/soccer/mexico/story/3536039/fifa-fines-mexico-federation-$10,000-for-chants-in-germany-match [Accessed 03 May 2019].

FIFA.com. (2017) 'Several Member Associations Sanctioned for Incidents During FIFA World Cup Qualifiers,' *FIFA.com*, 27 April, available: www.fifa.com/who-we-are/news/several-member-associations-sanctioned-for-incidents-during-fifa-world-2880775 [Accessed 11 Dec. 2019].

Gallardo, A. (2011) 'PUTO: The Almost Naked, Almost Communist Play,' *Remezcla.com*, 30 Sept., available: https://remezcla.com/culture/chi-puto-the-almost-naked-almost-communist-play/ [Accessed 10 Dec. 2019].

González, C. (2018) 'How Did Chivas vs América become the Classic of Classics?' *Latin American Post*, 03 Mar., available: https://latinamericanpost.com/19955-how-did-chivas-vs-america-become-the-classic-of-classics [Accessed 16 July 2020].

González, P.(2019) 'La palabra Puto no es un insulto (bajo estas circunstancias), de acuerdocon la RAE,' *GQ Mexico*, 7 Mar., available: www.gq.com.mx/entretenimiento/articulo/ la-palabra-puto-ya-no-es-un-insulto-de-acuerdo-con-la-rae [Accessed 15 Nov. 2019].

Grijelmo, Á. (2018) 'La palabra "puta" fue un eufemismo,' *El País*, 15 Dec., available: https://elpais.com/elpais/2018/12/14/opinion/1544785600_191059.html [Accessed 11 Dec. 2019].

Gutiérrez Chong, N. (2006) 'Patriotic Thoughts or Intuition: Roles of Women in Mexican Nationalisms,' *Nations and Nationalisms*, 12(2), 339–358.

Hidalgo, M. (1810) *Discurso de Miguel Hidalgo al Pueblo de Dolores para dar inicio a la independencia de México. Biblioteca.tv*, available: www.biblioteca.tv/artman2/publish/1810_115/Discurso_de_Miguel_Hidalgo_al_Pueblo_de_Dolores_pa_604.shtml [Accessed 15 Nov. 2019]

Irwin, R. M. (2003) *Mexican Masculinities*. Minneapolis: University Of Minnesota.

Jaramillo, J. J. (2014) 'What's the *Puto* Problem?' *Slate*, 24 June, available: https://slate.com/human-interest/2014/06/puto-world-cup-what-does-mexicos-anti-gay-world-cup-soccer-chant-really-mean.html [Accessed 12 Dec. 2019].

Kahn, C. (2014) 'Some Mexico Fans Feel Unfairly Targeted for World Cup Chants,' *NPR Code Switch*, 23 June, available: www.npr.org/sections/codeswitch/2014/06/23/324629058/some-mexico-fans-feel-unfairly-targeted-for-world-cup-chants.NPR.org [Accessed 11 Dec. 2019].

KTLA Channel 5. (2012) 'We Are the Raider Nation,' *Raiders.com*, 18 June, available: www.raiders.com /video/we-are-the-raider-nation-7487466 [Accessed 10 Dec. 2019].

Macias, A. (1980). 'Women and the Mexican Revolution, 1910–1920,' *The Americas*, 37(1), 53–82.

Macías-González, V. M. and Rubenstein, A. (2012) *Masculinity and Sexuality in Modern Mexico*, Albuquerque: University of New Mexico.

Mediotiempo. (2016) 'Así surgió el famoso grito de "eeh . . . puto",' *Mediotiempo*, 14 Jan., available: www. mediotiempo.com/*futbol*/liga-mx/asi-surgio-el-famoso-grito-de-eeh-puto. [Accessed 12 Dec. 2019].

Miller, L. S. (2017) '"Puta" Defined: "Narcos" Stars Debate the True Meaning of TV's Most Popular Spanish Curse Word,' *IndieWire*, 05 Sept., available: www.indiewire.com/2017/09/narcos-season-3-puta-pedro-pascal-interview-1201873241/ [Accessed 15 Nov. 2019].

Molotov. (1997) 'Puto,' Track 9 of *¿Dónde Jugarán las Niñas?* Polygram Records Latino.

Payne, M. (2017). 'Mexican Soccer Federation Begs Fans to Stop Homophobic Chant at Games,' *Washington Post*, 21 June, available: www.washingtonpost.com/news/early-lead/wp/2017/06/21/mexican-soccer-federation-begs-fans-to-stop-homophobic-chant-at-games [Accessed 15 Nov. 2019].

Paz, O. (1961) *The Labyrinth of Solitude*. New York: Grove Press [online], available https://archive.org/stream/labyrinthofsolit02pazo/labyrinthofsolit02pazo_djvu.txt [Accessed 12 Dec. 2019].

Planas, R. (2013). 'Molotov's Makes Major Announcement to LGBT Community,' *HuffPost*, available: www.huffpost.com/entry/molotov-puto_n_3678593?guccounter=1 [Accessed 15 Nov. 2019].

Real Academia Española. (2019) *puto,ta*, viewed 12 December 2019, *Real Academia Española*, available: https://dle.rae.es/puto [Accessed 15 Nov. 2019].

Smith, S. J. (2009) *Gender and the Mexican Revolution: Yucatán Women and the Realities of Patriarchy*. Chapel Hill: University of North Carolina.

Chapter 9

Regional politics of place-making and (un)belonging through language practices at a derby football match in the south of the Netherlands

Lotte Thissen and Leonie Cornips

Introduction

On Ascension Day 2017 (25 May), a football derby was played in Maastricht, the capital city of Limburg, located in the far southeast of the Netherlands. MVV, the football club of Maastricht, faced the football club of Kerkrade, Roda JC. Maastricht borders Belgium in the far southwest whereas Kerkrade borders Germany in the far southeast corner of the province. The distance between the two cities is only 35 kilometres. The stakes of the match were high: MVV aimed at promotion to the Dutch premier league, while Roda JC fought against relegation to the Dutch first division. In this chapter, we focus on how regional politics of place-making and (un)belonging were played out before, during and after the match.

Using sociolinguistic, anthropological and human geographical theories, this contribution addresses how language practices before and during the football derby match produced centre and periphery dynamics (Győri Szabó 2012) in a perceived peripheral province from a national perspective – that is, the south of Limburg (Cornips et al. 2016). The analysis of ethnographic, visual and audio-recorded data suggests that the language practices at the derby match produced place and achieved (un)belonging through the use of Dutch or local dialect. Limburg has a long history of dialect enregisterment (Cornips et al. 2016; Johnstone 2013) through which linguistic forms and its users have been associated with specific places and social (stereo)types, and people in Limburg are highly aware of these linguistic differences, in particular, at the phonological and lexical level (Hermans 2013). These differences for all forms of social semiosis are crucial in the process of place-making or (re)producing place in Limburg (Cornips et al. 2016). This chapter will show that by using Dutch, Roda JC and its fans were constructed as 'foreigners' in Maastricht, Limburg, and hence, as unbelonging (Christensen 2009) and *out of place* (Thissen 2018) in the Netherlands. At the same time, MVV and its fans were, through the use of the local dialect of Maastricht (Mestreechs), seen as belonging to local and regional levels in Limburg. This chapter, thus, shows how football and language choice in tandem contribute to making the MVV and Roda JC match a regional identity experience (Győri Szabó 2012; Shobe 2008) instead of a national one.

Limburg in the Netherlands: a piece of foreign country in the Netherlands[1]

Both MVV Maastricht and Roda JC Kerkrade are based in the southern part of Limburg. Thissen (2018) notes that the province of Limburg is imagined as an un-Dutch touristic paradise where other Dutch inhabitants can go if they want to escape the 'real' Netherlands. The idea that Limburg is regarded as not really being part of, and quite different from, the Dutch nation-state, is partly due to its tumultuous history in which different rulers came and went, and the shape of the province – as we know it now – changed several times. Its brief history is as follows: during the Eighty Years' War (1568–1648), most of the southern part of the Netherlands was under Spanish influence, and Catholicism was the only permitted religion (Cornips and Knotter 2017). Thereafter, the area now known as Dutch 'Limburg' was part of a larger territory including the modern-day areas of Luxembourg and Belgian Flanders, artificially created by the French administrative force, though it remained a highly contested area that was politically unstable and experienced Spanish and Austrian takeovers (Orbons and Spronck 2009, pp. 43–44). In 1815, the southern Netherlands became part of the United Kingdom of the Netherlands, under the rule of King William I. He decided that the areas of modern-day Dutch Limburg and Belgian Limburg should be called 'Limburg,' after the medieval duchy that was once part of the Spanish Netherlands and, later, the United Kingdom of the Netherlands. In 1839, the two Limburg areas were separated, after which the western part became Belgian while the eastern part became Dutch, though it remained a member of the German Confederation until 1867. From that time forward, Limburg became the 11th province of the Netherlands, though it retained the name 'duchy' until 1906 (Orbons and Spronck 2009, pp. 35–36).

Limburg's eventual and relatively late integration into the Dutch nation-state in 1867 fostered a strong regionally felt Limburgian identity based mainly on cultural, religious and linguistic differences (Thissen 2018) in comparison with the rest of the Netherlands. In the Dutch context, Limburg is (or used to be) peculiar for being homogeneously Catholic (Cornips and Knotter 2017) and for its vital use of local dialects (Cornips 2013). Knotter (2011) has called the integration of Limburg into the Netherlands 'negative integration': it was only after Limburg was absorbed into the Dutch nation-state that a distinct sense of regional identity could develop. Since then, inhabitants have experienced and imagined what they had in common and how they differed from the nation-state to which they, from that moment on, belonged: 'Limburgers' would cherish a joie-de-vivre lifestyle and certain traditions, such as carnival celebration (Cornips and Knotter 2017; Cornips and de Rooij 2015). The perceived differences and resulting dichotomy between Limburg and 'Holland' – as the rest of the country is often called in Limburg – is still of great significance in the province today (see Thissen 2018).

Centre-periphery dynamics

Portraying Limburg as a foreign country and distinct from the rest of the Netherlands feeds into centre-periphery dynamics in which 'centre' and 'periphery' refer to, relatively, the core or mainstream region of an area and the area that stands outside or at the edge of a defined space, respectively (Hall 2015, p. 162; Wall 2015, p. 180). Centre-periphery dynamics are driven by ideas that people in a particular place, region or country have about dominant power relations of who is or is not in charge (cf. Giddens 1984; Hannerz 1989; Kearney 1995); language practices may reproduce and express these power relations (Cornips et al. 2016). Centres and peripheries change, disappear and reappear (Harrison 2015, p. 173), and their dynamics tend to recur onto different levels (Thissen 2018). This chapter now examines how regional centre-periphery dynamics are played out within the nationally perceived peripheral province of Limburg between football clubs from the cities of Maastricht and Kerkrade.

The historical rivalry between MVV Maastricht and Roda JC

The province of Limburg has four football clubs that play in the professional divisions of the Netherlands. At the time of writing (2021), Fortuna Sittard and VVV Venlo both play in the premier league, while Roda JC Kerkrade and MVV Maastricht play in the first division.

Founded in 1902 as MCF/MVC, MVV Maastricht claims to be the oldest football club in Limburg. On its website and during the match, the club self-represents as 'the club of Maastricht.' This is also emphasised by the fact that its players are often called *De Sterrendragers* (The Star Bearers), thereby referring to the white star in the emblem of the club, which also symbolises the city emblem of Maastricht. Moreover, the fans call the club, in Maastricht dialect, *us MVV'ke*, which literally means 'our MVV' in a diminutive, hence, affectionate form (MVV n.d.). MVV's CEO and the members of the board are all locally bound, and the stocks of the club are property of local banks and entrepreneurs (Annual report MVV 2017–2018). Also, a major sponsor is *Veer zien MVV*, which is a foundation established by fans of MVV who aim to generate income for the club by providing catering, merchandise, and acquiring donations. Since its establishment in 2010, the foundation raised 748.741 euros to support MVV (Veer zien MVV n.d.). In its annual report, MVV prides itself for having positive financial capital (Annual report MVV 2017–2018).

Contrary to MVV, Roda JC does not emphasise its link to the city of Kerkrade so much in its self-representation but rather its connection to the coal mining history of the area of Southeast-Limburg. Until the 19th century, the southeastern part of Limburg was thinly populated, but when the coal mining industry took off and rapidly expanded between 1900 and 1930 in the so-called Eastern Mine district (*Oostelijke Mijnstreek*), communities were established around the mines.

The Dominiale Mine in Kerkrade was part of the German Aachen Mine District (Knotter 2014, p. 377). With coalminers settling in the Mine district at the beginning of the 19th century, football clubs and cultural associations were also founded to tie miners to the company (Beyers 2008, p. 179). According to Knotter and Mayer (2015, p. 10): 'histories of football as a miners' sport both in France and in Germany point to the ambivalent role of sport in inter-ethnic relations, ranging from the construction of ethnic identities to intercultural integration.' The club Roda JC as we know it now was founded in 1962 as a merger between Roda Sport (merger between Kerkrade FC from 1926 and SV Blijerheide from 1914) and Rapid JC (the merger between Juliana from 1910 and Rapid '54 from 1954). The coal mines were closed in the 1970s, and its history is still recalled through folk songs, miner stories, and through the football club Roda JC (Dolhain 2018; Hoekstra 2014; and see Schiering 2008 for the German Ruhr area). Roda JC's players are called and call themselves *koempels* 'coalminers' and in doing so probably mystify a glorious past during the peak of the mining industry when it 'guaranteed a bond among the members of the (masculine/authors) working class' (Schiering 2008, p. 227). Moreover, the club is referred to as 'the pride of the south' (*trots van het zuiden*).[2] In 2019, Roda JC faced financial hardships, and for some months, it was unclear whether they could survive financially. In October 2019, local entrepreneurs warranted 900,000 euros to bridge the deficiencies and save the club. Local entrepreneurs now have almost 80% of the club's stocks in their hands; the remaining 20% are in hands of a Russian investor (NOS 2019a).

In an article on the website 'Roda JC Live' that aims to inform reliably and objectively, 'yet from a Roda-perspective' about the dealings of the club, the author tries to explain the rivalry between Roda JC and MVV (De Regt 2017). The article starts with a disclaimer to emphasise that the objective descriptions of the origins of the rivalry should not be seen as the 'only true nature of the rivalry' and that 'personal ideas and feelings about the clubs can strongly differ.' The article describes an economic shift after the closing of the mines in the 1970s. During the heydays of the mining industry around Kerkrade, there was enough money to invest into Roda JC and its predecessors. Maastricht, on the other hand, played second fiddle (in an administrative respect) until the 1960s. After the closing of the mines, an economic shift took place in which the western part of South-Limburg developed with the strengthening of Maastricht as the administrative centre of the province and the establishment of Maastricht University and its medical centre. It is commonly thought that the investment of the Dutch government in South-Limburg to soften the effects of the closure of the mines never really arrived in the area where the closure was felt hardest. This has fed into centre-periphery dynamics between the eastern and western part of South-Limburg, with Kerkrade and Heerlen (eastern part) and Maastricht (western part) as the cities that stand in contrast to each other.

According to the Roda JC Live website, the rivalry is further strengthened by the fact that Maastricht is the capital of the province, making MVV the capital football club, while Kerkrade is still associated with its coal mining history, making Roda JC the labourers' football club. Roda JC is presumed as having a *koempel*

Figure 9.1 Photo of MVV fans bringing nine *tons* of euros to the stadium of Roda JC in Kerkrade (Angel-Side MVV 2019: with permission of Angel-Side MVV for using the photo).

('coalminer') mentality of hard work instead of whining, while MVV was associated with the bourgeoisie of the provincial government located in Maastricht. On top of this, the Roda JC Live article – not so objectively – claims that the rivalry from the perspective of MVV is also explained by the fact that Roda JC has played in the premier league more often than MVV.[3]

The rivalry between both clubs in recent times is also reproduced and kept alive by fans who engage in mockery of each other. For example, during the period in which Roda JC faced a financial gap of 900,000 euros, some fans of MVV brought nine barrels (to symbolize a *ton* of euros, which is in Dutch the equivalent of 100,000 euros) to the stadium of Roda JC with a banner saying: 'Here's 9 ton for Roda JC with greetings from MVV' (NOS 2019b; Figure 9.1). We will see shortly that mockery and hostility were also evident during the derby in 2017.

The derby match and fans' gathering

We now focus on the derby played between MVV and Roda JC in the Geusselt stadium in Maastricht on Ascension Day, 25 May 2017. As mentioned in the introduction, the stakes of the match were high. The two clubs would play the return match four days later in the stadium of Roda JC in Kerkrade.

When the draw for the play-offs of the Dutch competition was published, media in Limburg pointed to the possibility of a Limburgian final, a derby match between MVV and Roda JC (1Limburg 2017). The regional media not only highlighted the promotion and relegation stakes but also the historical rivalry between both clubs. MVV and Roda JC played their first derby match in 1963, a year after Roda JC originated out of a merger between two other clubs from Kerkrade. After that, the clubs played 46 derby matches of which Roda JC won 22 matches and MVV won 13 matches (Keukenkampioen Divisie). The last derby match had been played in the 2014/2015 season, so up until that derby in May 2017, the rivalry between both clubs was concealed for two seasons because the clubs played in different divisions of the league.

Coincidently, the first author of this chapter was dragged along to this very derby match by her partner. On the same day, she stumbled on a gathering of MVV fans, in the literature referred to as 'ultras' (Fuller and Junaedi 2018; Hodges 2016). The fans gathered in the city centre of Maastricht to start their march to the Geusselt stadium by foot (approximately a 40-minute walk). Before the march started, the leader of the fans used a megaphone to give a speech and to commemorate deceased fans, all in the Maastricht dialect (see Figure 9.2).

Figure 9.2 Fans gathering in Maastricht city centre during the commemoration of deceased fans (25 May 2017). The red flag with white star symbolises the city emblem of Maastricht.

Source: Photo reproduced by permission of Lotte Thissen©.

Before the match started, the MVV fans loudly sang along with the city anthem of Maastricht, which was performed by the famous singer Beppie Kraft. According to Schiering (2008, p. 225), the opening ritual of football matches provides the most optimal case of expressing regional identity. The singing in the dialect of Maastricht by Beppie Kraft, together with the communal singing of the MVV fans in the stadium, targets not only the MVV fans but also the opposing team's fans (Schiering 2008, p. 230) who speak a dialect that differs greatly (see below). At halftime, riots took place between the ultras of both sides. While the players and board members of MVV were mediating and calming things down, the match was delayed by half an hour. The match, watched by 8,800 spectators, eventually ended in a draw. Roda JC won the return match in Kerkrade four days later, in the process preventing Roda JC from being relegated and MVV from being promoted.

During the fans' gathering and the derby match, the first author immersed herself in the fans' practices. Although the researcher's participation remained low, this study could be seen as using (participant) observation in real-life practices (Shah 2017, p. 47). It is important to acknowledge the authors' bias. The first author viewed the match and the fans' gathering from the perspective of MVV and Maastricht, mainly because she lives in Maastricht, and her partner got tickets to the match via the website of MVV, meaning that she sat in an MVV section in the stadium. The second author mainly viewed the data from the perspective of Roda JC due to her interest in the club's association with the coal mining history of that region. In writing this article together, we noticed how the perceived centre-periphery dynamics influenced our own working with the data. For example, the first author's photos and videos of the derby match mainly focused on the practices of MVV fans in the stadium and not so much on the visiting Roda JC fans because they were located away from her section in the stadium.

Based on the data, we were able to describe the practices and transcribe the language used during the speeches in the fans' gathering and in the stadium. In the following sections, we will elaborate on the central theoretical notions of this paper.

Place-making and politics of (un)belonging

The construction of multi-level local and national identities through football is a globally recognised phenomenon (Győri Szabó 2012, p. 36), and place-making in these identities should be included (Shobe 2008, p. 330). Currently, the notion of place is highly politicised by the claiming of, and attaching meaning to, localities (Massey 2005; Paasi 2001; Pierce et al. 2010). People socially produce *places* (Cresswell 2009; Pred 1985) – that is, make social or 'lived' place through their practices (Lefebvre 1991) and the attachment of ideas to places about what behaviour is considered appropriate or not (Cresswell 1996, pp. 16–17). Language is regarded as being a vital aspect in these place-making processes (see Feld and Basso 1996; Cornips and de Rooij 2018;

Csordas 1994; Duranti 1997; Johnstone 2013; Low 2003; Valentine et al. 2008; Thissen 2018; Tuan 1991), since language 'not only represents or refers but "discloses" our being-in-the-world' (Csordas 1994, p. 11). This suggests that the study of language practices and place-making informs how places are endowed with meaning, such as conventions and rules of behaviour but also name-giving. In Limburg, historical name-giving practices turn dialects into indexes of places since dialects are named after locations; for example, the dialect of Maastricht is called Maastrichts (in Dutch) or *Mestreechs* (in dialect), the dialect of Kerkrade is called Kerkraads (in Dutch) or *Kirchröadsj* (in dialect) (Cornips et al. 2016, p. 190).

Consequently, cultural and linguistic place-making practices put forward ideas who and what is considered as *in place* and *out of place* (Cresswell 1996; Thissen 2018). Place-making processes seem to stimulate the creation of ideas and conventions about what practices and persons are regarded as appropriate, accepted and 'normal.' It is thus about who or what is considered to be *in* and *out of place*. This seems to be very relevant in these times when the question of who belongs to a place and who should be considered as 'the other' or 'outsider' is continuously raised (cf. Davis and Nencel 2011; Duyvendak 2011). We therefore argue that place-making practices and processes, while attaching linguistic meaning to places, simultaneously produce politics of belonging and, just as important (cf. Christensen 2009), unbelonging. In the following sections of this chapter, we will show how both MVV and Roda JC fans expressed belonging and unbelonging simultaneously.

Language choice in the city centre and stadium: the presence of Dutch and the dialect of Maastricht in place-making processes

Place-making practices were observed during the fans' gathering in Maastricht city centre before the derby match (see Figure 9.3) when the fans' leader gave a speech to warm up the crowd for the march to the stadium, the game against Roda JC, and to commemorate deceased fans. All this was done exclusively in Maastricht dialect, which presupposed that MVV fans can at least understand the local dialect, thereby revealing that the use of the Maastricht dialect and who is using it is considered *in place*.

The use of the local dialect of Maastricht, which is considered to be distinctive, may be understood as a resource from which the fans' leader draws when evoking 'the local' or a local identity (Cornips et al. 2016; Coupland 2007). Similarly, the stadium host of the match welcomed the fans in Maastricht dialect, showing that the use of this dialect is perceived *in place* during the match:

> Moog ich daovuur, Mestreechteneren, 'n applaus, veur uuch sowie g'r heij zeet, in us stadion De Geusselt, waant v'r staon es eine maan achter us klub, en dat is MVV Mestreech.

Figure 9.3 Fans' gathering in the city centre of Maastricht (25 May 2017).

Source: Photo reproduced by permission of Lotte Thissen©.

> Can I have for that, Mestreechteneren (i.e. people from Maastricht), an applause, for all of you as you are here now, in our stadium De Geusselt, because we stand as one man behind our club, and that's MVV Mestreech.
>
> (Stadium host before the derby match between MVV and Roda JC started, 25 May 2017).

Thus, this opening welcome from the stadium host can be analysed as a form of linguistic place-making. The host's use of Maastricht dialect underlines what is considered normal in this place and that the host expects the audience to understand this dialect. Tuan (1991, p. 685) emphasises that 'speech . . . direct[s] attention, organize[s] insignificant entities into significant composite wholes, and, in so doing, make[s] things visible, viable, and real.' When analysing the welcome, some words draw special attention from a place-making angle:

> Moog ich daovuur, **Mestreechteneren**, 'n applaus, veur uuch sowie g'r heij zeet, in **us stadion** De Geusselt, waant v'r staon es eine maan achter **us klub**, en dat is MVV Mestreech.

By the explicit use of the words *Mestreechteneren* ('people from Maastricht'), *us stadion* ('our stadium'), and *us klub* ('our club'), the host turns MVV, its fans, and the city of Maastricht into significant composite wholes that are seen as being directly linked to each other. Thereby, the city of Maastricht is appropriated as the place of MVV, behind which the *Mestreechteneren* stand as one man. Simultaneously, the Roda JC fans are excluded by the above phrases, which express local belongingness, and to some extent by the mere use of Maastricht dialect – although this might be intelligible for those who speak and understand a local Limburgian dialect.

Before the match started, the hosts also introduced the sponsors of the club and of the match ball in the Maastricht dialect:

> Autoschade Merkelbach en die zitte op de Molensingel 21. En dan höbbe v'r nog ein wedstrijdbal sponsor, det is de Gouverneur, mit Belgische speciaalbeere op de Boschstraot 105A in Mestreech.
>
> Car damage [repair] Merkelbach and they are located on the Molensingel 21. And then we also have the match ball sponsor, which is *De Gouverneur* [café], with Belgian specialty beers, [located] on the Boschstraat 105A in Maastricht.
>
> (Stadium hosts mentioning sponsors of MVV Maastricht, 25 May 2017.)

In this quote, the host mentions the sponsors by name, describes their product and gives their specific location in the city of Maastricht or in its near vicinity, all of which is done in Maastrichts. Besides this, the banners in the stadium also displayed local sponsors, such as the Maastricht-based parking company Q-Park. These commercials are exemplifying football's contemporary commodification (Giulianotti 2002) on a regional level while also showing how the tropes of local pride and profit are closely intertwined (Duchêne and Heller 2012; Del Percio and Duchêne 2012).

After the announcement of the sponsors and the entrance of the players, Beppie Kraft performed the anthem of the city of Maastricht in the Maastricht dialect. The use of Maastricht dialect by the host, the local sponsors, and the performance by the Maastricht singer can be regarded as place-making practices that are rooting or (re)producing MVV into Maastricht and vice versa. These place-making practices before and during the derby match therefore reveal routines and ideas about who/what is in place and out of place (Cresswell 1996; Thissen 2018).

Politics of (un)belonging at the derby match: producing Roda JC as 'foreign' in Maastricht, Limburg and the Netherlands

The fans and the stadium host of MVV construct a place where Maastricht dialect is considered *in place*, and simultaneously, everyone who identifies with that dialect is considered to belong in that place. This linguistic activity reveals power dynamics through which the Roda JC fans who could not/would not identify with the use of the Maastricht dialect were excluded and considered as *out of place* and as unbelonging. In this power dynamic, the Roda JC ultras (housed in the farthest corner away from the ultras of MVV) contested their marginalisation by turning their backs to the field when Beppie Kraft sang the city anthem (Figure 9.4).

Interestingly, during the riots at halftime of the match, the stadium host switched from Maastricht dialect to Dutch to remind the rioting fans in the stadium of the fact that football is played on the field and not through violence. In this case, the host probably selected Dutch to guarantee the full attention of the entire audience. In this respect, Dutch as the national language is used as a perceived 'neutral' variety, which overcomes socially and geographically distributed dialect differences between those from Maastricht and Kerkrade. There is a double-edge politics of unbelonging constructed in doing so. On the one hand, Dutch is used to address MVV fans who are nevertheless seen as *out of place* due to their inappropriately considered behaviour. By switching to Dutch and breaking the routine of using *Maastrichts*, it seems that the host aims to distance MVV and its 'proper' fans from the rioting fans. On the other hand, within the context

Figure 9.4 Photo of Roda JC ultras turning their backs to the field during the city anthem of Maastricht (Koempel.nl 2017).

of Limburg, switching to Dutch to address Roda JC fans seems to put forward a politics of unbelonging for fans from Roda JC.

Language choice between local dialect and Dutch in Limburg is never socially neutral. In particular, centre-periphery dynamics play out in how people consider and react to the dialect use of others. Maastricht is imagined as the centre of (south) Limburg: it hosts provincial dignitaries, including the king's commissioner seating in the provincial council and the provincial executive, which reside at the provincial government building, the so-called *Gouvernement*, representing a wide range of the province of Limburg's political, economic and cultural interests. Speakers of the Maastricht dialect evaluate the dialect of Kerkrade as being extremely funny and may laugh upon hearing someone speak in the dialect of Kerkrade in Maastricht (Cornips et al. 2016). The perception of Kerkraads as 'funny' or maybe 'weird' is based on it being perceived as the most deviant and exceptional dialect in the province. Kerkraads belongs to the Ripuarian dialects that were heavily influenced by the German city of Cologne. It is perceived as the dialect that is the hardest one to understand for people outside of the province and even for inhabitants elsewhere in Limburg (Cornips 2018). Its funniness is clearly based in its otherness, it being different from what most Limburgian dialects sound like. Aesthetic evaluations from a mental map drawing task have shown that the dialect in the capital Maastricht and immediate surroundings are evaluated as the most beautiful while the dialect in Kerkrade is perceived of as most ugly (ibid).

Someone who speaks in the dialect of Kerkrade is often associated with being German, and indeed, the MVV fans reproduced this association in one of their chants during the derby match. The Dutch song *'Wie niet springt'* ('Who doesn't jump') is a popular chant introduced by the football club Ajax from Amsterdam. Historically, Ajax was 'insulted' by other clubs for being a Jewish club on account of its supposed popularity among Jews (McVitie and Vos n.d.). Fans of Ajax turned this insult into a nickname of pride and now call themselves 'the club of Jews.' Originally, the song text is 'who doesn't jump, is no Jew,' encouraging every fan in the stadium to jump along to show their attachment to Ajax. Other clubs have made their own variants of this song. During the derby match with Roda JC, the MVV fans sang: 'who doesn't jump is a *mof*.'[4] *Mof* refers to the pejorative term used by the Dutch to refer to Germans. However, in this derby match, *mof* was used to refer to the fans and players from Roda JC, hence, linking Kerkrade to Germany emphasising their *foreignness* (Thissen 2018) within Limburg and the Netherlands. Roda JC's and Kerkrade's foreign image can only be understood from a historical, socio-economical and linguistic context in which the coal mining past of Kerkrade and its oddly perceived Ripuarian dialect (Cornips et al. 2016) are of significance.

Conclusion

This chapter showed how football is a vehicle for cultural and linguistic place-making practices, (re)producing tensions, thereby highlighting the politics of (un)belonging in a perceived peripheral region – that is, the province of Limburg in the Netherlands. In this chapter we have combined insights from anthropology, sociolinguistics and human geography to understand how regional identity politics manifested through the use of a local dialect and Dutch at a football match. We discussed how these linguistic place-making processes revealed what practice, and subsequently who, was considered to be *in* and *out of place*. Although we emphasised that the derby match between MVV (Maastricht) and Roda JC (Kerkrade) (re)produced centre-periphery dynamics, the chapter also underlined that historical, socio-economic contingencies influenced the politics of who belonged and who did not during this game in Maastricht.

To our knowledge, there are few in-depth and ethnographic studies (Warner 2007; Schiering 2008) of language practices before, during and after football matches (or any sports for that matter). In the current era, where major issues such as national identity politics, racism and loyalty issues are played out through football (and discussed in chapters in this volume), we argue that it is essential to consider the role of language in those processes.

Acknowledgements

Our gratitude goes out to the editors who included us in this exciting volume and the reviewers for their valuable feedback and comments on this chapter. We thank the organisers of the conference *Language, Place, and Periphery* at Copenhagen University (18–19 January 2018) for letting us present a first draft of this chapter and are grateful for the audience's input to improve the draft. Any shortcomings are, however, solely the responsibility of the authors.

Notes

1 See Thissen (2018) for more.

2 In 2018, Joris Hoefakker directed and made the promotional video *Roda JC: Are you with us!* to show the love of Roda JC fans for their club. The video caused some commotion; fans did not understand why the video was in English instead of Dutch or other dialect and some wondered why the ultra-fans, wearing balaclavas had been given such a stage (Dolhain 2018). See: www.youtube.com/watch?v=UaX_w0aoIMM.

3 Additionally, a historical religious division might have also fed into the rivalry between both clubs. Well into the 1960s, public life in the Netherlands was structured according to so-called religious pillars. During this time of pillarisation (verzuiling), institutions, such as schools, political parties, labour unions, radio, television and newspapers were compartmentalised according to their religious foundation: Protestant, Catholic, Social-democratic, or liberal/general (Schoffer 1956). This also held true for football clubs and unions. When looking into the histories of both clubs, we found that MVV was a member of the neutral Limburgian football union while Roda JC was a member of the Roman Catholic football union. Although we did not find evidence that this also contributes to the rivalry between the clubs, it would be interesting to examine this further in historical archives.

4 See www.youtube.com/watch?v=x7kkANdhnH8 from 9:56 onwards to see the footage of MVV fans singing *wie niet springt, dat is een mof.*

References

1Limburg. (2017) *Limburgse Derby Tussen Roda JC en MVV in Play-offs?* [online], available: www.1limburg.nl/limburgse-derby-tussen-roda-jc-en-mvv-play-offs [Accessed on 4 December 2019].

Angel-Side MVV (2019) *Photo of MVV Fans Bringing 9 Tons of Euros to the Stadium of Roda JC in Kerkrade* [online], available: www.facebook.com/angelsidemestreech/photos/384316415507450 [Accessed on 4 December 2019].

Beyers, L. (2008) 'From Class to Culture: Immigration, Recession, and Daily Ethnic Boundaries in Belgium, 1940–1990s', *International Review of Social History*, 53, 37–61. https://doi.org/10.1017/S0020859007003331.

Christensen, A. (2009) 'Belonging and Unbelonging from an Intersectional Perspective', *Gender, Technology and Development*, 13(21), 21–41. https://doi.org/10.1177/097185240901300102.

Cornips, L. (2013). 'Recent Developments in the Limburg Dialect Region', in Hinskens, F., and Taeldeman, J. (eds.) *Language and Space: Dutch. An International Handbook of Linguistic Variation*, Berlin/Boston: De Gruyter Mouton, 378–399.

Cornips, L. (2018) 'Social Meanings of the North-South Divides in the Netherlands and Limburg and Their Linkage to Standard Dutch and Dialect Varieties', in Evans, B., Benson, E., and Stanford, J. (eds.) *Language Regard. Methods, Variation and Change*, Cambridge: Cambridge University Press, 96–117. https://doi.org/10.1017/9781316678381.006.

Cornips, L. and de Rooij, V. (2015) 'Belonging through Languagecultural Practices in the Periphery. The Politics of Carnival in the Dutch Province of Limburg', *Anthropological Journal of European Cultures*, 24(1), 83–101. https://doi.org/10.3167/ajec.2015.240106.

Cornips, L. and de Rooij, V., eds. (2018) *The Sociolinguistics of Place and Belonging. Perspectives from the Margins*. Amsterdam: John Benjamins. https://doi.org/10.1075/impact.45.

Cornips, L., de Rooij, V., Stengs, I. and Thissen, L. (2016) 'Dialect and Local Media. Reproducing the Multi-dialectal Space in Limburg (the Netherlands)', in Thøgersen, J., Coupland, N. and Mortensen, J. (eds.) *Style, Media and Language Ideologies, SLICE Series Norwegian Novus Style*, Oslo: Novus Press, 189–216.

Cornips, L. and Knotter, A. (2017) 'Inventing Limburg (The Netherlands): Territory, History, Language, and Identity', in Helen, C., Gilles, P., and Purschke, C. (eds.) *Räume, Grenzen, Übergänge. Akten des 5. Kongresses der Internationalen Gesellschaft für Dialektologie des Deutschen (IGDD)*, Stuttgart: Steiner (ZDL. Beihefte. 170), 71–91.

Coupland, N. (2007) *Style: Language Variation and Identity*, Cambridge: Cambridge University Press.

Cresswell, T. (1996) *In Place/Out of Place: Geography, Ideology, and Transgression*, Minneapolis and London: University of Minnesota Press.

Cresswell, T. (2009) 'Place', in Kitchin, R. and Thrift, N. (eds.) *International Encyclopedia of Human Geography*, Volume 8, Oxford: Elsevier, 169–177.

Csordas, T. (1994) *Embodiment and Experience*, Cambridge: Cambridge University Press.

Davis, K. and Nencel, L. (2011) 'Border Skirmishes and the Question of Belonging: An Auto Ethnographic Account of Everyday Exclusion in Multicultural Society', *Ethnicities*, 11(4), 467–488. https://doi.org/10.1177/1468796811415772.

Del Percio, A. and Duchêne, A. (2012) 'Commodification of Pride and Resistance to Profit: Language Practices as Terrain of Struggle in a Swiss Football Stadium', in Duchêne, A. and Heller, M. (eds.) *Language in Late Capitalism: Pride and Profit*, New York and London: Routledge, 43–72.

De Regt. J. (2017) *Maastricht en Kerkrade: een bijzondere rivaliteit* [online], available: https://www.rodajclive.nl/maastricht-en-kerkrade-een-bijzondere-rivaliteit/ [Accessed on 4 December 2019].

Dolhain, P. (2018) 'Omstreden Roda-filmpje blijkt hit', *Regional newspaper De Limburger*, August 13, available: www.limburger.nl/cnt/dmf20180812_00070670/omstreden-roda-filmpje-blijkt-hit [Accessed 4 December 2019].

Duchêne, A. and Heller, M. (2012) *Language in Late Capitalism: Pride and Profit*, New York/London: Routledge.

Duranti, A. (1997) *Linguistic Anthropology*, Cambridge: Cambridge University Press.

Duyvendak, J. (2011) *The Politics of Home: Belonging and Nostalgia in Western Europe and the United States*, Basingstoke: Palgrave Macmillan.

Feld, S. and Basso, K., eds. (1996) *Senses of Place*, School of American Research Advanced Seminar Series, Santa Fe: School of American Research Press.

Fuller, A. and Junaedi, F. (2018) 'Ultras in Indonesia: Conflict, Diversification, Activism', *Sport in Society*, 21(6), 919–931. https://doi.org/10.1080/17430437.2017.1300392.

Giddens, A. (1984) *The Constitution of Society: Outline of the Theory of Structuration*, Oakland: University of California Press.

Giulianotti, R. (2002) 'Supporters, Followers, Fans, and Flaneurs: A Taxonomy of Spectator Identities in Football', *Journal of Sport and Social Issues*, 26(1), 25–46. https://doi.org/10.1177/0193723502261003.

Győri Szabó, R. (2012) 'Identity and Soccer in Corsica', *Soccer & Society*, 13(1), 36–55. https://doi.org/10.1080/14660970.2012.627166.

Hall, M. (2015) 'Elaborating Core-Periphery Relations in Tourism', in Singh, T. (ed.) *Challenges in Tourism Research*, Bristol/Buffalo/Toronto: Channel View Publications, 162–169.

Hannerz, U. (1989) 'Culture between Center and Periphery: Toward a Macroanthropology', *Ethnos*, 54(3–4), 200–216. https://doi.org/10.1080/00141844.1989.9981392.

Harrison, D. (2015) 'Vanishing Peripheries and Shifting Centres: Structural Certainties or Negotiated Ambiguities?', in Singh, T. (ed.) *Challenges in Tourism Research*, Bristol/Buffalo/Toronto: Channel View Publications, 170–175.

Hermans, B. (2013) 'Phonological Features of Limburgian Dialects', in Hinskens, F. and Taeldeman, J. (eds.) *Language and Space: An International Handbook of Linguistic Variation. Volume 3: Dutch*, Berlin: Walter de Gruyter, 336–356.

Hodges, A. (2016) 'The Hooligan as "Internal" Other? Football Fans, Ultras Culture and Nesting Intra-orientalisms', *International Review for the Sociology of Sport*, 51(4), 410–427. https://doi.org/10.1177/1012690214526401.

Hoekstra, I. (2014) 'Koempelmentaliteit Versus 2.0', Section Voetnoot, *Regional newspaper De Limburger*, January 4.

Johnstone, B. (2013) *Speaking Pittsburghese: The Story of a Dialect*, Oxford: Oxford University Press.

Kearney, M. (1995) 'The Local and the Global: The Anthropology of Globalization and Transnationalism', *Annual Review of Anthropology*, 24, 547–565.

Keukenkampioen Divisie. (n.d.) *MVV Maastricht-Roda JC: Historisch beladen duel in Maastricht* [online], available: https://keukenkampioendivisie.nl/mvv-maastricht-roda-jc-historisch-beladen-duel-in-maastricht [Accessed on 4 December 2019].

Knotter, A. (2011) 'Regional Character and Regional Stereotypes: Some Thoughts about Their Construction in Dutch Limburg', paper presented at workshop *The Construction of Local Identities through Language and Culture*, Netherlands Institute for Advanced Study in the Humanities and Social Sciences (NIAS), December 1.

Knotter, A. (2014) 'Changing Border Regimes, Mining, and Cross-border Labor in the Dutch – Belgian – German Borderlands, 1900–1973', *Journal of Borderlands Studies*, 29(3), 375–384. https://doi.org/10.1080/08865655.2014.938969.

Knotter, A. and Mayer, D. (2015) 'Introduction', *International Review of Social History*, 60, 1–11. https://doi.org/10.1017/S0020859015000450.

Koempel.nl. (2017) *Photo of Roda JC Ultras Turning Their Backs to the Field During the City Anthem of Maastricht* [online], available: https://koempel.nl/01fotos/2017/05_mei_2017/mvv-roda%20%20i.jpg [Accessed on 4 December 2019].

Lefebvre, H. (1991) *The Production of Space*, Oxford: Blackwell Publishing.

Low, S. (2003) 'Embodied Space(s). Anthropological Theories of Body, Space, and Culture', *Space & Culture*, 6(1), 9–18. https://doi.org/10.1177/1206331202238959.

Massey, D. (2005) *For Space*, London: Sage.

McVitie, P. and Vos, Y. (n.d.) *"Wie niet springt, is een Jood" – Buitenland kijkt raar op van Nederlandse 'voetbalcultuur'* [online], available: www.goal.com/nl/news/662/specials/2015/12/08/18112612/wie-niet-springt-is-een-jood-buitenland-kijkt-raar-op-van [Accessed on 8 December 2019].

MVV. (n.d.) *Club Historie* [online], available: www.mvv.nl/mvv-maastricht/club/clubhistorie [Accessed on 4 December 2019].

NOS. (2019a) *Roda JC lijkt gered door lokale ondernemers* [online], available: https://nos.nl/artikel/2308090-roda-jc-lijkt-gered-door-lokale-ondernemers.html [Accessed on 4 December 2019].

NOS. (2019b) *MVV-supporters doneren '9 ton' aan noodlijdend Roda JC* [online], available: https://nos.nl/artikel/2286483-mvv-supporters-doneren-9-ton-aan-noodlijdend-roda-jc.html [Accessed on 4 December 2019].

Orbons, P. and Spronck, L. (2009) 'Limburgers worden Nederlanders. Een moeizaam integratieproces', in Knotter, A. (ed.) *Dit Is Limburg! Opstellen over de Limburgse identiteit*, Zwolle: Waanders Uitgevers, 33–60.

Paasi, A. (2001) 'Europe as a Social Process and Discourse. Considerations of Place, Boundaries and Identity', *European Urban and Regional Studies*, 8(1), 7–28. https://doi.org/10.1177/096977640100800102.

Pierce, J., Martin, D. and Murphy, J. (2010) 'Relational Place-making: The Networked Politics of Place', *Transactions of the Institute of British Geographers*, 36, 54–70.

Pred, A. (1985) 'The Social Becomes the Spatial, the Spatial Becomes the Social: Enclosures, Social Change and the Becoming of Places in Skåne', in Gregory, D. and Urry, J. (eds.) *Social Relations and Spatial Structures*, New York: Palgrave MacMillan, 337–365.

Schiering, R. (2008) 'Regional Identity in Schalke Football Chants', in Lavric, E., Pisak, G., Skinner, A. and Stadler, W. (eds.) *The Linguistics of Football*, Tübingen: Narr Francke Attempto Verlag GmbH, 221–232.

Schoffer, I. (1956) 'Verzuiling, een specifiek Nederlands probleem', *Sociologische gids*, 7, 121–127.

Shah, A. (2017) 'Ethnography?: Participant Observation, a Potentially Revolutionary Praxis', *HAU: Journal of Ethnographic Theory*, 7(1), 45–59. https://doi.org/10.14318/hau7.1.008.

Shobe, H. (2008) 'Place, Identity and Football: Catalonia, Catalanisme and Football Club Barcelona, 1899–1975', *National Identities*, 10(3), 329–343. https://doi.org/10.1080/14608940802249965.

Thissen, L. (2018) *Talking in and Out of Place: Ethnographic Reflections on Language, Place, and (un)belonging*, unpublished thesis (Ph.D.), Maastricht University.

Tuan, Y. (1991) 'Language and the Making of Place: A Narrative-Descriptive Approach', *Annals of the Association of American Geographers*, 81(4), 648–696.

Valentine, G., Sporton, D. and Bang Nielsen, K. (2008) 'Language Use on the Move: Sites of Encounter, Identities and Belonging', *Transactions of the Institute of British Geographers, New Series*, 33(3), 376–387.

Veer zien MVV. (n.d.) *Activiteiten and De Financieën* [online], available: www.veerzienmvv.nl/visie-en-activiteiten [Accessed on 4 December 2019].

Wall, G. (2015) 'Tourism in Peripheries', in Singh, T. (ed.) *Challenges in Tourism Research*, Bristol/Buffalo/Toronto: Channel View Publications, 180–184.

Warner, K. (2007) 'Soccer Fans, Language Politics, and the Ambivalence of Nationalism in Galicia', in Geōrgiadēs, K. (ed.) *Proceedings of 14th International Seminar of the International Olympic Academy*, Athens: Livani Publishing Organization, 320–331.

Chapter 10

Rescuing football clubs by supporters

The role and forms of social capital

Radosław Kossakowski and Mateusz Grodecki

Introduction

The issue of football fan activism has been present in research on football fandom for a considerable time (Lomax 2000). During this period it has grown to become one of the major topics in the field. Football fan activism is quite a capacious term; it refers to different endeavours of supporters, including different kinds of protests (Numerato 2018), involvement in local community issues (Totten 2015), charity and educational actions (Kossakowski 2017a; Grodecki 2018a) and broadly understood political engagement (Doidge et al. 2020). It also refers to activity undertaken by organised football supporters for the sake of their clubs. This paper proposes the term 'pro-club activism' to describe this dimension of football fan activism and to differentiate it from its other aspects. Pro-club activism usually emerges as a response to various consequences of commodification of football and progressive inequalities (Kennedy 2012, p. 410). On the one hand, it can take the form of protests against the relocation of clubs (Fitzpatrick 2013), club ownership changes (Brown 2007; Millward 2012) or changing the name of the club (Hayton et al. 2017). On the other hand, in situations when football clubs are in financial crisis or on the verge of bankruptcy, it can take the form of active engagement of their fans, including financial support (eg Lomax 2000) or even rebuilding the club altogether (Numerato 2018).

This study fits into the 'pro-club activism' dimension of football fan studies: it explores cases where Polish football supporters have rescued/rebuilt their clubs. As approached here, rescuing a club from collapse is the takeover of, or involvement in, its management by supporters in the situation of a financial crisis, a move that helped to avoid bankruptcy. Rebuilding a club, in turn, is defined here as a process whereby fans established or co-established a new entity that evoked or continued the tradition of their club. However, this analysis focuses only on those cases in which supporters were (formally or informally) responsible for rebuilding clubs. As used in this study, the term 'supporters' refers to people who define themselves as supporters of a particular club and who had not worked for it (or for football structures in general) until they became involved in the rescue/rebuilding process.

What makes Polish examples distinct from previously explored cases (mostly from the British context) is their systemic transformation background. In general, it translates into a different economic and political environment, into a lack of institutional support for football clubs and thus into a vital role of internal community resources of supporter groups. The aim of this article is to explore and analyse the various forms of mobilisation of a particular internal resource of supporter circles – social capital. We argue that social capital was crucial for these initiatives because due to the lack of external support, they were pursued using the existing (informal or formal) internal structures and networks in the world of supporters. The study of how they were used is crucial for understanding the mechanisms of rescuing/rebuilding football clubs and their effectiveness.

The paper opens with a discussion of previous research on fan activism and the concept of social capital applied in the study. The research methods section is followed by a description of three ways of using social capital by supporters aiming to rebuild their clubs. The final section presents a summary of our analysis.

The activism of football fans

As it is today, the issue of fan activism is one of the most current topics in international sociology of sport (see Martin 2007; García and Welford 2015; Hodges 2018; Numerato 2018; Cleland et al. 2018). Fans who are involved in various initiatives for the sake of the club are called 'active' (Cleland 2010), 'activists' (Kossakowski 2017a) or 'new activists' (Grodecki 2018b). These categories are mainly defined in terms of contrast to 'consumer fans' (Giulianotti 2002), whose activity is limited to the consumption of club products, the purchase of tickets and souvenirs. 'Active fans' engaging in initiatives aiming to reinforce the influence of supporters on managing the club are described as 'stakeholders' (García and Welford 2015). The 'shareholders,' in turn, are a particular category of 'stakeholders' (ibid.): they are fans who are formally involved in club governance. In this classification, joining a supporters' association (aiming to incorporate fans into management or to undertake other community actions) is the important moment of transition from a 'passive' to 'active' fan.

The emergence of supporter activism, as Jamie Cleland notes, is associated with wider social changes – that is, the transformation of the economic system from industrial to post-industrial. The result of this change was the increase in the size and importance of the middle class, which began to transform traditional working-class relations with clubs. The process was primarily related with more prosumer attitudes (creating fan magazines or websites devoted to club issues) and a growing civic involvement of supporters in issues related to clubs, apparent as the emergence of supporters' associations (Cleland 2010).

Changes in the economic system have had a great impact also on football clubs. They have undergone a gradual transformation from local (communal) institutions towards companies that are attractive in terms of investment and provide new opportunities to generate profit. The most popular clubs gained the status of 'transnational brands' (Giulianotti and Robertson 2009). In recent years, there has been a real revolution in the sphere of club ownership. Especially in England, some clubs with a great local tradition have been taken over by international companies without any ties with the local community, and sometimes even without any previous connections with football. Clubs have become corporations with global ambitions and a typical corporate structure and style of management. Many 'new managers' of football clubs have started to explore new ways of increasing revenues and potentially extracting profits from football (Millward 2012). On the other hand, the growing income from various sources (TV broadcasting rights, sponsorship deals, etc.) has been unequally distributed among clubs, which has resulted in huge financial inequalities. In consequence, sports competition on the pitch has become unequal as well. Some football clubs – in accordance with the logic of the capitalist market – could not withstand this race and faced serious financial problems, often functioning on the edge of bankruptcy. The logic of the free market (which, although present in football for several decades, has gained momentum since the 1990s) is contrary to the traditional communitarian spirit of football (especially in England), assuming that football clubs are a common asset of local communities (see Antonowicz et al. 2015). Therefore, football clubs with certain traditions and significance for the local community were supported in times of financial crisis or rebuilt by the communities of their supporters. The first case of such activity described in the literature is the English club Northampton Town. When it faced bankruptcy, it was financially supported by the Supporters Trust, an organisation founded for this purpose by the fans, who gained the right to co-manage the club in return (Lomax 2000).

What makes Polish examples distinct from previously explored cases is their systemic transformation background. It translates into a different economic and political environment, into a lack of institutional support and thus into a vital role of internal community resources of supporter groups. Until the systemic transformation, which began in 1989, all Polish sports clubs operated under the patronage of state-owned companies or public institutions (eg the police, the army). After 1989, market logic resulted in the breakup of relations particular to the socialist economic model and forced the clubs to look for other financial resources. Suffering from the lack of sufficient external resources and the inability to accommodate to the new market order, some of them declared bankruptcy. The breakup of patronage relations often stemmed from transformations of the entire economy (the collapse of many state-owned companies). The restructuring of the mines, one of the most powerful patrons in the previous system, inevitably affected the financial situation of the clubs that they supported. Other clubs, in turn, suffered from the lack of appropriate institutional solutions: they were exposed to the practices of 'wild' capitalism and eccentric owners; often merged with larger commercial enterprises, sometimes they were exploited and left to their own devices. The transformation period proved to be destructive to most sports clubs (not only football ones). The scale of this phenomenon can be illustrated by the decline in their number: out of 33,000 sports organisations active in 1988, only 11,000 operated in 1996, seven years after the change of the political system (Mańkowski 2020).

Just like the whole country, in the first years of transformation to free market economy, Polish football experienced an era of 'wild capitalism.' During this period, the first 'new owners' – mostly Polish entrepreneurs who set up their businesses in the early 1990s – started to invest in Polish clubs. One example of this unprecedented change in the first half of the 1990s (there were no clubs owned by private individuals or companies in communist times) is Sokół Pniewy, a local football club from a small town in central-western Poland. Following investments made by a 'new' Polish entrepreneur, it quickly gained promotion to the top league. Between the 1990/1991 season and its organisational collapse in 1996/1997, the club was renamed five times and even changed its location from Pniewy to Tychy (in the south of the country). Owing to financial problems, it was withdrawn from competition in 1997. Kornelia Sobczak writes that 'the story of Sokół Pniewy could be a metonymic story about the adventures of Polish clubs in the times of capitalism and chimeric owners-presidents, about ownership changes, mergers, title sponsors, buying licences, changing names, relocation, abandoning fans' (2017, p. 92).

In terms of football supporters' involvement in clubs, the decade can be characterised as quite passive. Supporter groups pursued their hooligan rivalry and did not show any interest in making an impact on structural changes in football clubs. During the first years of transformation, fans were not involved in any formalised resistance movements that would be active when clubs collapsed or were subject to organisational transformation. The first fan initiatives devoted to rebuilding clubs appeared in the early 2000s. In many cases, supporters decided to rebuild their clubs by means of grassroots activity (Kossakowski 2017b). In the early days, they most often followed the 'call to arms' scheme, as there were no institutional rules, sports associations or legal frameworks supporting such initiatives. Moreover, fans did not have any experience in managing clubs or functioning in democracy as such. Later on, the democratisation and bureaucratisation of state institutions induced the emergence of formal representation of football supporters. As a result, many groups established their supporters' associations – legal entities formed to represent the interests of the fan community. They provided essential structures for legal action and for supporting insolvent clubs. They also became the structural and legal basis for rebuilding bankrupt clubs and continuing their traditions. The latter was fostered especially by the 'democratic' experience of supporters, an important factor at play that contributed to establishing new legal entities that took over or evoked those traditions (Grodecki 2015). This clearly shows that the mobilisation and adaptation of internal structures and external networks – that is, social capital – played an enormous role in the success of initiatives aiming to rescue/rebuild clubs.

Social capital as a theoretical frame

Participation in sports organisations and competitions has been proved to foster the emergence of social capital among their members (eg Burnett 2006; Skinner et al. 2008; Tucker 2016). Such activity is also considered to be a 'school for democracy' (Putnam 1995), as it translates into engagement in other forms of civic involvement (eg Perks 2007). Therefore, sport has found its place in public policies as a tool for community building and has been explored in this function in several studies (eg Jarvie 2003; Persson 2008; Włoch and Gołdys 2015). Social capital has also been examined as a resource influencing the governance of sports organisations (Groeneveld et al. 2010), both as a factor aiding effective management (eg Numerato 2008) and in the context of abuse of institutional resources (eg Numerato and Baglioni 2012).

However, the role of sports fan communities in creating social capital and its potential for further use is still underexplored. Existing studies have demonstrated that fan communities supporting teams in various disciplines can be a source of both bridging and bonding social capital (Palmer and Thompson 2007; Phua 2012). What is more, recent studies on organised Polish supporter groups have established that the bonding form of social capital is what makes these groups so effective in different areas of social life (Grodecki 2018a, 2019). This form of social capital originally developed in the course of intergroup rivalry (involving group fights, choreographies, etc.), which created structures based on reciprocity, internal trust and organisational ability (ibid.). Then, as an internal resource, it has been effectively transferred to other spheres of social life, as can be seen in establishing formal associations, organising fund-raising and charity actions, protests, and so on. Other studies demonstrated that supporters also mobilise their private networks to provide financial support to clubs (Kossakowski 2017b) and to reduce costs in some areas of club activities (Grodecki 2018b). Therefore, skilful mobilisation of personal networks by members of supporter groups may also be a key factor for the effectiveness of their initiatives.

Considering these findings, in order to describe and explain the processes of rescuing/rebuilding football clubs by their supporters, this chapter draws on two different intellectual traditions in which social capital has been developed: the network approach and the structural approach. The former is based on network concepts of social capital derived from Pierre Bourdieu (1986). In his view, social capital is primarily an attribute of individuals; it is a potential for interaction that – in an instrumental way – can be translated into personal gain (Bourdieu 1986, p. 249) and other forms of capital. On the other hand, the 'structural' tradition was initiated by James Coleman (Coleman 1990) and continued in various interpretations by other researchers (Putnam 1993; Fukuyama 1995). In Coleman's approach, social capital is a product/property of a social structure, which involves certain specific features (including trust, reciprocity norms and their social control), which in turn promote effective cooperation of individuals for the common interest (Coleman 1990, p. 302). The strength of this concept is primarily its emphasis on the organisational aspects of social structure that promote the effectiveness of collective action for common interest. Coleman distinguishes three organisational forms of social capital: (1) 'authority relations,' referring to structures in which access to resources is entrusted to particular individual(s) by other actors; (2) 'appropriable social organisation,' describing those structures that were established for a specific purpose and that can successfully achieve other goals thanks to the creation of sufficiently large resources of social capital; and, on the other hand, (3) 'intentional social organisation,' the result of planning social structure in such a way that it creates social capital and more effectively achieves the set goals (Coleman 1990, pp. 311–313).

The form that social capital takes – that is, for what aims and how it is used – is strongly correlated with the institutional and organisational environment (eg Putnam 1993; Berman 1997; Letki 2008). Putnam observes that a democratic setting is conducive to the emergence of social capital at the macro level (society). This means that social capital is not concentrated only in small structures (usually family) but is transferred also to the public sphere (Putnam 1993). In other words, the social environment (legal regulations, institutions, culture) determines the perception of common interest – whether it is narrow, limited to small groups, or wide, extending beyond moral obligations to one's own family. It needs to be emphasised, though, that such a conceptualisation involves an implicit assessment that public aims are generally more positive and therefore considered more desirable (Woolcock 1998). To avoid this, our analysis is situated beyond the public-private good controversy, and thus, it does not situate football clubs in this dichotomy. Rather, rebuilding/rescuing a football club is defined as a collective aim that mobilisation of social capital – as one of internal resources – makes possible to achieve.

Social capital is thus an internal resource embedded both in the social environment (Coleman 1990) and in social networks (Bourdieu 1986), whose presence determines organisational efficiency and the potential to mobilise other resources. It is a key attribute that determines the possibilities of achieving specific goals. This is important because, as we have already mentioned, in the case of Poland, most initiatives aiming to rebuild/rescue football clubs were pursued by already existing informal and formal groups of supporters who had to rely on their internal resources (unlike, for instance, in Britain, where the government organisation Supporters Direct was established to support fan initiatives, see Martin 2007). This is why research on how social capital was used seems to be extremely important for understanding the success of supporters' initiatives aiming to rescue clubs.

Methods of data gathering

The findings presented here are based on a pilot qualitative study aiming to explore the phenomenon of rescuing/rebuilding football clubs by supporters in Poland. The objective was to identify all cases in which Polish football clubs had been rescued/rebuilt by their fans after 1989 and to establish details that would help to describe the process. In order to achieve these aims, we relied on desk research and re-analysis of semi-structured interviews. They were analysed in order to gather data that would make it possible to (1) map such cases; (2) reconstruct the general economic, structural and institutional background of each case; and (3) indicate the mechanism that contributed to the success of football supporters.

Specific information on the process of rescuing/rebuilding clubs was collected using a mix of sources, including: (1) the fanzine *To My Kibice* ('It's Us, Fans,' published monthly since 2002); (2) press articles from sports media and sports web portals, club websites; (3) interviews with 15 supporters of six clubs that had been rescued/rebuilt by their fans, conducted in previous research projects: Odra Opole, Widzew Łódź, Lechia Gdańsk, Hutnik Kraków, Chrobry Głogów, ŁKS Łódź. It is important to note that the cases of rescuing/rebuilding football clubs by supporters had taken place at different times and under different circumstances. Thus, we used different sources of data and applied a purposive sampling strategy. We examined these sources for specific articles, reports or statements concerning the issue and providing any information on the analysed process.

The initial analysis revealed the vital role of internal resources and different strategies of their mobilisation. The concept of social capital was applied as a theoretical frame providing an adequate explanation and interpretation of supporters' actions in this respect. As a result, it was possible to distinguish and provide a detailed description of three forms of mobilisation of supporters' social capital. All of them are investigated in the following sections.

Three ways of rebuilding clubs by fans

The results of our analysis indicate that Polish fans have rescued or rebuilt 18 football clubs. On the basis of preliminary analyses of each of these cases, we have distinguished three basic mechanisms of mobilising the social capital of supporters. Each form of social capital mobilisation will be illustrated by one case. For the analysis, we have selected the most typical cases, those that exemplify each mechanism of mobilisation of resources most fully.

Call to arms

The first form of use of supporters' social capital is characterised by reactivity and spontaneous rather than planned action. Fans react to the current problems of the club (eg they organise transport for players, raise funds for bonuses for footballers, etc.) almost exclusively based on the internal resources of their environment, with a more important role of personal networks than of organised structural forms. It is a commonly known strategy, as it mobilises fans' resources in a spontaneous, informal way. There are many examples of such actions across Europe. In one of them, supporters of Bohemians Prague collected 102,000 euros to prevent the collapse of their club (Numerato 2017). In the case of Real Oviedo, in turn, each fan could buy a share in the club at the price of 10.75 euros in order to save it from bankruptcy; after a few days from the official announcement, fans bought shares worth 750,000 euros (Wilson 2012). In Polish cases, however, this strategy has not been limited only to fund-raising; it went much further.

One great illustration of this form of mobilisation of social capital is the story of the collapse of Lechia Gdańsk. Today, the club competes in the top division and plays in a modern arena built for the UEFA Euro 2012. However, the road to this success was a hard one, with many failures on the way. In 1989, the year that marked the beginning of Polish transformation, Lechia was relegated from the First League (level 1 at the time), which was to be only the first step on a slippery slope. In the early 1990s, a new company set up to run the club failed to meet expectations, and Lechia found itself in the Third League. Hopes for a revival came with mergers, first with Olimpia Poznań football club and then with Polonia Gdańsk. Those initiatives also failed. Relegation to the Third League, instead of the expected promotion to the Ekstraklasa, was a major blow.

In 2001, the club broke up its association with Polonia: Lechia was left only with the football team, a few coaches working on a voluntary basis, and a group of talented young players. Following the decision of the Polish Football Association, the club joined the competitions in the sixth level of the league system. With practically no financial resources available, even paying for a coach trip to away games was a problem. Under the circumstances, the supporters started to drive players in their own cars. The number of Lechia supporters at away matches was unprecedented for this level of competition nationwide (most games took place in local rural area around Gdańsk).

The club urgently needed financial resources for its current activities, because the immediate help of the most engaged supporters did not guarantee stability. Some stories have become a legend: wealthy supporters – local entrepreneurs – brought plastic bags with cash so that the club could pay for renting the pitch or buy jerseys for players. One of the fans recalled this as follows:

> We had a fan who was a big baker in Gdańsk. When things got really bad, we used to call him to ask for help and he brought money in a bag. Once, it was as much as 20,000 złotys.
>
> (Lechia Gdańsk, personal interview)

The chaotic, 'all aboard' form of mobilisation of individual networks and resources took a more organised form. Trying to rescue the club, local supporter circles established an organisation called 'White and Green' Lechia Gdańsk Supporters' Association (*Stowarzyszenie Kibiców Lechii Gdańsk 'Biało-Zieloni'*). The fans alerted the local authorities to the tragic situation of the club. They stood up for the 2002 local elections as 'Come on Lechia' (*Naprzód Lechio!*) movement, which received 3.14% of votes, thus failing to pass the 5% threshold, but coming to the attention of Gdańsk authorities. In a meeting with fans, the mayor of Gdańsk, Paweł Adamowicz, promised help and financial assistance to the club (he kept his promise until his tragic death in January 2018). Supporters officially supported the mayor in the following local elections.

As a result of fan involvement, three representatives of supporters were appointed as members of the managing board in 2003. Fans helped to clean the stadium and joined the security team, which meant that the club had their organisational assistance and was able to make some savings. In the same year, one of the most engaged fans (a well-known local entrepreneur today) became the managing director of the club. In 2008, Lechia management (including representatives of supporters as board members) and the city council decided to set up a limited company with the council as a majority shareholder. The move meant that the club had a guarantee of financial stability and met formal requirements for a football licence. This made it possible to attract new investors. The club won successive promotions to higher divisions, reaching the level of Ekstraklasa in 2008. Lechia moved to a new stadium with a capacity of 44,000. In 2014, the majority of shares was taken over by a German-Swiss consortium. Lechia gained momentum when it won the Polish Cup, took the third place in the Ekstraklasa and played in European cup games for the first time since 1983.

Appropriable social organisation

Based on the typology of organisational forms proposed by Coleman (1990), this form of mobilisation of social capital refers to structures established for a specific task that have generated a sufficiently large amount of social capital during its implementation and can thus be used also for other purposes. In the case of football fan activism, this form is characterised by the use of existing supporters' associations – legal entities established to represent the interests of the supporters' community in other tasks. This was, for instance, observed in the case of Hajduk Split, where fans used their association (called 'Our Hajduk') to put political pressure on local authorities and to become the second-largest official club shareholder (after the city council, see Glaurdić 2019). These organisations can provide fans with the structural basis for rescuing/rebuilding clubs. In this model, supporters mostly use internal resources, networks and organisational skills and combine their roles of fans and club managers. In the Polish context, one case in point is Odra Wodzisław.

It is a club with a rich history, which will celebrate its centenary in 2022. In 1996–2010, Odra played at the top level of competition, and in the 1996/1997 season, it took the third place in the Polish Ekstraklasa. In 2010, despite contracting many famous players, the club was relegated to the First League, which – as it turned out – was the beginning its serious problems. In the following season, due to financial reasons, Odra was relegated again (to the Second League) and was refused licence to enter the competition. The indebted club was put into bankruptcy. A new entity was created in its place – KP Odra 1922 Wodzisław; its organisation was taken care of by fans, represented by Odra Wodzisław Supporters' Association, founded in 2008, when Odra still played in the Ekstraklasa. The club run by fans started from playing in Class C (level 9, 2011/2012 season). Following a merger with Start Bogdanowice, Odra returned to the Third League; the name was changed to Odra Wodzisław Śląski, and the club was transformed into a limited company. In 2014, after relegation to the Fourth League, it was refused licence to play. As a result, the well-deserved club disappeared from the football map of Poland for the entire 2014/2015 season.

It is worth mentioning that for over a year the fans struggled not only with the Silesian Regional Football Association but also with local municipal authorities, which hindered the functioning of the club they rescued. Consequently, the club could not play in its own stadium for two years. In Wodzisław, the situation was doubly complicated because apart from the club run by fans, there is also another club, called MKS Odra Centrum Wodzisław; although it focuses on training children and youth, it also has a senior team. The authorities of this club were not interested in cooperation with the club run by fans. As a result, there are currently two football clubs in Wodzisław playing in the same division (Fourth League): MKP Odra Centrum and MKS Odra (with the supporters' association as a majority shareholder). The former receives greater support from local municipal authorities. Problems with the external environment were mentioned by one of the supporters of MKS Odra:

> We have problems because we're not part of the system. We are not like those old guys who have their posts in local football . . . and we don't have any connections. The town hall is very unfriendly to us, to say the least. We get all sorts of inspections all the time and we have practically no support, and our rivals have jobs in municipal institutions or schools for their activists and they have connections everywhere.
>
> (*To My Kibice* 2017, p. 48)

Great differences in views on the role of fans can be seen in the statements of the president of MKP Odra Centrum and the president of MKS Odra, respectively:

MKP ODRA CENTRUM: We don't like what sometimes happens in the other Odra; there were flares fired recently. Fans shouldn't take responsibility for managing a club.

MKS ODRA: We feel heirs to the tradition of Odra, although there is actually no legal continuity. This Odra is run by fans for fans. We work mainly as volunteers. The MKP [the other Odra club, ed. authors] receives support from the town hall, and we have fans. People say that one Odra is municipal and the other is fan-based. We have the support of fans who cheered this team in the Ekstraklasa.

(Łączy nas Piłka 2018)[1]

The case of the fan-based Odra (MKS) shows the importance of supporters' resources in the absence of help from important external actors. MKS Odra fans have organised many actions to support their club, such as internet fundraisers, the 'One Odra for Wodzisław' action (held in 2016 in the presence of the mayor of the town), the poster campaign called 'No way out if they got clout' (*Na układy nie ma rady*) and the campaign promoting season tickets called #action attendance.

The case of Wodzisław indicates that without the existing organisational resources (an association), initiatives aiming to revive the club would have been extremely difficult, and probably completely ineffective, especially given that there is another club in the town and that it has the ambition to gain the sympathies of local residents.

Intentional social organisation

Intentional social organisation is also based on an organisational form of using social capital (Coleman 1990). It refers to structures established in order to effectively achieve specific objectives. In the context of mobilising social capital to rebuild/rescue clubs, this form refers to cases where fans have established a new legal entity – most often an association – which has taken over or evokes the tradition of the club. These structures were created solely for the purpose of managing the club. In this model, supporters selected from their environment (broadly understood as the whole community of supporters of the club) people who had the skills required to manage the club.

Setting up a supporters' association is the most widespread form of institutionalisation of fans' activities aimed at rescuing/rebuilding their club. This path was followed, for example, by supporters of Sambenedettese Calcio in Italy (Croci 2017). Fans of Bohemians Prague raised funds for the rescue of their club and established a cooperative called *Družstvo fanoušků Bohemians*. Apart from paying off the debt of the club, the organisation also aimed to secure rights to the use of its symbols (Numerato 2017). Another form – particularly important in the UK – is supporters' trusts. In general, the idea behind most of these organisations is to increase fans' influence, especially when clubs face a difficult financial situation (Martin 2007). In some cases, supporters' trusts own and fully manage the clubs, while in others, they operate as a communication platform between the club and the fans (Cleland et al. 2018). Unlike in Britain, football supporters in Poland did not have any external institutional support or a framework that would provide assistance to their initiatives (as mentioned in previous sections of the chapter).

One typical example illustrating this form of mobilisation is the case of Hutnik Kraków. The history of the club is inseparably linked to Nowa Huta, a district of Kraków that takes its name from the steelworks (*huta* in Polish) built there by communist authorities in 1949. The Hutnik sports club was established following the initiative of its employees. Thanks to state funding, in its heyday, it had as many as 20 different sports sections. The greatest period of the Hutnik football team was the mid-1990s, when they played in the Ekstraklasa for seven consecutive seasons. In 1996, they won the third place, which qualified them for the UEFA Cup (where they played against such teams as Monaco). Paradoxically, the best season in the history of Hutnik marked the beginning of its demise (Gliksman 2010). Nowa Huta steelworks, the main sponsor, was privatised, but the state authorities did not make provisions obliging the new owner to support the club. Hutnik management had become used to the assistance of the former sponsor and were not able to stand up to the new situation. In consequence, the club went down the hill in the league system. In the middle of the 2009/2010 season, it turned out that the players had not been paid for months and the club was six million złotys (about 1.5 million euros) in debt. The supporters had made some donations to the budget even before: they sponsored bonuses for the players (as it turned out in 2010, it was the only money received by the team members), bought equipment for junior teams, sponsored longer away trips and even arranged a flat for a foreign player. All this was done without any formal representation in the management of the club.

In 2010, supporters lost their trust in the club authorities: they decided to take matters into their own hands, and they established a new association called 'New Hutnik 2010' (*Nowy Hutnik 2010*), which ran a boycott of the matches played by the team. As a result, the old Hutnik disintegrated, and the fans entered a new club in the competition. Although it was meant to continue the old traditions, the new name, Hutnik Nowa Huta, stressed its local character. One of the supporters explained: 'Hutnik has always been a club that belongs here in Nowa Huta. Whatever level of the league we play in and whatever match turnout there is, Hutnik has always been and will always remain a showpiece of this district' (*Hutnik Nowa Huta* 2012, p. 46). The regional football association accepted the team for the Fourth League competition (level 5). Today, a decade since it was established, the club plays in the Third League and is still managed by the fans' association. Its former deputy president, and a founding member of the association, recalled the difficulties of the early days as follows:

> It was a really difficult thing to do and even today it's hard to believe that we managed to do so much. . . . It was an association which had just started, which had no resources, which had only begun to accept its first members. The task ahead was really hard: for an association like that, it was quite a challenge to maintain the team in the Fourth League. Even more so, that the financial expectations of footballers are quite high even in the lower leagues, a fact that tends to be overlooked. Apart from this, there were also the costs of hiring a stadium and a training pitch, and buying the equipment. It's quite easy to calculate, we had to spend a few thousand złotys just on the equipment. So, we ran up expenses and we had to finance the junior team on top of that. It was our success that we got people interested and they were generous with their money. And we really did manage to join the competition and, after two years, win promotion to the Third League, which meant a return to the level the old Hutnik had played when it collapsed.
>
> (Hutnik Kraków, personal interview)

The idea of a new club was accepted by the local community: over 2,000 fans turned up at the 60th anniversary of the club in July 2010 (a friendly match with 1. FC Magdeburg) and the figure for away matches in the league has sometimes been as high as 600. For four years, the supporters have had to prove their own value to themselves and, even more so, to the world in general and the football and local authorities in particular. One of the fans commented:

> In general, the old-style football associations look askance at young, energetic people who want to change something, to promote development and innovation. . . . We don't have any backup or informal connections, so we have to achieve everything ourselves. Of course, they look at us as hard-core fans, but it gives us even more boost. We just have to be even more diligent, trustworthy and competent.
>
> (*To My Kibice* 2012, p. 46)

The club receives support from local sponsors, often small entrepreneurs, and membership fees in the *Nowy Hutnik 2010* association are an important position in the budget. The entire management team (the board of the association is at the same time the board of the club) work on a voluntary basis, and their main principle is not to overspend. Running an own club stimulates a kind of reflexive approach to fandom:

> Of course, the approach of a supporter who is an executive and a supporter who is a fan will never be exactly the same. Still, we think that even when you run your own club, take responsibility for it and want it to move on as high as possible, you can keep up your independent approach with a touch of a wild spirit. It can all be negotiated. We have all known everyone around here very well for years and we can notice there is a will to come to an agreement and to work together for the glory of Hutnik.
>
> (*To My Kibice* 2012, p. 47)

The management of the club is composed of fans and meets with the rest of supporters for consultations. The executive board is elected from among members of the association.

Since 2016, the club has been operating under its traditional name – Hutnik Kraków. As it is today, fans no longer have to struggle with the burden of the past, but are developing the club. In 2017, the city of Kraków provided the association with funding for an artificial pitch, which came as a sign of commitment to fan activism. Hutnik is the operator of its stadium; the club has also reactivated the handball section.

Conclusions

Our analysis has revealed three different forms of social capital mobilisation by football supporters in order to rescue/rebuild their football clubs. Each of them has been illustrated by one case: call to arms by Lechia Gdańsk; appropriable social organisation by Odra Wodzisław; intentional social organisation by Hutnik Kraków. Each of these forms is based on a different dimension of the use of social capital. Call to arms refers to spontaneous and reactive use of mostly individual social networks. Appropriable social organisation involves the use of existing supporters' associations, in the frame of which supporters rely mainly on internal resources, networks and organisational skills and combine their roles of fans and club managers. Intentional social organisation involves building new formal structures designed only to manage clubs, whereby supporters with appropriate management skills are elected to the board of the club.

These forms developed in the process of mobilisation of internal resources of supporters' community in the context of a lack of institutional support for football clubs during the transformation period. On the other hand, the distinctive features of the Polish fan world – its inaccessibility, strong internal rivalry and lack of trust towards 'others' – seem to rule out any external aid based on enforced organisation. However, an extremely high social cohesion and a strong sense of brotherhood in this world (Kossakowski et al. 2020) have facilitated collective action and mobilisation of social capital to pursue objectives related to commonly accepted principles, which the survival of a club fits perfectly. Its demise can be devastating to supporters' identity and to the local community, as can be seen from the recent case of Bury FC (Beal 2020).

These three forms of social capital also have another common feature: they have been built upon spontaneous relations and identities developed in the course of intergroup rivalry. Originally, social capital (strong relations and group cohesion) only enabled chaotic collective mobilisation of individual networks with a view to pursuing common goals. Later on, democratisation and bureaucratisation of the public sphere forced supporters to establish official associations – the next, and more advanced step of organisation. The emergence of associations as a response to the new democratic order fits in with well-established explanations according to which the way of using social capital is strongly connected to the wider institutional setting (eg Putnam 1993; Fukuyama 1995; Woolcock 1998; Letki 2008). However, what made these associations effective in their rebuilding/rescue efforts (both in the case of those already in place and those established for the purpose) was the adaptation of existing informal structures based on reciprocity, internal trust and organisational ability (Coleman 1990) – in other words, on bonding social capital established in the course of intergroup rivalry. Moreover, these associations were strictly limited to internal human resources of fan circles – no external actors were allowed to be involved in the decision-making process. These characteristics, combined with the mobilisation of individual networks, made internal resources of supporter groups sufficient to rescue/rebuild their football clubs.

The typology presented in this article – based on a combined, two-dimensional (individual and structural) approach of social capital – is an analytical tool that can be useful in research on the process of mobilisation of internal resources of supporter circles in their struggle to rescue/rebuild football clubs. Its particular value lies in its analytical potential: it can reveal how supporters' communities mobilised their internal resources to cope with the reality without any assistance from the state.

Note

1 www.laczynaspilka.pl/rozgrywki2/nizsze-ligi/nizsze-ligi-odra-wodzislaw-ktora-trafila-na-meandry (accessed 11.07.2020).

References

Antonowicz, D., Kossakowski, R., and Szlendak, T. (2015). *Aborygeni i Konsumenci. O kibicowskiej wspólnocie, komercjalizacji futbolu i stadionowym apartheidzie*. Warszawa: Wydawnictwo IFiS PAN.

Beal, T. (2020). *Bury FC: The Football Fans without a Team*. Available at: www.bbc.com/news/stories-51134707 (accessed 1 May 2020).

Berman, S. (1997). Civil society and the collapse of the Weimar Republic. *World Politics* 49(3): 401–429.

Bourdieu, P. (1986). The forms of capital. In: J. Richardson (ed.), *Handbook of Theory and Research for the Sociology of Education*. New York: Greenwood.

Brown, A. (2007). 'Not for sale'? The destruction and reformation of football communities in the Glazer Takeover of Manchester United. *Soccer and Society* 8(4): 614–635.

Burnett, C. (2006). Building social capital through an active community club. *International Review for the Sociology of Sport* 41(3–4): 283–294.

Cleland, J. (2010). From passive to active: The changing relationship between supporters and football clubs. *Soccer & Society* 11(5): 537–552.

Cleland, J., Doidge, M., Millward, P., and Widdop, P. (2018). *Collective Action and Football Fandom: A Relational Sociological Approach*. Basingstoke: Palgrave Macmillan.

Coleman, J.S. (1990). *Foundations of Social Theory*. Cambridge, MA and London: Harvard University Press.

Croci, O. (2017). Football supporters' trusts in Italy: A horizontal survey and the case of sambenedettese. In: B. Garcia and J. Zheng (eds.), *Football and Supporter Activism in Europe. Whose Game Is It?* Basingstoke: Palgrave Macmillan.

Doidge, M., Kossakowski, R., and Mintert, S. (2020). *Ultras. The Passion and Performance of Contemporary Football Fandom*. Manchester: Manchester University Press.

Fitzpatrick, C. (2013). The struggle for grassroots involvement in football club governance: experiences of a supporter-activist. *Soccer & Society* 14(2): 201–214.

Fukuyama, F. (1995). *Trust: The Social Virtues and the Creation of Prosperity*. New York: Free Press.

García, B., and Welford, J. (2015). Supporters and football governance, from customers to stakeholders: A literature review and agenda for research. *Sport Management Review* 18(4): 517–528.

Giulianotti, R. (2002). Supporters, followers, fans and flaneurs: A taxonomy of spectator identities in football. *Journal of Sport and Social Issues* 26(1): 25–46.

Giulianotti, R., and Robertson, R. (2009). *Globalization and Football*. London: Sage.

Glaurdić, J. (2019). Football activism as political contention: Contextual determinants of membership in the association of supporters of Hajduk Split. *International Review for the Sociology of Sport* 55(7). https://doi.org/10.12690219889565.

Gliksman, A. (2010). Historia Hutnika Kraków. *Suche Stawy* 13(1): 8–11.

Grodecki, M. (2015). The third side of the stands. Activity of supporter trusts in Poland. *Miscellanea Anthropologica et Sociologica* 16(4): 100–115.

Grodecki, M. (2018a). *Życie po meczu. Formy wykorzystania kapitału społecznego kibiców piłkarskich w Polsce*. Warszawa: Wydawnictwa Uniwersytetu Warszawskiego.

Grodecki, M. (2018b). Nowi aktywiści. Polski ruch 'socios' jako nowa forma relacji kibiców z klubem. *Przegląd Socjologii Jakościowej* 14(2): 30–49.

Grodecki, M. (2019). Building social capital: Polish football supporters through the lens of James Coleman's conception. *International Review for the Sociology of Sport* 54(4): 459–478.

Groeneveld, M., Houlihan, B., and Ohl, F. (2010). *Social Capital and Sport Governance in Europe*. New York: Routledge.

Hayton, J.W., Millward, P., and Petersen-Wagner, R. (2017). Chasing a Tiger in a network society? Hull City's proposed name change in the pursuit of China and East Asia's new middle class consumers. *International Review for the Sociology of Sport* 52(3): 279–298.

Hodges, A. (2018). *Fan Activism, Protest and Politics: Ultras in Post-Socialist Croatia*. Abingdon: Routledge.

Jarvie, G. (2003). Communitarianism, sport and social capital: Neighbourly insights into Scottish sport. *International Review for the Sociology of Sport* 38(2): 139–153.

Kennedy, P. (2012). Supporters Direct and supporters' governance of football: A model for Europe? *Soccer & Society* 13(3): 409–425.

Kossakowski, R. (2017a). *Od chuliganów do aktywistów. Polscy kibice i zmiana społeczna*. Kraków: Universitas.

Kossakowski, R. (2017b). From the bottom to the premiership: The significance of supporters' movement in the governance of football clubs in Poland. In: B. Garcia and J. Zheng (eds.), *Football and Supporter Activism in Europe. Whose Game Is It?* Basingstoke: Palgrave Macmillan.

Kossakowski, R., Antonowicz, D., and Jakubowska, H. (2020). The reproduction of hegemonic masculinity in football fandom. An analysis of the performance of Polish ultras. In: R. Magrath, J. Clelenad, and E. Anderson (eds.), *The Palgrave Handbook of Masculinity and Sport*. London: Palgrave Macmillan.

Łączy nas Piłka. (2018). *Odra Wodzisław, która trafiła na meandry*. Available at: www.laczynaspilka.pl/rozgrywki2/nizsze-ligi/nizsze-ligi-odra-wodzislaw-ktora-trafila-na-meandry (accessed 11 November 2018).

Letki, N. (2008). Does diversity erode social cohesion? Social capital and race in British neighbourhoods. *Political Studies* 56(1): 99–126.

Lomax, B. (2000). Democracy and fandom: Developing a supporters' trust at Northampton town FC. *Soccer and Society* 1(1): 79–87.

Mańkowski, D. (2020). *Społeczne czynniki upadku i trwania klubów sportowych w okresie transformacji ustrojowej w Polsce*. Unpublished PhD thesies. Gdańsk: University of Gdańsk.

Martin, P. (2007). Football, community and cooperation: A critical analysis of supporter trusts in England. *Soccer & Society* 8(4): 636–653.

Millward, P. (2012). Reclaiming the Kop? Analysing Liverpool supporters' 21st century mobilizations. *Sociology* 46(4): 633–648.

Numerato, D. (2008). Czech sport governing bodies and social capital. *International Review for the Sociology of Sport* 43(1): 21–34.

Numerato, D. (2017). Between civic engagement and politics: A case study of bohemians prague 1905 supporters' trust. In: B. Garcia and J. Zheng (eds.), *Football and Supporter Activism in Europe. Whose Game Is It?* Basingstoke: Palgrave Macmillan.

Numerato, D. (2018). *Football Fans, Activism and Social Change*. Abingdon: Routledge.
Numerato, D., and Baglioni, S. (2012). The dark side of social capital: An ethnography of sport governance. *International Review for the Sociology of Sport* 47(5): 594–611.
Palmer, C., and Thompson, K. (2007). The paradoxes of football spectatorship: On-field and online expressions of social capital among the 'Grog Squad'. *Sociology of Sport Journal* 24(2): 187–205.
Perks, T. (2007). Does sport foster social capital? The contribution of sport to a lifestyle of community participation. *Sociology of Sport Journal* 24(4): 378–401.
Persson, H.T.R. (2008). Social capital and social responsibility in Denmark: More than gaining public trust. *International Review for the Sociology of Sport* 43(1): 35–51.
Phua, J. (2012). Use of social networking sites by sports fans: Implications for the creation and maintenance of social capital. *Journal of Sports Media* 7(1): 109–132.
Putnam, R. (1993). *Making Democracy Work: Civic Traditions in Modern Italy*. Princeton: Princeton University Press.
Putnam, R. (1995). *Bowling Alone: An Interview with Robert Putnam about America's Collapsing Civic Life*. American Association for Higher Education. Available at: xroads.virginia.edu/~hyper/DETOC/assoc/aahe.html (accessed 4 May 2020).
Skinner, J., Zakus, D., and Edwards, A. (2008). Development through sport: Building social capital in disadvantaged communities. *Sport Management Review* 11(3): 394–404.
Sobczak, K. (2017). W składzie węgla i papy. Cudowne lata dziewięćdziesiąte polskiej piłki nożnej. *Kultura Współczesna* 94(1): 89–103.
To My Kibice. (2012). Hutnik Nowa Huta. *To My Kibice* 6(129): 46–48.
To My Kibice. (2017). MKS Odra Wodzisław. *To My Kibice* 2(185): 46–49.
Totten, M. (2015). Sport activism and political praxis within the FC Sankt Pauli fan subculture. *Soccer & Society* 16(4): 453–468. https://doi.org/10.1080/14660970.2014.882828
Tucker, L. (2016). The football club: Spaces for capital accumulation. *Soccer & Society* 17(4): 555–570.
Wilson, J. (2012). *Fans try to save Spanish football club Real Oviedo from bankruptcy*. Available at: www.independent.co.uk/sport/football/european/fans-try-to-save-spanish-football-club-real-oviedo-from-bankruptcy-8307125.html (accessed 4 May 2020).
Włoch, R., and Gołdys, A. (2015). The transformation of the public sports policy: Politics, grassroots management and social capital of the Orlik programme in Poland. *Miscellanea Anthropologica et Sociologica* 16(4): 31–45.
Woolcock, M. (1998). Social capital and economic development: Toward a theoretical synthesis and policy framework. *Theory and Society* 27(2): 151–208.

Chapter 11

The political economy of grassroots football

From obscurity to austerity

Daniel Parnell, Danny Fitzpatrick, Anthony May and Paul Widdop

Introduction

On a pleasant enough evening in early Autumn (15 September 2008), a football match was being played between two of England's historic clubs on the site of one of London's oldest and most famous stadiums, White Hart Lane. Tottenham Hotspur were the hosts, welcoming Aston Villa. The victors that night were Aston Villa, beating the home team 2–1. By the end of the night, the world was on the brink of an economic disaster. Indeed, New York City was waking up to the news that one of the world's largest banks, Lehman's, had filed for bankruptcy with $639 billion in assets and $619 billion of debt (Corelli, 2019). This set in motion a cascading domino effect, as bank after bank collapsed under the weight of debt. Entire national economies failed, and many experienced suffering as a result of mortgage foreclosures, job layoffs and the decimation of pension funds and savings accounts (Peck, Theodore, and Brenner, 2010). The fallout saw the world teetering on the brink of a deep recession and resulted in the imposition of austerity policies by the governments of many of the world's largest economies (Parnell et al., 2019; Webber, 2018).

Much has happened in the 12 years since Tottenham Hotspur faced Aston Villa. The United Kingdom (UK) has experienced more than a decade of fiscal austerity and has left the European Union, the consequences of which appear unlikely to be positive for many of the it's poorest citizens. Meanwhile, the wealthiest English Premier League (EPL) clubs have spent heavily, seemingly insulated from the impacts of austerity by the wealth of their billionaire owners (Webber, 2018). Despite the spending power of a few elite clubs, the grassroots of the game is struggling with the burden of austerity, and the trickle-down economic tap has failed to permeate down the lower echelons of the game (Parnell et al., 2019). To that end, this chapter aims to address a gap in the literature on grassroots football. It has a geographical focus on the English game. The authors acknowledge this narrow perspective may reinforce the tendency towards ethnocentrism and English exceptionalism in writing about the history of football (Mason, 2011). Nevertheless, the following is intended to provide an analysis of the governance and political economy of the grassroots game in England, up to the emergence of the COVID-19 pandemic. This will serve as a departure point for further study, including comparative research.

Given that the gaze of the global media is increasingly fixed on the narrow stratum of elite professional football, it is easy to forget that football continues to be an activity and 'source of invigoration in the social lives of millions of people' (Kennedy and Kennedy, 2016: 497). As Walvin (2001: 215) expounds:

> *There is another football story to tell; about ordinary, run-of-the-mill football, about boys in the park schoolchildren driven to games by their parents, older men (long past their prime) struggling on bleary-eyed Sunday mornings to recapture their footballing best, and millions more simply kicking a ball against a wall.*

This 'massive, incalculable substratum of popular football' has been left largely unexamined by academic research. Although scholarship on football is now well established (Giulianotti and Robertson, 2009; Chadwick et al., 2019), this literature has invariably focused on the elite professional level in terms of its governance and/or spectatorship. Despite the growing body of critical academic research on the political economy of football, the grassroots level has been 'ignored almost without exception' (O'Gorman, 2011: 5). The study of grassroots football has tended to fall between two stools: the burgeoning interest in the commercialisation of the professional game and the research into the wider participation and health benefits of various types of football. More recently, there has been increased interest in junior grassroots football from a policy perspective (Pitchford, 2007; O'Gorman, 2011), with particular attention focused on the impact of the respect agenda (Cleland, O'Gorman, and Bond, 2015), child welfare and safeguarding and equality and diversity (Lusted, 2014). Additionally, there has been an emergence of studies that use grassroots football as the primary unit of study, exploring a wider range of sociological topics, such as race and discrimination (Kilvington and Price, 2013) and even the sound of grassroots football (Sound Diaries, 2020). Notwithstanding this contemporary interest, the study of grassroots football from a socio-political perspective remains woefully underdeveloped.

The paucity of academic research belies the prominent position of grassroots football in the cultural life and leisure of contemporary Britain. Approximately 8.2 million people – one in five adults – play football in some form (FA, 2015); 1.8 million do so on a weekly basis (Sport England, 2016b). Despite the popularity of the sport at grassroots level, it is surprising how little research has actually been conducted into the sub-culture(s) of grassroots football. This seems ever more anomalous, given the 'everyday turn' in the social sciences and the interest of sociologists and political scientists in the seemingly trivial phenomena of normal life (Sztompka, 2008). Even where there has been a deliberate attempt to shift research focus to the mundane and everyday nature of people's cultural participation beyond the orthodox arenas of 'legitimate culture' (such as museums, galleries and exhibitions), this has tended to neglect grassroots football. Where sport has been included, the focus has been on more 'marginal' sporting activity, such as martial arts, gymnastics and synchronised swimming. As such, the contribution of grassroots football to communities has generally fallen outside the purview of research councils and bodies, such as the Arts and Humanities Research Council. This is ironic, given the cultural significance of football and its relationship to self-reflection and identity.

What is grassroots football?

One of the key issues with the current research on grassroots football is definitional. The phrase is oft cited, but rarely explicitly defined. It is applied to a wide range of football, from games played and watched informally in improvised spaces, such as a street corner or park, all the way through to established non-league clubs competing in the national league (Kerrigan, 2014). Each of these levels is appealed to at different times, by different people, as the essence of 'real' or 'proper' football. Indeed, the concept is quite vague. This may be one significant reason behind the relative lack of published research into grassroots football.

Perhaps more than any other sport, football is characterised, and often caricatured, by the impromptu nature of its play in places and circumstances that were not designed for it. The ingenuity of football games, in the face of a lack of proper facilities, is celebrated in the global cultures of football: from Maradona's 'keep-ups' with oranges and tennis balls to the cliché of 'jumpers for goalposts' (Amis, Slack, and Hinings, 2004). Indeed, the apparent loss of these street games in the UK is lamented and attributed to the demise of home-grown talent almost as frequently, and somewhat paradoxically, as the failure to invest in facilities and coaching. Arguably, the most gifted English player of his generation, Wayne Rooney, was venerated as 'the last of the street footballers,' implying that at least a part of his precocious genius was derived from the football he played in the streets of Croxteth in Liverpool, as much as the coaching instruction he received as an Everton academy prospect from the age of nine. Such is the romanticism of the street footballer, and indeed, its myth has seen some more professional footballing bodies seek to replicate the grassroots street environment, albeit in a sanitised way.

Part of the ambivalence surrounding what constitutes the 'grassroots' is derived from its elision with 'amateur' football. Although they are seen as interchangeable in contemporary usage, the political and social history of football reveals fierce contestation about their meaning and significance. The ideal of the amateur is inextricably linked to the development of the sport and the internecine struggle between the ancient universities and public schools on one side and the emergent professional clubs, players and supporting industrial interests on the other. It is important to note that it was only in 1974 that the FA abolished the distinction between professionals and amateurs, thereby denoting all participants as simply 'players.'

Whether formally organised in a league structure or more impromptu and recreational, grassroots football can be seen as an example of collective consumption (Castells, 1977) – it is consumed by a group or the entire community rather than individuals and relies on (indirect) state provision, through subsidies and regulation. Conventionally, the market has played little to no role in grassroots football, although these dynamics are shifting, especially given its perceived power to generate social capital and other social benefits (Parnell and Richardson, 2014). From the perspective discussed by Castells (1977), sport can be seen as part of the extended reproduction of labour power through the provision of public facilities and green space to ensure healthy, skilled and socialised workers and the long-term interest of the capitalist economy as a whole.

What is the politics of grassroots football?

The importance of football, as the national game, for understanding wider patterns of politics and power in British society is largely ignored in the political science and public policy literature (Houlihan, Bloyce, and Smith, 2009). Football is not an isolated sphere of activity, but as King (2010: 890) observes, 'a public ritual [that] is deeply embedded into the wider institutional and political realities of which it is a conscious reflection and manifestation.' Before the 1960s, the state was a marginal force in the governance of sport at elite and grassroots levels. The autonomy of the governing bodies in their own sphere was treated as 'almost a sacred principle' (Wolfenden-Committee on Sport, 1960: 12).

The otherness of sport in the wider context of British politics is derived from its inception in a pre-democratic context, in which the ideal of the 'gentleman amateur' was privileged. This 'amateur ideal' was embedded in the corridors of Whitehall, where the imagery of the 'non-specialist' or 'all-rounder' resonated as much as in the clubhouses and boardrooms of British sport. Historically, the administrative elite in Britain has been disproportionately represented by men from a narrow social and educational background, particularly Oxbridge and the major public schools, which was steeped in the late Victorian belief in amateurism, in government as well as sport (Polley, 2006). What Allison (1986) refers to as the 'amateur hegemony' was manifested in the relations between the state and sport in three ways: an instinctive aversion on behalf of politicians and officials to intervene in the 'voluntarisitic fabric of British sport,' preferential treatment for the 'gentlemen amateur' (athlete, cricketer, rugby union player) over the 'unsportsmanlike behaviour' of professionals (particularly footballers) and the informal and private nature of 'official' involvement of the state in sport (Polley, 2006: 457, 461). Where the state did seek to enable participation in sport, via public bodies such as the Central Council of Physical Recreation set up in 1935, the focus was on the provision of courses to enable novices to take up new sports, such as climbing, gliding, archery or badminton rather than sports with a more developed professional identity, such as football.

The prevailing sporting and governing cultures, therefore, inhibited the development of a coherent programme of state intervention in football. Like so many other aspects of economic and social life in Britain, the experiences of World War II led to a (partial) recalibration of these dominant traditions. Football figured prominently in the rhetoric of post-war reconstruction. A series of matches were played between domestic and overseas teams as part of the Festival of Britain in 1951 (Mason, 2011). By this point, football rather than cricket, could confidently declare itself as the national game.

The creation of the Sports Council in 1965, following the recommendation of the 1960 Wolfenden Report, was designed to provide strategic direction to the aim of 'promoting the general welfare of the community' (CCPR, 1960). This reflected a shift in rhetoric and policy style, if not substance. At the heart of the establishment of the Sports Council was the egalitarian value to create equal opportunity to participate in sport and recreative activity. The agency of individual politicians and officials was also important. Denis Howell – MP for Small Heath, Birmingham, and former referee – was chosen as the first minister for sport. Howell was close to key figures in football, including Sir Stanley Rous (former FA secretary and then head of FIFA) and Walter Winterbottom (the general secretary of the CCPR and former professional football player and first full-time England manager, who would be appointed by Howell to be the first director of the Sports Council). These football administrators played a pivotal role in advising Howell and steering the state's gaze to a focus on football. Howell's appointment was instrumental in the commissioning of the first substantive inquiry into football, led by Sir Norman Chester, the first recognised football scholar. The terms of reference of the inquiry – which sought to develop the game for 'the public good' – represented a shift to a more social democratic, welfarist approach to football (Hargreaves, 1985). The report was wide ranging, covering issues that would be reprised several times thereafter, including the corporate structure of the FA, industrial relations between players and the clubs, the standard of stadium facilities, on-field discipline as well as crowd behaviour and the transfer system.

The Chester Report represented the first official recognition of the 'makeshift or poor conditions' of the playing facilities on offer to those in the community (1.68, para 73). It highlighted key problems of access, citing a 1967 survey by Lancashire County Council, which revealed that less than a quarter of its maintained grass pitches were open to the public. The differential standard of football facilities reflected the enduring influence of the amateur vs professional struggle. Well-established amateur leagues, such as the Isthmian League, were well equipped (with floodlighting) due to healthy attendances and wealthy patrons; this contrasted sharply with the situation in the rest of the country relying on public provision. The in-built privileging of amateur football in the FA was responsible for a decoupling of grassroots football from the professional elite.

The recommendations of the Chester Report met with inevitable resistance from some of the all-too-amateur worthies in positions of power within the game.

As ever, this was a question of political will rather than feasibility. In the House of Commons debate on the 1968 Chester Report, Denis Howell (HC Deb 5 October 1969: 564) himself stated:

> *I must emphasise that most of these matters are for the sporting bodies. The Government cannot instruct them. We have no power to instruct, nor would we want power to instruct, the sporting bodies. Our influence is brought about by persuasion, by co-operation, by conversation and by trying to convince them of the logic of the Chester Committee's Report.*

The putative social democratic period of state intervention in sport was short-lived and failed to ingrain itself in the psyche of the British state. It is revealing that in the aforementioned Commons debate, not a single member of the Conservative opposition was present. Sport, including football, continued to be peripheral to matters of the state, with its place on the political agenda contingent on the personal interests of individual MPs. Direct management and control from the centre as such is still largely absent; it is at the local level that this aspect manifests itself in the main and where the major proportion of state expenditure has taken place.

The election of Margaret Thatcher in 1979 and the subsequent imposition of neoliberal policies in the UK changed the direction of policy in sport. Indeed, the hegemonic position of neoliberalism in leading world economies by the 1990s changed the nature of politics not just in the UK but also across the developed world. Successive neoliberal governments since 1979 have been elected in the UK, and the political landscape has been dramatically altered as a consequence of the rollback of the state and the foregrounding of the market. Indeed, despite a brief resurgence of recognisably left-wing politics within the Labour Party following the surprise election of Jeremy Corbyn as leader, when in government from 1997–2010, Labour (rebranded as New Labour under Tony Blair) pursued a neoliberal policy agenda, just as the Conservative Party has done in its periods in power (1979–1997, 2010–2015 as part of a coalition with the Liberal Democrats, and 2015–present as sole party of government).

It is important to define at this stage what we mean by neoliberalism, as there is a danger that the term itself has become almost meaningless due to its extremely wide application, not all of which can be considered helpful. Peck et al. (2010: 96) refer to neoliberalism as a 'rascal concept' due to its association with 'an almost bewildering array of local trajectories, contingent forms, and hybrid assemblages.' While many scholars see the not-so-hidden hand of neoliberalism everywhere (Peck et al., 2010 discuss more than 90 articles on neoliberalism in one journal, *Antipode*, alone, and there have been hundreds more produced globally since 2010), others deny its utility. As long ago as 2005, Barnett (2005: 9) argued that there is no such thing as neoliberalism, in the sense of it being a useful term for analysing social, political and economic change. To be clear, we do not agree with this assessment, but we do acknowledge that the term can lack utility when stretched to the point of incoherence.

Our understanding of neoliberalism derives from the analysis of tangible changes in the ways that states are governed. As Ferguson (2010) argues, in policy terms, neoliberalism involves the deployment of mechanisms developed in the private sphere within the functions of the state itself. Within sport, as in other areas of policy, services that were previously provided by the state have been subcontracted out to private providers and run along the same lines as a private business (Parnell et al., 2019 explore this neatly, as do Walker and Hayton, 2018). The pursuit of profit fundamentally changes the dynamics of state policy. Whereas liberalism (classically, at least) considered both the state and the market, and the public and the private to be separate spheres, neoliberalism privileges the market above all else, and the state is consequently managed according to the rules and whims of the market (Ferguson, 2010). When the market fails, as it did in 2008, the state also suffers (Peck et al., 2010).

In terms of the role of citizens (post British Nationality Act of 1981), neoliberal doctrine tends to promote the idea of individuals as a 'miniature firm,' assessing opportunities and responding to risks according to a rational assessment of the possible courses of action available (Ferguson, 2010: 172). Margaret Thatcher's consistent railing against what she termed 'the nanny state' is revealing – the individual is encouraged to be self-reliant rather than be reliant on the state for opportunities and financial support. The state's role in this doctrine is not to provide rights, but to provide opportunities for individuals within the market. As Parnell, Millward, and Spracklen (2017), Webber (2018) and Parnell et al. (2019) discuss, the British state's role in providing social welfare has been drastically reduced, in keeping with the doctrine that the individual should be responsible for themselves.

Despite this, sport has been cast as a vehicle for social change, albeit with relatively little fiscal support from the state, in keeping with the broader neoliberal ideology (King, 2009). In the 1990s, sport was considered to have the potential to impact social welfare and regeneration (Coalter, 2007). Sport was also considered as an instrument to deliver upon multiple agendas, such as increasing income and jobs and improving education, health and social inclusion (Coalter, 2007; King, 2009). Given the widespread appeal and reach of sport, some have suggested that it may provide a more effective vehicle in reaching those at risk who may not be reached by traditional political or civic activities (Bloyce and Smith, 2009; Collins and Kay, 2014; Parnell and Richardson, 2014; Parnell et al., 2015). In contrast, several authors have challenged the social impact of sport, citing a lack of empirical evidence (Smith and Waddington, 2004; Collins and Kay, 2014). Despite this lack of evidence, policies have continued to endorse sport as a vehicle to attend to social agendas and change (Coalter, 2007).

In the mid-1990s, the FA surrendered much of its power over the professional game to the Premier League and recast its role with a much bigger focus on grassroots and, in particular, junior football. This coincided with the coming to power of New Labour, with its modernising agenda for sport and football in particular (Hudson, Hardy, Henwood, and Wistow, 1999). Political pressure to increase participation rates in sport to achieve wider social policy objectives has become enforced by a regime of key performance indicators, whereby funding is allocated on the basis of meeting targets. This is a classic case of mechanisms developed in the private sphere being deployed within the functions of the state, a core element of the neoliberal policies adopted both by New Labour and the Conservatives. As highlighted by O'Gorman et al. (2018), football authorities, through new public management techniques have attempted to incentivise stakeholders to systematically increase participation in the game. Despite this, English football has faced an ongoing battle with a decline in funding from central funding to local authorities as a result of the economic downturn and the subsequent austerity policies (Parnell et al., 2017; Widdop, King, Parnell, Cutts, and Millward, 2018).

Evidence suggests that there has been an historic mismanagement of sport facilities, most notably playing fields – and resultantly football pitches, which are a vital resource for community participants to play the game (see King, 2009). This previous policy disorganisation has resulted in lost playing fields and lack of maintenance, certainly over the past 50 years. Subtle changes over times such as shifting the protected area from 6 hectares to 0.2 hectares at present may well have had a significant impact on practice (see King, 2009). This would suggest that despite the political hyperbole around sport, and particularly football, little genuine value has been placed on sport locally and nationally, historically and geographically over time.

Despite growing regulation (King, 2009), there is an absence of rigid, coherent and effective statutory law related to playing fields, which has resulted in a decline in the spaces available to play. Evidence details a lack of coordination and collaboration between central government, national governing bodies for sport, Sport England, other major stakeholders and local government. Alongside this, there is a lack of decision-making and power at a national level to influence local decisions. In this respect, local governments can make their own arrangements to sell playing fields outside of the control of the central government (King, 2009). This is often led by real fiscal and housing stock dilemmas, brought about both by austerity policies and central government inaction. This decline in playing fields has developed over time, despite many local governments' previous support for football (and sport). Indeed, many local governments remain inclined to support the benefits of football today (Krustrup and Parnell, 2019). However, in England, the current political and fiscal climate has heightened the ongoing decline and worsened the state of play for community and grassroots football.

In May 2010, a Conservative Party–led coalition government assumed political leadership of the UK. The new government initiated considerable cuts to public spending, including a raft of austerity measures in its 'Comprehensive Spending Review,' which outlined £81 billion cuts to government departments. This meant that public spending was reduced on a national scale, leaving few government departments untouched. By the end of 2013, almost three and a half years after the introduction of austerity-driven policy measures, it was estimated that £64 billion had been wiped from public expenditure (The Centre of Welfare Reform, 2013). There has been no easing of the fiscal constraints placed onto local councils. The cuts detrimentally impacted upon the provision of services such as libraries, clubs for disabled children, leisure centres and community sport facilities (Blyth, 2013; Parnell, Millward, and Spracklen, 2015; Parnell et al., 2019). Importantly, these cuts were primarily focused on social benefits and local government budgets (The Centre for Welfare Reform, 2013).

The Department of Communities and Local Government's funding was cut by 51% between 2010 and 2015, resulting in grants to local governments falling by 27% (Parnell, Widdop, and King, 2015). As a consequence, discretionary services, such as sport, leisure and culture faced funding uncertainty (Collins and Haudenhuyse, 2015; Parnell et al., 2019). Political commentary from the then prime minister (David Cameron) highlighted that austerity, or leaner practice, might be around for longer (Krugman, 2015). Lowndes and Gardner (2016) term this period 'super austerity' (ie further cuts upon already financial constrained services – 2015 onwards). The enduring nature of austerity for local governments is likely to have profound consequences for grassroots football and the broader participation targets for football authorities.

In terms of local government expenditure, the annual spending commitment to services categorised as 'sport development and community recreation' are important to consider, as these services primarily aim to raise and widen participation among socio-economic groups considered to be the most excluded and tend to be subsidised in order that income is not a barrier to participation (King, 2009). It is recognised that the Chartered Institute of Public Finance and Accountability category for expenditure on 'indoor and outdoor facilities' is also critical for participation as is the expenditure on 'parks and open spaces.' In fact, research outlined that although reductions in expenditure on maintaining and servicing facilities have occurred and were likely to continue, it is community-based programmes that have been disproportionately affected, whether these services are a component of direct local authority provision, funded from local budgets and delivered by local authority staff, or are funded by central government agencies and delivered in a partnership arrangement locally.

There is a lack of research on the impact of these cuts on sport and grassroots football (O'Gorman et al., 2018). However, recent evidence of the impact on a range of sport contexts and services is starting to emerge, including in the third sector (Walker and Hayton, 2017, 2018; Kenyon, Mason, and Rookwood, 2018; Parnell et al., 2015; Parnell et al., 2019), public sector services (Ramchandani, Shibli, and Ping Kung, 2018) and sports participation (Widdop et al., 2018). This is of particular importance for football, as playing fields and football pitches often fall under the leadership of local government or third-sector organisations. Moreover, football, as the national game, is a significant contributor to sport participation and physical activity, but its grassroots facilities are often at the mercy of local governments working in an environment of austerity (Parnell et al., 2019).

In the few research papers surrounding this topic, only one (to our understanding) examines the impact of funding cuts on sport participation longitudinally. By comparing the Active People data in 2008–2009 with 2013–2014, Widdop et al. (2018) noted that sport participation among socio-demographic groups defined as 'hard to reach' has not altered significantly. The study revealed that only marginal differences can be identified across the five-year time span (during the period of intense austerity), which is perhaps unsurprising, given the difficulties of raising and widening participation among the low-income and socially excluded in a context of disinvestment through austerity policies. This is important, as a recent government strategy (Cabinet Office, 2015; Sport England, 2016b) has specifically focused on 'social and community development,' implying that a commitment of resources to raising and widening participation among 'hard-to-reach' groups is needed. Through austerity and public spending reductions, it appears that investment has not followed these policy aspirations to date, in that participation has not increased among these priority groups (Widdop et al., 2018). Indeed, central government has a commitment to 'distribute funding to focus on those people who tend not to take part in sport, including women and girls, disabled people, those in lower socio-economic groups and older people' (Cabinet Office, 2015: 10). In order to achieve this, local governments are viewed as critical in delivering policy in this respect. However, it appears investment needs to follow policy statements for any tangible change in participation to result.

Austerity cuts have created major challenges for community sport facilities that have had to manage both their financial viability and sustainability during this period of fiscal constraint (Parnell et al., 2019). An Association for Public Service Excellence report (2012) anticipated falling revenue budgets, staff cuts, increased charges, reduced opening hours, facility closures and reduced commitments to parks and pitches utilised for organised and casual participation in the light of changes to public funding levels. Some of these predictions have been reported through case studies on reductions to sport and leisure services and their impact on a range of sports from swimming facilities (see Parnell et al., 2015) to municipal golf courses (Widdop and Parnell, 2015). The question remains how this may impact the potential for football to deliver for participation, but the evidence is suggesting that facilities and grass pitches are systematically being downgraded (Parnell and Widdop, 2015).

Despite austerity, football remains one of the most popular sports in England, with a reported 1.8 million participants on a weekly basis (Sport England, 2016a). While there is an absence of longitudinal data, evidence suggests a decline in the number of people playing 11-a-side competitive football (Lusted, 2009; Koutrou, Pappous, and Horne, 2016). The data suggests that this decline accelerated between 2005 and 2015, showing the number of people playing affiliated 11-a-side football fell by 180,000 (The FA, 2015). Indeed, in 2014, Sport England imposed a £1.6 million cut from the £30 million four-year investment into the FA. At the time, poor weather conditions and facilities and decreased clubs and the end-user (ie community players) were factors for this decline. A recent analysis on contemporary issues in grassroots and community football suggests we should anticipate a further reduction in the quality of football playing facilities, increased costs, overuse of pitches, less funding available from constrained local businesses to sponsor grassroots football clubs, more matches cancelled and potentially poorer experiences for players and, subsequently, less players involved in the game (O'Gorman et al., 2018).

The importance of driving participation has become a growing need for football authorities. Utilising the UK's most popular sport to drive participation is important to tackle inactivity (Krustrup and Parnell, 2019). Given the cost of lifestyle-related diseases and inactivity alongside the abundance of evidence for the role football can play towards the health agenda, it would make a reduction in funding for grassroots football appear counter-productive. It could be argued that these cuts are a false economy. Given the relatively low estimated costs for grassroots football pitch development, whether grass or artificial grass surfaces, it offers an opportunity to design and deliver programmes to reduce inactivity and increase sport participation. The cost of upkeep and enhancing grassroots and community football is insignificant when compared to the potential public health benefits of football and the financial burden of inactivity (see Krustrup and Parnell, 2019).

Given the potential ongoing threat of austerity-driven policies in England, alongside the absence of rigorous protection for sport and leisure services and playing fields, it would appear that we may be missing out on an opportunity to capitalise on the evidence that football works (Krustrup and Parnell, 2019). However, the reductions in funding are consistent with government policy since the start of the Thatcher era. The expectation that people should be self-reliant certainly impacts the extent to which possibly beneficial, but publicly funded, schemes are supported. Ideologically, consecutive governments in the UK have not supported increased state funding for sport and have encouraged private businesses to take an increasing role in provision (Parnell et al., 2019; Walker and Hayton, 2018). Arguably, opportunities to improve participation and public health are being missed because of ideological opposition to the means by which these improvements could be achieved.

The ecosystem of grassroots football has undoubtedly worsened as a consequence of COVID-19. The centrality of football – in terms of both professional football clubs and grassroots football – to people's everyday lives has been brought into focus by the pandemic. Yet, to date, the response by government and the football authorities has privileged the narrow stratum of the elite professional game (ie the English Premier League [EPL]) to the detriment of other levels, notably grassroots football. This is in keeping with the dominant neoliberal ideology in operation, that football is viewed in terms of the revenue it generates; as such professional football has been prioritised. In the short-term, the pandemic is likely to have a disproportionately negative impact on the physical and mental well-being of those adults and children in the most deprived communities in England (Clarkson, Culvin, Pope, and Parry, 2020; Parnell, Widdop, Bond, and Wilson, 2020).

Much of the attention in England has been focused on '*Project Restart*' (Mohr et al., 2020; Parnell et al., 2020). The widening gap between the wealth in the English Premier League and vast majority of the football pyramid has been put into stark reality by the COVID-19 pandemic. It has exposed the great inequalities that exist within the professional game and the unsustainable management practices that pervade its corporate governance (Parnell et al., 2020). On 13 March 2020, the EPL was postponed, and three days later, English football authorities also postponed all grassroots football. On the 27 March 2020, this decision evolved, and non-league football and grassroots football were confirmed as 'null and void' and are yet to have a confirmed full return-to-play date; at the same time many facilities and pitches have been left untouched during this period, degrading them further (Parnell et al., 2020).

The early postponement and accelerated return of the English Premier League demonstrates the preoccupation of football authorities with the top level of men's professional football as well as the gulf in resources between the elite and the rest of the English game (including women's football, see Clarkson et al., 2020). It is also the case that the women's game has been heavily impacted by COVID-19 and an approach that has heavily privileged the EPL (and the Championship, to a lesser extent). The relative lack of funding to the women's game has seen clubs such as Liverpool in the invidious position of having their men's team complete their season and win the EPL title, while the women's team had their season voided and were at the bottom of the Women's Super League (WSL). While Liverpool were by no means by the only club that experienced this disparity in outcomes, the stark difference between the fortunes and funding of their men's team and women's team reveals wider inequalities in the current system (Clarkson et al., 2020).

The media has also had an almost exclusive focus on the return of the men's professional game, predominantly the EPL and Championship. The financial resources to provide the testing regime required for Project Restart has been the key factor in this discrepancy. The estimated weekly cost of £30,000 to test an average squad and backroom staff of 50 people three times per week is clearly beyond the means of most professional clubs (Delaney, 2020). In this respect, COVID-19 has shown us that in addition to the clear chasm in financial might between the EPL (and, to a lesser extent, the Championship) the debate about Project Restart has also revealed the extent to which football in England is viewed by the media and football authorities as an exercise in mass consumption, rather than mass participation.

In contrast, grassroots football constitutes a complex but delicate ecosystem of volunteers, private businesses, and local authorities sitting at the heart of communities around the country. While football, an important vehicle for delivering several public health outcomes (Krustrup and Parnell, 2019), faces multiple challenges, the lack of an effective governance regime to protect and develop the infrastructure of grassroots football has left it in a perilous state. It appears that we require a fundamental transformation of the governance of football and priorities of English football in order to save it.

Conclusion

This chapter provides an analysis of the governance and political economy of grassroots football in England. There appears to be little genuine value placed on grassroots football, and indeed wider grassroots sport, by the central government, in line with the wider neoliberal ideology that underpins policy. There are tensions between local authorities and the central government, and drastic funding reductions in the context of austerity have made it difficult for local authorities to privilege sport over other discretionary services, despite the possible public health benefits. Evidence also points towards the mismanagement of policy with relation to playing fields, and there seems to be little joined up working between key football stakeholders and local and central governments.

Existing issues in the governance of grassroots football have been exacerbated by austerity and now COVID-19:

- A reduction in funding for local government, resulting in decisions made at a local level becoming complicated and politically loaded, especially for discretionary services like the maintenance of football pitches.
- These processes have ultimately increased the cost for football players in terms of club membership.
- As the quality of pitches continues to be downgraded, participation is systematically reduced, which has influence on their consumption behaviour.
- Fewer players play football and engage in sport participation.

As grassroots football returns post-COVID-19, it is not enough to hope for football to return to its previous state. The current trajectory for grassroots football is that of a serious decline. Given the relative lack of research in this area, we call for more empirical research to better understand the issues facing grassroots football, alongside further discussion and analysis of existing evidence (see Parnell et al., 2019) to better inform and influence policy-makers. We hope this chapter stimulates interest, ideas and further research by colleagues in the academy.

References

Allison, L. (1986). *The Politics of Sport*. England: Manchester University Press.
Amis, J., Slack, T., and Hinings, C.R. (2004). Strategic Change and the Role of Interests, Power and Organizational Capacity. *Journal of Sport Management*, 18: 158–199.

Barnett, C. (2005). The Consolations of 'Neoliberalism'. *Geoforum*, 36(1): 7–12.
Bloyce, D., and Smith, A. (2009). *Sport Policy and Development: An Introduction*. Abingdon: Routledge.
Blyth, M. (2013). *Austerity: The History of a Dangerous Idea*. Oxford: Oxford University Press. Retrieved from https://www.amazon.co.uk/Austerity-History-Dangerous-Mark-Blyth/dp/019982830X
Cabinet Office. (2015). *Sporting Future: A New Strategy for an Active Nation*. London: Cabinet Office.
Castells, M. (1977). *The Urban Question: A Marxist Approach* (Translated by Alan Shendan). Cambridge, MA: MIT Press.
CCPR. (1960). *Sport & The Community: The Report of the Wolfenden Committee on Sport 1960*. London: CCPR.
The Centre of Welfare Reform. (2013). *A Fair Society? How the Cuts Target Disabled People*. Duffy: Author.
Chadwick, S., Parnell, D., Widdop, P., and Anagnostopoulos, C. (2019). *Handbook of Football Business and Management*. London: Routledge.
Clarkson, B.G., Culvin, A., Pope, S., and Parry, K.D. (2020). Covid-19: Reflections on Threat and Uncertainty for the Future of Elite Women's Football in England. *Managing Sport and Leisure*: 1–12.
Cleland, J., O'Gorman, J., and Bond, M. (2015). The English Football Association's Respect Campaign: The Referees' View. *International Journal of Sport Policy and Politics*, 7(4): 551–563.
Coalter, F. (2007). *A Wider Social Role for Sport: Who's Keeping the Score?* London: Routledge.
Collins, M., and Haudenhuyse, R. (2015). Social Exclusion and Austerity Policies in England: The Role of Sports in a New Area of Social Polarisation and Inequality? *Social Inclusion*, 3(3): 5–18.
Collins, M., and Kay, T. (2014). *Sport and Social Exclusion*, 2nd edition. New York: Routledge.
Corelli, A. (2019). *Understanding Financial Risk Management*. London: Emerald.
Delaney, M. (2020). Coronavirus Testing Costs Pose Problem for Sport's Restart Plans. *The Independent*, Thursday 30 April 2020. Available at: www.independent.co.uk/sport/football/premier-league/premier-league-news-coronavirus-testing-2019-20-season-restart-table-a9493041.html
Ferguson, J. (2010). The Uses of Neoliberalism. *Antipode*, 41(1): 166–184.
Football (Chester Committee Report) C Deb 15 October 1969, vol: 788: 559–570.
The Football Association. (2015). *Football Participation Continues to Rise in England* [online]. Available at: www.thefa.com/news/2015/jan/29/football-participation-on-rise [Accessed 26 October 2020].
Giulianotti, R., and Robertson, R. (2009). *Globalization and Football*. London: Sage/Theory, Culture & Society.
Hargreaves, J. (1985). The Body, Sport and Power Relations. *The Sociological Review*, 33(1): 139–159.
Houlihan, B., Bloyce, D., and Smith, A. (2009). Developing the Research Agenda in Sport Policy. *International Journal of Sport Policy*, 1(1): 1–12.
Hudson, B., Hardy, B., Henwood, M., and Wistow, G. (1999). In Pursuit of Interagency Collaboration in the Public Sector: What Is the Contribution of Theory and Research? *Public Management: An International Journal of Research and Theory*, 1(2): 236–260.

Kennedy, P., and Kennedy, D. (2016). *Football in Neo-Liberal Times: A Marxist Perspective on the European Football Industry*. London: Routledge.
Kenyon, J.A., Mason, C., and Rookwood, J. (2018). Emerging Third-sector Sports Organisations and Navigating Uncertainty in an 'Era of Austerity': A Single Ethnographic Case Study from Liverpool. *International Journal of Sport Policy and Politics*, 10(1): 25–42.
Kerrigan, D. (2014). Languaculture and Grassroots Football: 'Small Goal' in Trinidad. *International Review for the Sociology of Sport*, 51(6): 735–751.
Kilvington, D., and Price, J. (2013). Tackling Social Media Abuse? Critically Assessing English Football's Response to Online Racism. *Communication & Sport*, 7(1): 64–79.
King, A. (2010). After the Crunch: A New Era for the Beautiful Game in Europe. *Soccer & Society*, 11(6): 880–891.
King, N. (2009). *Sport Policy and Governance: Local Perspectives*. London: Routledge.
Koutrou, N., Pappous, A., and Horne, R. (2016). *Keeping Up Participation Levels in Adult 11V11 Football in Kent*. Kent FA.
Krugman, P. (2015). The Austerity Drive in Britain Isn't Really About Debt and Deficits at All; It's All About Using Deficit Panic as an Excuse to Dismantle Social Programs. *New York Times*.
Krustrup, P., and Parnell, D. (2019). *Football as Medicine: Prescribing Football for Global Health Promotion*. London: Routledge.
Lowndes, V., and Gardner, A. (2016). Local Governance Under the Conservatives: Super-austerity, Devolution and the 'Smarter State'. *Local Government Studies*, 42(3): 357–375.
Lusted, J. (2009). Playing Games with 'Race': Understanding Resistance to 'Race' Equality Initiatives in English Local Football Governance. *Soccer & Society*, 10(6): 722–739.
Lusted, J. (2014). Equality Policies in Sport: Carrots, Sticks and a Retreat from the Radical. *Journal of Policy Research in Tourism, Leisure and Events*, 6(1): 85–90.
Mason, T. (2011). *Sport in Britain: A Social History*. Cambridge: Cambridge University Press.
Mohr, M., Nassis, G.P., Brito, J., Randers, M.B., Castagna, C., Parnell, D., and Krustrup, P. (2020). Return to Elite Football after the COVID-19 Lockdown. *Managing Sport and Leisure*: 1–9.
O'Gorman, J. (2011). Where Is the Implementation in Sport Policy and Programme Analysis? The English Football Association's Charter Standard as an Illustration. *International Journal of Sport Policy and Politics*, 3(1): 85–108.
O'Gorman, J., Fitzpatrick, D., Sibley, J., Hindmarsh, M., Saskova, Z., and Parnell, D. (2018). 'Contemporary issues in the management of grassroots football'. In S. Chadwick, D. Parnell, P. Widdop, and C. Anagnostopoulos (Eds.), *Routledge Handbook of Football Business and Management*. London: Routledge.
Parnell, D., Buxton, S., Hewitt, D., Reeves, M.J., Cope, E., and Bailey, R. (2015). The Pursuit of Lifelong Participation: The Role of Professional Football Clubs in the Delivery of Physical Education and School Sport in England. *Soccer & Society*, 17(2): 225–241.
Parnell, D., May, A., Widdop, P., Cope, E., and Bailey, R. (2019). Management Strategies of Non-Profit Community Sport Facilities in an Era of Austerity. *European Sport Management Quarterly*, 19(3): 312–330.
Parnell, D., Millward, P., and Spracklen, K. (2015). Sport and Austerity in the UK: An Insight into Liverpool 2014. *Journal of Policy Research in Tourism, Leisure and Events*, 7(2): 200–203.
Parnell, D., Millward, P., and Spracklen, K. (2017). Sport Management Issues in an Era of Austerity. *European Sport Management Quarterly*, 17(1): 67–74.

Parnell, D., and Richardson, D. (2014). Special Issue: Football and Inclusivity. *Soccer and Society*, 15(6): 823–827.

Peck, J., Theodore, N., and Brenner, N. (2010). Post Neoliberalism and Its Malcontents. *Antipode*, 41(1): 94–116.

Parnell, D., Widdop, P., Bond, A., and Wilson, R. (2020). COVID-19, Networks and Sport. *Managing Sport and Leisure*: 1–7.

Parnell, D., Widdop, P., and King, N. (2015). Local Authority Cuts Loom Large Over Community Sport. *ConnectSport*. Available at: www.connectsport.co.uk/academic-research/localauthority-cuts-threaten-community-sport

Pitchford, A. (2007). Youth Football. In C. Brackenridge, A. Pitchford, K. Russell, and G. Nutt (Eds.), *Child Welfare in Football: An Exploration of Children's Welfare in the Modern Game*. London: Routledge.

Polley, M. (2006). The Amateur Ideal and British Sports Diplomacy, 1900–1945. *Sport in History*, 26: 3.

Ramchandani, G., Shibli, S., and Ping Kung, S. (2018). The Performance of Local Authority Sports Facilities in England During a Period of Recession and Austerity. *International Journal of Sport Policy and Politics*, 10(1): 95–111.

Smith, A., and Waddington, I. (2004). Using 'Sport in the Community Schemes' to Tackle Crime and Drug Use Among Young People: Some Policy Issues and Problems. *European Physical Education Review*, 10(3): 279–298.

Sound Diaries. (2020). *Football Not Happening at Brightwell Recreation Ground* [online]. Available at: www.sound-diaries.co.uk/2020/05/football-not-happening-at-brightwell-recreation-ground/ [Accessed 26 October 2020].

Sport England. (2016a). *Annual Report & Accounts*. London: Sport England.

Sport England. (2016b). *Towards an Active Nation. Strategy 2016–2021*. London: Sport England.

Sztompka, P. (2008). The Focus on Everyday Life: A New Turn in Sociology. *European Review*, 16(1): 23–37.

Walker, C.M., and Hayton, J.W. (2017). Navigating Austerity: Balancing 'Desirability with Viability' in a Third Sector Disability Sports Organization. *European Sport Management Quarterly*, 17(1): 98–116.

Walker, C.M., and Hayton, J.W. (2018). An Analysis of Third Sector Sport Organisations in an Era of 'Super-austerity'. *International Journal of Sport Policy and Politics*, 10(1): 43–61.

Walvin, J. (2001). *The Only Game*. Oxford: Blackwell.

Webber, D.M. (2018). Feasting in a Time of Famine: The English Premier League, 'Conspicuous Consumption' and the Politics of Austerity. *Journal of Consumer Culture* (Online First).

Widdop, P., King, N., Parnell, D., Cutts, D., and Millward, P. (2018). Austerity, Policy and Sport Participation in England. *International Journal of Sport Policy and Politics*, 10(1): 7–24.

Widdop, P., and Parnell, D. (2015). *Consumption and Class: The Curious Case of Golf*. Leeds Beckett University, The Media Centre. Available at: http://mediacentre.leedsbeckett.ac.uk/post/consumption-and-class-the-curious-case-of-golf/

Wolfenden-Committee on Sport. (1960). *Sport and the Community*. London: Central Council of Physical Recreation.

Index